D1191902

The Writing Life of Hugh Kelly

The Writing Life of Hugh Kelly

Politics, Journalism, and Theater
in Late-Eighteenth-Century London

Robert R. Bataille

Southern Illinois University Press
Carbondale and Edwardsville

Library of Congress Cataloging-in-Publication Data
Bataille, Robert R., 1940–
    The writing life of Hugh Kelly : politics, journalism, and theater in late-
eighteenth-century London / Robert R. Bataille.
        p. cm.
    Includes bibliographical references and index.
    1. Kelly, Hugh, 1739–1777. 2. Politics and literature—Great Britain—History—
18th century. 3. Journalism—England—London—History—18th century. 4. Great
Britain—Politics and government—18th century. 5. Theater—England—London—
History—18th century. 6. Dramatists, English—18th century—Biography.
    7. Journalists—Great Britain—Biography. I. Title.

PR3539.K2 Z59 2000
822'.6—dc21
[B]
ISBN 0-8093-2288-9 (alk. paper)
                                                                99-045455

The paper used in this publication meets the minimum requirements of American
National Standard for Information Sciences—Permanence of Paper for Printed
Library Materials, ANSI Z39.48-1992. ∞

Contents

Preface

Some years ago, when delivering the yearly speech that all presidents of the American Society for Eighteenth-Century Studies give upon the occasion of the Society's annual meeting, Prof. Henry Snyder noted that much work remained to be done in writing the history of eighteenth-century British journalism. The present study is an attempt to contribute modestly to that task, for one of my arguments is that Hugh Kelly was one of the most important and prolific journalists of his time. During the period in which he edited or wrote for a number of London periodicals (roughly between 1760 and 1776), he self-consciously reflected on the new profession of journalism itself; contributed significantly to the discussion on manners, morals, and the theater; and finally, as a major propagandist for George III and his ministers, participated importantly in the public discourse on a number of the controversial political issues of his time. These issues involved him both in local London politics and in the larger world of the Empire itself. It is in connection with this last role that I have uncovered a large body of heretofore unknown work.

When I began my research on Hugh Kelly over ten years ago, I gradually discovered what paths of inquiry earlier researchers had followed with little or no success. I saw no reason to duplicate their searches and sought instead to uncover new sources of information about Kelly's life. I had noticed in cursorily reading through newspapers from the period of Kelly's greatest activity, roughly from 1767 to 1776, that his name came up often enough to encourage the feeling that an intensive reading of such papers might yield me information about Kelly that I could glean no other way.

Somewhat ironically then, it is to journalism itself, although indeed journalism often hostile to Kelly, that I owe much of the new knowledge I have been able to uncover about Kelly's writing life. Because archival and manuscript materials pertinent to Kelly's life are so few in number, my method of investigation has been to read carefully and widely in the periodicals of Kelly's time, mainly in the newspapers, in order to (re)construct his writing career. It is often Kelly's political enemies, writing in newspapers, who provide hints about his journalistic career. Often taking a hint from a hostile source, I have been able to locate Kelly's journalistic contributions and have in some cases been able to verify such contributions through a consideration of internal evidence.

Yet the uncovering of Kelly's writing life has not yielded much in the way of biographical information, and this study is clearly not an attempt at a biography. What biographical facts I have uncovered ought to be seen as incidental or supplementary to my major purpose, which is to trace Kelly's public life, his life of writing. The one exception to my concentration on Kelly's writing life is my consideration of his law career, the reconstruction of which, once again, I owe to newspaper accounts.

In his own time and in our own, Kelly was known chiefly as a major practitioner of sentimental drama, and to the extent that he has received modern critical attention, much of that attention has focused on estimating the kind and degree of his sentimentality. I confess that this focus is not a major one in this study; to be sure, I feel it necessary to consider Kelly's place in sentimental drama. But his drama is only one of my concerns. Rather, I am more interested in viewing Kelly as part of that larger movement of sensibility, one of whose aims was to reform what G. J. Barker-Benfield has called the "hard male culture," than I am in defining in some narrower fashion Kelly's place in sentimental drama. Here Barker-Benfield's *Culture of Sensibility* has been invaluable to me.

I examine how Kelly's interest in didactic literature, whether essayistic, novelistic, or dramatic, was tied to sensibility as a movement of reform. But I also view Kelly as a pragmatic writer of popular culture, as a rhetorician, in other words, who in attempting to earn his living as a fully professional writer (despite his own misgivings about such a profession) understood full well the implications of Samuel Johnson's statement that "he who lives to please must please to live" ("Prologue"). That is, I argue that Kelly was the complete professional. To succeed in his art, he knew he had to cater to audience needs and desires, and to succeed as a polemicist for political causes often unpopular with the London masses, he had to employ the rhetorical skills of a propagandist. At the same time, however, I also emphasize that, at least in his early writing career, when journalism alone sustained him and his family, Kelly expressed more than a little anxiety and ambivalence about the life of writing and that this ambivalence sometimes seems to have pressed him to engage in fantasies in which he escapes from Grub Street drudgery.

In constructing my view of Kelly as a propagandist and a popular writer, I have relied on the work of two sociologists, Jacques Ellul and Herbert J. Gans. In particular, Ellul's extensive discussion of the structure of propaganda systems has enabled me to illuminate the propaganda machines of both the Wilkites and the Courtiers of George III, while Gans's distinction between the audience-centered popular writer and the creator-centered artist has helped me to a deeper understanding of Kelly's career. In arguing for the sophisticated qualities of the Wilkite propaganda system, I rely in turn on the valuable work of George Rudé, John Brewer, and Lance Bertelsen, each of whom has written extensively on the political and popular culture of the 1760s; Gerald Newman's study of English nationalism allowed me to put the political tensions of the 1760s into a broader perspective. In attempting to situate Kelly in the new commodity culture of writing and in comparing his situation to Samuel Johnson's, I have learned much from the scholarship of Alvin Kernan in his *Printing Technology, Letters & Samuel Johnson.*

To delineate Kelly's role in the interrelated worlds of journalism, politics, and theater, I often discuss people and events in the microworld of this complicated, local London culture that broader studies or those dealing with more major figures might normally ignore or minimize. I contend that most of these normally marginal figures and events are important in understanding Kelly's situatedness. In some ways, Kelly himself was perhaps a marginal man. But if so, he was also one who succeeded and embodied in his success the myth of rising in the world so dear to the popular, sentimental culture to which he contributed. If this study contains a master narrative, then Kelly's triumph, his success at wresting a comfortable living from his writing, is that central story.

Acknowledgments

This study was completed with the help of a considerable number of fellow scholars. Throughout my work, I have been indebted to several who have written dissertations about Kelly: to William W. Watt, Thomas K. O'Leary, and Jean-Michel Lacroix I owe much. Among others who responded to specific requests were Bertram Davis, who kindly answered my inquiries concerning the intersection of Sir John Hawkins's and Kelly's legal careers; James Aikman Cochrane, who aided my search for further connections between Kelly and William Strahan; Samuel H. Woods Jr., who responded to my queries concerning the nature of the Goldsmith–Kelly relationship; and John C. Greene, who graciously made his work on the eighteenth-century Irish theater calendar available to me. My colleague William McCarthy read early versions of the first three chapters and suggested valuable changes. Larry Carver and Betty Rizzo read the entire draft of the study; I owe much to their judicious criticism and kindly encouragement. Betty Rizzo has been especially helpful to me over many years.

A number of libraries here and in the United Kingdom have allowed me to use their collections. Among these were the British Library, the Victoria and Albert Museum, the Bodleian Library at Oxford, and the Cambridge University Library. I have also benefited from research carried out at the Princeton University Library during a summer spent at an NEH seminar led by Alvin Kernan and at the University of Pennsylvania Library during another NEH seminar led by John Richetti. At the Harvard Theatre Collection, I was kindly allowed to read a number of rare materials related to the Kelly–Garrick connection, while the Spencer Library at the University of Kansas and the Department of Special Collections at the University of Illinois Library permitted me to consult their extensive holdings on the eighteenth century. Early in my work, I consulted materials at the Boston Public Library, the New York Public Library, and the Library Company of Philadelphia. The copies of Kelly's plays from the Larpent Collection at the Henry E. Huntington Library in Pasadena were invaluable in my attempt to compare the acted with the printed versions of his plays. Finally, I would especially like to thank the interlibrary loan staff of the Parks Library of Iowa State University; they searched far and wide for rare materials, usually with a high degree of success and always with good humor.

The Writing Life of Hugh Kelly

1

❧

Beginnings

To attempt to compose even an overview of the life of Hugh Kelly is to confront a bewildering and often contradictory array of anecdotes and myths and, at the same time, to lament the scarcity of hard facts. This is particularly true of Kelly's early life, for what public records and documents exist have to do with his later life after he had achieved some success in London. Even after Kelly became not only a well-known dramatist but also a professional journalist pensioned by the ministers of George III, his life must be traced in part using anecdotes often circulated by hostile sources. For his early life, we owe almost all of our information to four contemporary sources: Capt. Edward Thompson, William Cooke, John Taylor, and the anonymous biographer of the *Town and Country Magazine*.[1] The three identifiable biographers all knew Kelly personally, but the degree of knowledge each possessed about Kelly is uncertain.

Each biographer's general narrative is illuminated by the anecdote: it is this form that provides each biographical sketch with the persuasive specificity of detail about characters and events that, in novelizing the material of Kelly's life, compels belief. In his introduction to *Minor Lives,* Edward L. Hart reminds us of the importance of the anecdote and the ana to the writing of eighteenth-century biographers. He points to the rich seventeenth-century examples of Thomas Fuller, John Aubrey, and Anthony à Wood; notes the anecdote's importance to our biographical understanding of major writers like Alexander Pope and Samuel Johnson; and cites the achievements of anecdotists in the later part of the century, including Horace Walpole, William Seward, John Almon, Thomas Percy, Hester Thrale, and the most indefatigable of all, John Nichols.[2]

In our own time, the anecdote, partly from the influence of the new historicism and partly from the relatively new interest in marginal discourses, has gained new attention from scholars and critics. Joel Fineman, in arguing that the anecdote is the "literary form or genre that uniquely refers to the real," suggests that it has a twofold usefulness:

It reminds us, on the one hand, that the anecdote has something literary about it, for there are, of course, other and non-literary ways to make reference to the real. . . . On the other hand, it reminds us also that there is something about the anecdote that exceeds its literary status, and this excess is precisely that which gives the anecdote its pointed, referential access to the real. (56)

Fineman goes on to define the anecdote as a "*historeme,* i.e., as the smallest minimum unit of the historiographic fact" (57). For Stephen Greenblatt, the anecdote speaks both to the singularity of the contingent as well as to the representativeness of larger patterns (2–3). I mean to employ anecdotes about Kelly in what I take to be both senses of Greenblatt's usage: that is, as somehow like a snapshot of a moment but also as emblematic of a larger pattern.

The anecdotes that help construct the narrative of Kelly's early years are of several kinds and may be said to resemble generic formulas insofar as they echo similar occasions in the life stories of other eighteenth-century writers, particularly those writers of humble origins. The circumstances of the writer's family, his education, his first and usually unsatisfactory occupation, his early manifestations of genius that suggest his true calling, and his difficulties when initially attempting to establish himself in London are all important narrative sites in such biographies and are often given realistic concreteness through the anecdote. In Hugh Kelly's case, the narrative of his youth in Dublin is presented by his biographers with a minimum of anecdotal drama; we learn that his father was a Dublin tavern keeper, that Kelly received a "tolerable school education" (Thompson, "Life" iii–iv), and that, because of his father's financial difficulties, he was removed from school abruptly and apprenticed to a staymaker. Later anecdotes— as well as attacks on Kelly many years later—will highlight the staymaker event as part of the generic "genius" narrative: obviously a literary talent cannot be allowed to suffer long at such a menial occupation.

What may be termed the early-detection-of-genius formula is variously represented by Kelly's biographers. One claims Kelly spent some time as a youth working in his father's tavern and there became acquainted with actors from the local theater, while another maintains that it was at the theater itself that young Kelly spent his leisure hours during his staymaker apprenticeship. And it was the actors who, struck by Kelly's earliest journalistic efforts, first urged him to seek his fortune in London.[3]

Accordingly, most narratives relate that Kelly, when reaching London, first tried staymaking but was told by his master that he lacked skill. Thus this false-career-step anecdote concludes with Kelly freed to pursue his true calling, the life of writing; and just how he started down that right path is the site of one of the first important anecdotes of Kelly's early years in London. William Cooke relates what may be termed Kelly's initiation anecdote by locating him in the Black Lion public house on Russell Street soon after losing his staymaker's position. Cooke relates how Kelly, looking dour, had been questioned by a friendly attorney who was then eager to offer Kelly a position as scribe because he could write a fair hand and spell "transubstantiation" ("Hugh Kelly," Nov. 338). After this, Kelly was soon able to begin part-time work in journalism, adding to his law clerk's salary by "occasional essays and paragraphs in the newspapers" (338). The hack legal work was no more suitable to Kelly's talents, however, than staymaking, so another biographer, combining the false-career and true-genius thematics, comments that "this employment, though profitable could not long be agreeable to a man of his original genius, and lively turn of mind" (Thompson, "Life" v). Finally, the narratives of Kelly's life begin to include factual information along with the anecdote, and the *Town and Country Magazine* "Memoirs" writer identifies Kelly's first extensive journalistic employment by specifically connecting him to Charles Green Say's *Gazetteer* (87).

Because these four contemporary narratives of Kelly's early life cease to approximate each other even in general outline after tracing Kelly's career to about 1762, I must pause here to see what modern scholars of Kelly have to say about the worthiness of these earlier accounts and then decide which aspects of these narratives seem most credible. There are only three modern, comprehensive studies of Kelly: William W. Watt's unpublished 1935 dissertation, "Hugh Kelly and the Sentimental Drama," Thomas K. O'Leary's unpublished 1965 dissertation, "Hugh Kelly: Contributions toward a Critical Biography," and Jean-Michel Lacroix's 1984 dissertation, *L'oevre de Hugh Kelly (1739–1777): Contribution à l'étude du sentimentalisme anglais* (The works of Hugh Kelly: Contributions to the study of English sentimentalism). All three of these modern scholars did extensive research in attempting to uncover more information about Kelly's birth and early life.[4] But they all were generally unsuccessful and hence, for the data in their own studies of Kelly's early life, rely almost exclusively on the four major, contemporary accounts just reviewed, as well as on some lesser materials, such as Kelly's obituaries and biographies of Kelly's contemporaries, especially those of Oliver Goldsmith, Samuel Johnson, and David Garrick, whose lives touched Kelly's in some way.[5]

What then can be trusted of the various and sometimes conflicting views of Kelly's life up until early 1762 when he would seem to be firmly established as a London journalist? Part of the answer lies in looking for those larger narrative elements that the biographical accounts have in common. The father's economic difficulties, his keeping a tavern, young Kelly's brief but successful education, his departure for England in the spring of 1760—all are mentioned to some degree by all of the major eighteenth-century versions of his life. Yet these general phases of Kelly's life seem to be at least partially paralleled in the life stories of other young Grub Street writers. One is left with the inability to disentangle life from art. A similar difficulty arises in connection with the more specific anecdotes that are employed to illustrate some of these general phases; these anecdotes occur primarily after Kelly's arrival in London, and here William Cooke and the *Town and Country Magazine* "Memoirs" author not only provide more details of Kelly's early London days but illustrate these phases with anecdotes complete with dialogue.

One very much wants to believe in the Cooke—"Memoirs" anecdotal versions of Kelly's early London days if for no other reason than these versions, with their dramatic features and realistic detail, are so much more entertaining than the less novelized narratives of Thompson and John Taylor. But these anecdotes are not merely entertaining; rather, as Fineman suggests in his definition of the form, they are the "smallest minimum unit of the historiographic fact" (57). Let us look more closely at the anecdote that describes what we can call the true-calling phase of Kelly's life in William Cooke's narrative. Cooke tells of how Kelly first obtained employment as a copyist for the attorney during a meeting at the Black Lion:

> The manner of his engagement with this Attorney, Kelly used often to tell with some pleasantry: "I was sitting one evening at the Black Lyon, rather a little out of spirits at the gloomy prospect before me, when I was observed by my friend, who asked me what was the matter? We were alone, I ingenuously told him; adding, I was willing to do any thing within the reach of my abilities for an honest livelihood. 'Can you write a good hand?' says the Attorney.— 'I believe pretty tolerable, Sir,' says Kelly. 'Well, come let's see. Here (calling for pen and ink, and a slip of paper), write me down the word "Transubstantiation."'" Kelly instantly complied;—when the other taking it to the light, and looking at it, exclaimed, "Very well indeed, well written and well spelled; come, my Lad, don't despond, I'll give you a place in my office directly till something better turns out, and here's a Guinea earnest." ("Hugh Kelly," Nov. 338)

The details make the narrative seem credible and authentic (in the mode of realistic fiction), especially the opening of the first sentence, "Kelly used often to tell," which suggests that Cooke had heard this story so many times as to make audience incredulity impossible. The problem, beyond the possibility that Cooke wrote with just such a purpose in mind, is that the narrative was written some sixteen years after Kelly's death, the events themselves having taken place some thirty-two years previously. To accept all this quotation as precisely true would require a suspension of all skepticism, skepticism that may be well warranted, as the very next paragraph begins with a sign of fictionalized framing: "Our hero waited on his benefactor next morning" ("Hugh Kelly," Nov. 338).

Nevertheless, it is with the last stage of the Cooke—"Memoirs" accounts of the beginning of Hugh Kelly's career in journalism that we can begin to provide at least some measure of external supporting evidence. We can attempt to reconstruct Kelly's career at this point with some measure of independence from the contemporary narratives and can take issue with these sources when they can be shown to be either erroneous or problematic. Thompson asserts, for instance, that Kelly, "in 1762, became the Editor of the *Lady's Museum*, the *Court Magazine*, and other periodical publications" ("Life" v), but this assertion can be shown to be inaccurate by simply recalling that the *Museum* ran from March 1760 to January 1761.

Other problems involving the chronology of Kelly's early work in journalism, however, are not so easily resolved. The meeting with Say and the subsequent work for the *Gazetteer* are presented as the beginning of Kelly's London career, but hard evidence of the sort that could be obtained only by examining the paper for the years 1760–61 is impossible to obtain because there are few numbers of the paper extant before July 1762. I am inclined to accept the claim made by Cooke and the *Town and Country* "Memoirs" author that Kelly first worked for Say's *Gazetteer* because of the specific evidence presented in their narratives, but because Kelly's labors for this paper definitely continued through 1762 while the *Lady's Museum* ceased publication with its January 1761 number, it is with this latter journal that my discussion needs to begin.

Early Magazine Journalism: Lessons and Directions

Nearly all contemporary biographical accounts of Kelly's life mention his work on Charlotte Lennox's *Lady's Museum*, but no Kelly or Lennox scholar has been able to decide the degree of Kelly's participation, and conjectures about his specific contributions seem hazardous, lacking as we do any sort of external evidence and no previous examples of Kelly's writing to form a basis for comparison. One commentator has noted that the "Trifler" essays in the *Museum* were probably Kelly's, as he reprinted some of them two years later when he was editing the *Court Magazine* from 1761 to 1765 (O'Leary 27), but a comparison between the two series reveals that they shared a title only, the contents being entirely different (see Bataille, "Hugh Kelly's Journalism"). Thus, despite the listing of Kelly by some bibliographies as coeditor, because he was newly arrived in London when the magazine was first published and probably but twenty or twenty-one years old with no experience in journalism, it is doubtful that Kelly did much more than follow Lennox's directions.

Still, the claim that Kelly played a part in the *Museum* persists even today. Duncan Isles, in a study of Lennox's letters, notes that the 1760–61 period produced no professional correspondence and maintains that this absence of correspondence "may perhaps be explained by, or give support to, the already-attractive hypothesis that Mrs. Lennox's editorship of *The Lady's Museum* was titular, the day-to-day organization being conducted by Hugh Kelly" (323). But that "organization" most probably did not include much writing of the actual material that formed the contents of the magazine.

We may infer the value to Kelly of this work on behalf of the *Museum*. Apart from introducing him to the general problems associated with editing periodicals, his work for the *Museum* was valuable as an object lesson in what *not* to do if one wanted to produce a successful, long-running periodical with broad appeal. No doubt Kelly learned that a variety of material was needed to attract the kind of large audience necessary to ensure a magazine's existence during the 1760s, a time when competition between magazines, both new and old, was severe.[6] The *Museum,* which never numbered more than nine different items per issue, was hardly in a position to achieve that kind of variety. Brevity is a corollary of variety; yet too many of the *Museum's* prose pieces ran as multi-issue features, and even those that did not were often six, seven, or more pages in length, far greater than the average length of items in other periodicals of the 1760s.[7] Finally, Kelly learned that magazines were popular-culture vehicles that, in order to be successful, had to become what Herbert Gans has called user centered (see Gans 70), certainly more so than the *Museum* ever was.[8] That need meant, among other things, that a periodical had to respond to its own milieu, to reflect its own times, but the *Museum* failed to be timely in any consistent fashion. In fact, only the June 1760 issue contained any reference at all to contemporary events; in this issue were two letters referring to the trial and execution of Earl Ferrers for murder. Kelly, when he began to edit the *Court Magazine* in late 1761, produced a product far different in format from the *Museum.*

Kelly's editorship of Israel Pottinger's *Court Magazine* (Sept. 1761–Nov. 1765) is mentioned in all contemporaneous biographical accounts. In addition, there is substantial internal evidence that Kelly wrote for this magazine: a number of items, mainly poems, are signed "H. K." and other poems, not signed, appear in the *Court* and then are later identified as Kelly's by his editor and biographer, Capt. Edward Thompson, in the collected *Works.* It is probable that Kelly edited the *Court* from its inception until its final number. Throughout the four years of its existence, the content and format remained remarkably consistent even for a medium where consistency was not unusual: the domestic moral tales, the essays of advice to young women, and the occasional pieces about journalism and the plight of the journalist are sprinkled throughout the run of the magazine and bear the stamp of Kelly's tone and values. The didactic material, in particular, he wrote using the same themes and genres (the framed tale with middle-class, urban-humor characters was one of these genres) that he also employed while conducting his essay series, "The Babler," which for the first two years of its life, 1763–65, coincided with the publication of the *Court.* In fact, there are numerous reprints of individual "Babler" essays in the *Court* beginning in the April 1764 number of the magazine and continuing intermittently until the journal ceased publication. Then, too, the interest in dramatic criticism found in a regular column called the "Green Room" strongly suggests Kelly's hand, as drama and dramatic criticism were two of his sustained interests.

Modern commentators have not had much to say about the *Court,* although they have selected different aspects of the magazine to emphasize. Walter Graham simply notes that it is "worthy of remark chiefly because of its theatrical department called the 'Green Room'" (178); while Alison Adburgham, writing from a feminist perspective, calls the *Court* a woman's magazine (264), presumably because of the large number of items dealing with courtship, marriage, and general domestic conduct. Even Kelly specialists have not felt it necessary to examine the periodical very carefully. William Watt sees it as important only insofar as it looks forward to Kelly's career as a playwright; he comments on the poetry and fiction Kelly wrote for the magazine, particularly examining the elegies, but views the poems as important only "as the young Journalist's first steps in the realm of the sentimental Muse" (13). Even the theatrical criticism—an interest that was eventually to lead Kelly to compose *Thespis* (the poetic satire in imitation of the *Rosciad* by Charles Churchill), which first gained Kelly literary notice and attracted the attention of Garrick—does not receive much analysis. William Watt only mentions that the "Green Room" looks at drama with the same moral tone that Kelly later exhibited in his plays (17). Watt does make one observation that is of importance in light of the charges that later in his career Kelly was always puffing Garrick and Drury Lane: he notes that in the *Court* Kelly had not "yet begun the humble vein of flattery and hero worship" toward Garrick but rather cautioned the public against Garrick idolatry (W. W. Watt 30).

One possible reason Kelly had not begun to flatter Garrick in his *Court Magazine* reviews could well have been because of the magazine's printer, Israel Pottinger, whose house is not listed by Plomer but who was working at the sign of the Royal Bible on Ave-Maria Lane in September 1761 when the *Court* was first published.[9] Pottinger was also a sometime playwright who led for a short period of time a group of writers who were antagonistic to Garrick (Stone and Kahrl 343). Cooke reports that Kelly later in life told many "pleasant Anecdotes" of Pottinger and suggests that the two men got along well ("Hugh Kelly," Nov. 339), but even Cooke does not associate Pottinger with the *Court Magazine*.

My focus in studying the *Court Magazine* is twofold. First, I examine how Kelly attempted to attract and hold his women readers, saving an analysis of his general inscription of a middle-class audience for chapter 2, where I focus on "The Babler" essay series. Second, I am also concerned with the microview of the practices of the journalist that the magazine provides. In "The Babler," Kelly was to bring a somewhat broader perspective to his musings and stories about the writer; his "Babler" pieces on writing are more reflective and often attempt a larger view of the professional writer's social situatedness. On the other hand, in most of the self-reflexive journalistic pieces in the *Court,* the focus is on the nuts and bolts of the practicing journalist, and in these pieces Kelly's persona seems most eager to expose—even to boast about—the textual practices of periodical writers.

Surveying the entire run of the *Court Magazine* from September 1761 until November 1765, we view Kelly attempting to attract a female audience through a selection of materials appealing to what he felt were its taste and interests. Over the fifty-month period, the magazine published some two hundred thirty-five major essays and pieces of short fiction. Of this total, some twenty items dealt at least in part with sex or with sexual morality; another twenty depicted husband-wife relationships; and about nine pieces featured concerns we should today identify as feminist in nature. These last included attacks on the parent and, especially, the father who refuses to allow his daughter to marry a man of her own selection or forces her to marry against her will (Dec. 1761, 161–64; Dec. 1764, 487–89) and advice on sensitive marital conduct provided young men by an older woman (Dec. 1764, 505–6). Another thirty items were concerned with parenting and the idea of the family; and thirty-four pieces had to do in some respect with marriage itself. Even after allowing for some overlapping—certain items dealt with more than one subject and hence can be classified under two categories— what remains is a large body of material centered on what would have been traditionally seen as the interests of the female reader. This was an important achievement in the 1760s before magazines intended mainly or exclusively for women had firmly established themselves and when dual-audience publications tried to appeal to both sexes, usually to the neglect of women's interests.[10]

That this appeal to women readers, long lasting as it was, must have been a self-conscious strategy seems evident. Just as self-conscious were Kelly's attempts, sometimes serious and sometimes comic, to explore the practices of journalism. The terms *journalist* and *journalism* were but rarely employed in eighteenth-century British discourse about periodicals and periodical writers: the *OED* records the first appearance of either term in 1710 and notes no further use, although Kelly himself used the term *journalist* in the *Court*. Joseph Addison preferred the term *periodical author,* which occurs in the *Freeholder* (no. 45, 1716); but even *editor,* meaning one who conducted a newspaper or other periodical, was not often employed, and the general term *author* was used instead. Even as late as the 1770s, letters addressed to newspapers were much more often directed to the papers' printers than they were to their editors. Part of the reason journalism discourse had not developed its own distinct vocabulary by the time Kelly began to write in the 1760s, despite the fact that the century was in many ways the first great age of journalism, can doubtless be found in the low status accorded the occupation and those who pursued it. (The details of the status of the journalist need not concern us now but are taken up in chapter 2.) Students of the age are familiar with the Grub Street myth, invented primarily by Jonathan Swift and Alexander Pope and carried on through the century often by the very people, Kelly among them, who were themselves earning a living from journalism.[11] Another reason that journalism discourse had not developed its own vocabulary can perhaps be found in the blurred distinction between it and other forms of writing, including fiction itself, as Lennard J. Davis has recently shown in his concept of the news-novel discourse. This blurring is suggested by the prevalence of the omnibus term *author,* which appears everywhere in journalism discourse and is surely reinforced by many of the century's finest writers' continuing to produce journalism throughout their careers. Still, in writing about the life of an author, these very writers did not accord the periodical author much status. If, as Charles Knight maintains, Johnson attempted to develop an image of the writer as hero in some of his journalism ("Writer"), and if, as Edward Bloom notes, Johnson often protested against the poor rewards accorded writers *(Samuel Johnson)*, he nevertheless pointed to the large number of those whom he considered to be incompetent to write and thus reinforced the Grub Street myth.[12]

Kelly's view of journalism comes from a perspective somewhat different from Johnson's. Instead of looking down from Olympian heights upon the hordes of Grub-Streeters and condemning their existence, he presents a microview that brings into detailed focus the rough-and-tumble world of midcentury periodical writing. During the first six months of the *Court Magazine*'s existence, Kelly devoted five pieces to the subject of journalists and journalism, omitting only September, the first month of publication. In a tone composed partly of self-mockery and partly of bravado, Kelly's persona in these pieces develops an insider's view of the profession. Functioning almost as exposés, these essays highlight the more scandalous practices of the journalist, noting some of the tricks employed by hack writers in gathering and preparing material for the periodical press. In an October 1761 piece, framed as so many of Kelly's essays were by a letter to the editor, the persona writes first of his experience ("I have wrought for several magazine-shops . . .") and of his reputation before writing of his sources and methods of operation:

> Once a week I change cloaths, whip to the Bedford, assemble with the wits, and deliver my opinion with as much confidence as the best of them. Very often I converse with some of the principal actors of either house, and am generally once a season admitted into that *sanctum sanctorum* of the playhouse, the green-room. An humble bottle of port will entitle me to a room at the Shakespear; I am respected by the waiters, saluted by the master, and distinguished by the appellation of the captain, or his honour, by every chairman round the garden. By this means, I am become acquainted with the most necessary articles of magazine—intelligence; the cabals of politicians, the disputes of wits, the wrangling of authors, and the secrets of the theatres. (68–70)

This reductionist view creates some self-satire, but there is also some literal truth to this broad outline of a journalist's ritualistic procedures and his patronizing of his sources. Kelly engages in a gentle self-mockery here, but what is described other than the processes of interviewing and information gathering, what we today should view as the basic operations of the investigative—or at least diligent—reporter? Somewhat ironically, Kelly has also pinpointed the three areas on which much of his own future newspaper journalism for the *Public Ledger* and the *General Evening Post* would focus: politics, literature, and the theater. And contesting the satirical tone is a contrary one that almost demands the reader be impressed with the professional skill involved in such journalistic success and with the mind who can reduce all this necessary professional effort to a formula he self-reflexively articulates.

In November's number, Kelly complains about the entire profession of writing, considering the "republic of letters as a commercial state" and viewing the "different professions as a kind of mechanics" (Nov. 1761, 122). The major evil in the profession he ascribes to the author-bookseller relationship: writing has little merit because the "principal consideration of both the author and the bookseller" is "quantity, and not the quality of the work." It is difficult to decide how much of this piece is lament and how much boast. But if we look at these journalism essays as somehow both an embrace and a satire of this emergent discipline, then we see Kelly expressing the attitude that several modern critics perceive in his stance toward sentimental drama: that is, he simultaneously practices it and mocks it. Additionally, it is problematic whether such a stance is meant to keep others from the field (and hence is to be seen as a kind of "gatekeeping") or whether it is merely Kelly's version of the ritualistic attack on Grub Street leveled many times since Pope's *Dunciad,* an attack that was expected to view commercial writing as venal, crude, and formulaic.[13]

The final piece of self-reflexive writing about journalism in the *Court Magazine* that I consider here concerns the receipt for success that "Tom Tell-Truth," one of the "most considerable news-paper authors in town," details in the January 1762 issue. It might arguably be entitled The Art of Sinking in Journalism. Reminiscent of the October piece's "insider's" view of the magazine writer, this letter to the author of the *Court* outlines the strategies used by Tom during his forty-three years' practice in "periodical literature" (209). First, he maintains, "I abuse every other paper, and positively assert, that there is not a single grain of understanding to be found in any but that which I am immediately concerned in" (209). The second strategy is to write letters to himself from fictitious sources:

> If the mails should happen to be delayed . . . , I receive a private letter written with my own *proper manner,* from an officer in the army, or a lieutenant aboard a man of war; and, from the very situation of affairs, draw some probable relation, which is gulped down with the greatest avidity by the unthinking multitude. (209)

The third ploy focuses on the manufacturing of news events, for which he commands a "maker of paragraphs to draw up occasional *good things,* in a manner so natural, that the most piercing eye can never discover the fallacy" (209). He then relates one of these pseudoevents and the effects of its publication. The event concerned a porter eating beefsteaks in competition with a butcher's dog; the porter beat the dog by "several mouthfuls." The writer claims that the readers of the paper thought the incident true because it appeared in the *Gazetteer,* "which was the principal reason why they should not believe a single syllable of it" (209). In this context, the writer also mentions the fabrications of duels, false advertising for nonexistent items, and love affairs that make up other fictional elements of a newspaper.

Kelly wrote other essays and letters on the life of the journalist for the *Court Magazine*. In the May 1764 issue, for instance, there is a piece on the hardships of a periodical writer seeking work; and in the February 1762 number, there is a lament on the sorry state of magazine journalists, especially reviewers. But after mid-1762, these pieces become much less frequent, although he would write self-reflexive pieces on the life of writing for "The Babler" that take a broader perspective than those in the *Court* did. Perhaps the note of self-exposure we feel emanating from these *Court* satires was due in part to the scorn the young Kelly, still a poorly compensated novice, felt for the entire Grub Street world. Editor or not, it is not likely that Kelly was paid much for his work on the *Court,* and in order to survive he worked for more than one periodical during a number of years in the 1760s. But as Kelly became more centrally connected to the world of London journalism and began to write for the *Gazetteer* and to establish "The Babler" series, he perhaps thought better of exposing its methods of operation, methods on which he was now so dependent for his livelihood. Nevertheless, taken together, Kelly's essays and letters about journalism in the *Court* during 1761 and 1762 make up a most revealing and detailed source of information about how the entire field conducted its work and furthermore provide a view of the complex feelings of ambivalence that many reflective journalists must have harbored at the time.

What then did the experience of writing for and editing the *Court Magazine* mean for Hugh Kelly? As William Watt has noted, it provided him the opportunity to discover some of the themes and concerns that he was later to develop in his drama, although the writing of sentimental tales and elegies was hardly unique to Kelly; a number of periodicals in the 1760s were printing much the same fare. Then, too, the theatrical criticism of the "Green Room" section, despite appearing only sporadically after the fall of 1762 and often containing little more than a calendar of play dates, shows the same moral preoccupation that the fiction and poetry did.[14] The column's concern with the actors and actresses deserves noting; on many occasions—the February 1763 review of Frances Sheridan's *Discovery* is a case in point—the "Green Room" reviews assess the quality of the acting rather than comment extensively on the drama itself. This emphasis certainly prepared Kelly to compare critically the players in his important poem, the satirical *Thespis,* which upon appearing suddenly in November 1766 plunged Kelly into the midst of London theatrical politics from which he really never escaped.

2

Newspaperman and Essayist:
The *Gazetteer* and "The Babler"

I
t is not clear why the *Court Magazine* ceased publication in November 1765;
but even while editing this magazine, Kelly continued to have other journalistic employment. One such position had Kelly supplying Charles Say's
Gazetteer with news paragraphs probably a few months after Kelly's arrival in
London during the spring of 1760. Alexander Andrews, the mid-nineteenth-
century historian of journalism, went so far as to suggest that Kelly had a specific contract to supply news to Say, and certainly the Cooke anecdote noted in
chapter 1 concerning Kelly and Say would seem to support Andrews's contention (Andrews 1: 220; Cooke, "Hugh Kelly," Nov. 338). A modern student of
the *Gazetteer*, Robert Haig, has even stated that Kelly, along with John Almon,
furnished the Say paper with essays about politics and manners couched in a
favorite Kelly mode, the familiar letter-to-the-editor form (71), but unfortunately so few numbers of the paper exist for the 1760–61 period that verifica-
tion of these claims seem impossible.

The first evidence of Kelly's work on the *Gazetteer* from the extant numbers
of the paper occurs in early August 1762 and consists of three poems by Kelly
that appeared in the *Gazetteer* on 4 August, 9 August, and 10 August entitled,
respectively, "Epistle from a Lady in the Country," "Spatter's Rambles," and
"Flavella to Beverley, An Epistle from the Country," but few additional attributions are possible.[1] This is unfortunate because were we to know more about
the nature of his contributions to this newspaper—as we know, for example, of
his efforts on behalf of the *Court Magazine* during the same period—we would
be in a better position to judge what Kelly learned from the *Gazetteer* experience that enabled him by 1765 to become editor of the *Public Ledger*, one of
the most prominent pro-Court newspapers of the 1760s. His work for this paper brought Kelly into the Wilkite conflicts on the eve of the American Revolution. Surely Kelly wrote more than just some occasional poetry for the Say
paper—we have a hint of more from Haig's comment about the political es-

says—and it was probably here and not with the *Court*, which contains little political material, that Kelly cut his political journalist's teeth.

While editing the *Court Magazine* and presumably still writing for the *Gazetteer*, Kelly began yet another journalistic effort on 12 February 1763. On that day appeared in *Owen's Weekly Chronicle* the first number of what was his most successful and certainly his most sustained journalism. "The Babler" essay series continued to be published every Saturday until 5 June 1767, its run of some four years and three months making it one of the longest-lived series in the century. When this series was finally concluded and published in book form as *The Babler* by John Newbery in 1767, it contained 123 numbers, or only a little over one-half of what had probably been the original total of approximately 220, assuming that one number was published each week during the series' existence.[2] Much of "The Babler" series will be familiar to students of the *Tatler–Spectator* tradition.[3] But Kelly does not slavishly imitate his predecessors; he slants his advice much more toward the middle-class, urban, merchant audience than those before him had done and explores domestic life with a homey realism, including an implicit acknowledgment of what his audience needs to learn in order to rise in the world, not always found in this genre. This realism, combined with a candid treatment of sexual morality and a self-conscious, self-reflexive treatment of the life of the journalist, makes "The Babler" essays worth a modem reader's attention.

That Kelly reprinted many numbers of "The Babler" in both the *Court Magazine* and the *Public Ledger* suggests that he had a certain fondness for this essay series. That in book form the series went through four and possibly five editions before the end of the century and that at least some numbers were being reprinted by American magazines as late as 1790 argue a degree of general popularity.[4] One modern Kelly scholar, O'Leary, even claims that "The Babler" may have had additional circulation in the form of individual half-sheets distributed to London clubs. O'Leary relies on a letter to the editor of the *Public Ledger* written by "Crazy Grub" (O'Leary 29, note 63). As this letter is a puff for the entire "Babler" series and may have been written by Kelly, the claims it makes for the half-sheet distribution (as well as the claims for the series' enormous popularity) ought to be received with skepticism.[5]

That Kelly owed much to Joseph Addison and Sir Richard Steele in his overall conception of "The Babler" seems clear.[6] Structurally, Kelly employs the letter-to-the-editor formula used by Addison and Steele and also borrows the extended or composite eidolon of Mr. Spectator and his Club. But with a more focused concentration on domestic life than used by Addison and Steele, Kelly creates a fictional family rather than a social club; these family characters consist of Mr. Babler himself, an avuncular figure of late middle age who is the chief persona of the series; his sister, Mrs. Rattle; and her son and key example of the younger generation, Harry Rattle. Other related characters are occasionally introduced to create what may perhaps be best called a neighborhood community. Two of the most important are Richard Bumper, a libertine who eventually reforms, and Cornelia Marchmont, a model young woman who eventually is to marry Harry Rattle. The family image here created by Kelly seems to resemble that new affectional family that Lawrence Stone finds developing in the later part of the eighteenth century (413–14). Certainly the family members in "The Babler" exhibit an emotional commitment to each other; there is additionally less patriarchal domination (gentleness is indeed one of Mr. Babler's key traits) and a clear concern for the children and their needs. Stone also notes that, with the new affectional family as it developed among the urban middle classes, there was some loss of the "intrusive and inquisitorial function of village or parish community" (246). However, with Kelly's attempt to bring neighbors into his admittedly urban-family context, he may be seen to maintain some semblance of rural ethos by importing village-community values into his city setting.[7]

From the essay-series tradition, Kelly also takes the humor names endemic to "The Babler"; names such as Frank Surly, Tom Giddy, Ned Headstrong, and the like abound. The comic humor names, to an extent, distance the reader from the characters and prevent their realistic problems from becoming overbearingly heavy. Then, too, Kelly's sentimental morality doubtless owes something to the *Tatler–Spectator* example, as do some of his subjects and thematic concerns, among them the issues of dueling, proper dress, and affable temperament. But by and large, Kelly sets his own agenda in "The Babler," an agenda much narrower in focus than those of his predecessors. Foremost, Kelly is concerned with domestic manners and morals, particularly with regard to courtship, marital relationships, and the training of children. This agenda is focused on a middle-class, urban, merchant audience, the class most frequently inscribed through the essays' characters.[8] Finally, as in the *Court Magazine,* Kelly carries on his self-reflexive discourse about journalists and journalism.

Of the 123 "Babler" essays that were reprinted in the 1767 edition, twenty-one treat in some fashion marriage and courtship, while another seven deal explicitly with the related subject of sexual morality. Kelly's ideas here, though hardly original, illustrate not only his view of the importance of what Lawrence Stone has called the companionate marriage but also show how Kelly feels he can best serve his middle-class audience by consistently dwelling, more than Addison and Steele ever did, on those institutions of family and marriage that so dominated that audience's moral universe.[9] One idea constantly reinforced is that marriage for love ought to govern in all cases and that the marriage of convenience is doomed; this stance emerges in the second "Babler" and is repeated in several subsequent numbers where winter-spring alliances are criticized (in nos. 15, 16, 26, and 40). In otherwise urging filial obedience, however (as in nos. 83 and 84), Kelly seems to complicate his stance against marriage undertaken for any reason but love because obviously to marry in obedience to one's parents may also compel one to marry for reasons other than affection.

We may explain this contradiction by simply deciding not to expect either deep or consistent thinking from a harried Grub-Streeter, but generally popular periodicals—indeed all popular-culture vehicles—attempt to flatter all sides on a particular issue, especially in major conflicts over manners, perhaps counting on the serial nature of their publications to disguise the contradiction, hiding it from their audiences. This is not the place to document how popular culture performs propaganda functions, but a similar pattern can be noticed, for instance, in the way many magazines of the 1760s and 1770s treated those issues that we should call feminist or prefeminist today.[10]

Kelly's sexual morality is reformist, and he clearly exemplifies what Barker-Benfield has described as the attack on "hard" male culture that was central to sensibility (239–48). Kelly assails the double standard practiced by predatory males. In no. 54, for instance, the family frame is established, as in the eidolon itself, so that the attack on the double standard is presented in the context of another Kelly concern—the education of children:

> I have frequently remarked what a degree of nicety is requisite in the education of young women; and delivered it, as my opinion, that those parents were very fortunate, who, from the sex of their children, had none of the various consequences to apprehend, which the least indiscretion in the ladies is constantly sure of bringing on a family. I have said that the same levity of conduct which would steep a woman in the grossest lees [sic] infamy, is entirely overlooked, if not publicly approved, in a man; and that the meerest circumstance of sex gives him a kind of privilege to practice a number of irregularities, that would render an uncultivated female the scandal of society. (*Babler,* Harrison 82)

Kelly goes on in this number to attack male sexual license, as he will in his novel *Memoirs of a Magdalen,* calling it the "depravity of custom," and reprints a supposed journal of a libertine to show how the double standard produces a life that is "nothing but a repetition of cruelty and lust" (84). In no. 56, Kelly reprints a letter to a rakish colonel from a woman who assails him for his presumption and vanity in assuming that she would be flattered into a liaison with him merely because of his military rank. She concludes by telling him that she will remain a dutiful daughter and resist all such solicitations. In yet another "Babler," no. 43, a guilty libertine expresses remorse at having seduced a tenant's daughter; happily, he has reformed (the converted rake is to make his appearance in more than one Kelly play), married his victim, and now cautions others about careless passion. It is only to be expected that an author whose plays are later to be both praised and attacked for their sentimental ethos should attack the libertine creed; and with regard to sexual morality in general, Kelly maintains throughout his writing career a consistent commitment to male reform.

That Kelly consciously sought to make clear his audience and his purposes is made obvious by framing devices. In "Babler" no. 41, he has a letter simply begin, "Seeing a variety of letters in your entertaining paper from husbands and wives, I have taken the liberty of adding to the number of your matrimonial correspondents" (62). In no. 7, Mr. Babler himself introduces a letter: "The subject of my correspondent's letter in a former number, has procured me a very sensible complaint from an honest buckle-maker near Cornhill" (14). Nor is Kelly above reminding his audience of the image he expects them to perceive in his eidolon; in a letter that constitutes no. 35, the writer begins:

> You seem a friendly good-natured sort of a man; and I have often heard my grandson repeat, with a great deal of satisfaction, many pretty things out of your writings; and Tom, though I say it, is a very sensible lad, has been three years at a Latin school, and is, moreover, as dutiful a child as any in England. (54)

It is as if the "Babler" readership were all one large, extended family of middle-class citizens situated in real neighborhoods throughout London. This attempt to construct an in-text audience, a virtual community, occupying recognizable space in real time, enhances the entire series' verisimilitude and hence its authenticity with its actual audience.

Recent work by Charles Knight and by Michael G. Ketcham has described from different vantage points how the *Spectator* achieved a similar intimacy with its audience through spatial relationships in which, for example, the coffeehouse and its clientele in Knight's view become the important focus of audience identification ("Bibliography" 242–43). Knight usefully suggests that the work spoke to the audience about itself, and this important gesture, I would repeat, is simply another kind of the necessary audience flattery I have already noted as central to the success of the popular-culture writer-propagandist. Kelly attempted to create the kind of environment that Addison did, where spatial familiarity bred an intimacy between eidolon and audience. But in Kelly, instead of the coffeehouse, it is the atmosphere of the middle-class home and neighborhood (*neighborhood* is a word used extensively in "The Babler"); his space is thus more intimate and less public than that of Addison, and it is an atmosphere appropriate to the domestic thrust of sensibility's didacticism.

What Kelly accomplishes is unlike the defamiliarization that the Marxist formalists found so valuable in Jonathan Swift and Laurence Sterne. That is, instead of making the familiar strange, Kelly is refamiliarizing his middle-class audience with their world not only in hopes of gaining their readership by flattering that world through a recreation of it but also by regularizing their recourse to print by making it less foreign to them through habituation. That is why, I suggest, so many of the "Babler" essays are framed with reference to family members in a domestic setting—"My nephew Harry called on me this morning" (*Babler* no. 56, Harrison 86) and "I was sitting at home the other morning ruminating on a subject for my next paper, when the penny-post-man stopped at the door" (no. 57, 87). It is this consistent attempt at constructing domestic realism (despite its orality—the "surrogate of space," in Knight's phrase ["Bibliography" 240]) that some have seen as looking back to the qualities of pre-print culture (240) and that reminds one of the connections between jour-nalism and the novel recently pointed out by Lennard Davis.[11] In addition, the site of these essays is clearly a domestic one; if, as I have suggested, Kelly was in sympathy with the reformist nature of sensibility, then it is clear why he would prefer to situate his males at home rather than in the coffeehouse or tavern. These public sites would merely recall the old public culture of the hard male, but it was part of Kelly's agenda to attract males to domesticity.[12]

The Rattle family is the collective eidolon Kelly employs as a first step in creating intimacy, and the family image is one of the chief strategies Kelly uses to inscribe his audience. That image is strengthened on those occasions when one of the Rattles is not the narrator and Kelly instead employs a letter-to-the-editor framing device written by a character who nevertheless identifies herself as a member of yet another family who reads the series faithfully. Kelly thus moves out from the "Babler" family to the local community, which can be dem-onstrated by examining "Babler" no. 3 (*Babler,* Harrison 8–9). Here a letter written by Winifred Tapely is the central narrative. Mrs. Tapely writes to com-plain about her fashionable husband (a haberdasher) who instead of paying at-tention to his business talks to his customers of operas and plays. He will not disturb his dinner even if a customer enters his shop, refusing to inconvenience himself in the slightest manner. In addition, he has recently purchased an ex-pensive house just to go riding in a fashionable neighborhood on Sundays. "'Pray, Mr. Babler,' Mrs. Tapely concludes, 'print this letter: your writings are much read in our neighborhood; and my husband condescends to say you are a very sen-sible fellow.'"

Reading Kelly, one is reminded of Walter Ong's statement that a writer's audience is always a fiction. And certainly Kelly, in a very specific sense, may be said to imagine, to inscribe, or to write his audience. But if he does so, he cre-ates this specific fictional readership only to mirror and thus to attract that very audience as readers; these he desires as real readers, not as ideal ones. Perhaps one of the values of an audience analysis of journalism like Kelly's is to remind us that there *are* often specific audiences for texts, audiences other than those ideal readers created by alienated post-eighteenth-century writers hostile to "real" audiences. Even in the eighteenth century, the completely imagined, fully ide-alized reader constructed by a Henry Fielding or by a Sterne, existing nowhere but in the text, can be compared to the empirically constructed audience who receives a modern business communication. Kelly's situation is possibly best seen as somewhere between these polarities of ideal and empirical audiences. His audience is both invented and real, both in the text and out of it, and "The Babler" itself is situated between the elite artist's creator-centered fictions and the popular writer's audience-centered persuasions.

Finally, in "The Babler," Kelly maintains the conversation on writing that he began with his *Court Magazine* essays about journalism and the journalist. Even in the preface to the collected *Babler*, Kelly touches upon the particular problem of the "news-paper writer"; here he compares his own work, which appeared first in a newspaper *(Owen's Weekly Chronicle)* and not as a separate publication, to other essay series. He is aware of his form's limitations and traditions: "Small as the boundaries of a *Spectator*, a *Rambler*, a *World*, an *Adventurer*, or a *Connoisseur*, may seem, the news-paper writer is under a necessity of moving in a still more contracted circle" *(Babler*, Harrison i). Kelly later claims in this preface that the reason so many of his essays are couched in "little histories" rather than in "regular argument" is that he is at the mercy of a printer, who

> does not so much consider the importance of a writer's subject, as the immediate profit of the partners; it is not the improvement of the reader which he consults, but the interest of the paper, or the topic of the day, and therefore often stints the essayist in room, to advertise a parcel of stolen goods, or to epitomize the trial of some remarkable murderer. (iii)

Here and elsewhere in his self-conscious discussions of the periodical writer, Kelly exhibits his understanding of what happens to the professional writer in the middle of the eighteenth century as he participates in what Alvin Kernan has recently called the beginning of the "print culture" (49).[13] Aware of the writer's new master, the marketplace, Kelly realizes the economic complexities of periodical publishing and how those complexities affect, in turn, not only his work space, as we saw above, but even choices of mode and genre. He points out specifically in this preface that he was forced to compose narratives ("little histories") when he would have preferred to employ argumentation.

It is worth noting, too, Kelly's address to his audience, always a point of attention to him. Aware that in the new economic order of print the writer owed allegiance first to his readers—his consumers—Kelly asks for his readers' indulgence, claiming that "tenderness in criticism is the next virtue to generosity," and that he "shall scarcely feel a greater share of gratitude for those, who kindly discover any little merit in the following Essays, than for those who benevolently overlook their numerous imperfections" *(Babler*, Harrison iv). Although the tone here may be too imploring, perhaps in consideration of Kelly's historical and rhetorical situation, one should view his attitude as the stance of the humble professional writer who knows he must please his new patrons, the audience who buys his wares. Of this new situatedness of the writer in the middle of the century, Kernan has this to say about Samuel Johnson, who lived out, in an intense and dramatic manner, the social mutation of writers from an earlier role as gentlemen-amateurs to a new authorial self based on the realities of print and its conditions of mechanical reproduction. His struggle to create dignity for himself and his writing in new economic conditions that tended to make the writer only a paid worker in the print factory, and his work only a commodity . . . shows in the most immediate terms the power of technology over life and belief, even as it dramatizes human resistance to absolute mechanical determinism. (5–6)[14]

Kelly also inhabited this world, yet his attitude was certainly different from Johnson's, at least Kernan's Johnson. Certainly Kelly was aware of mechanistic aspects of his trade, for in an essay, "The Motives for Writing" (*Court Magazine,* Dec. 1761, 167–69), Kelly refers to fellow journalist Edward Purdon as a "magazine builder," and he had his fictional persona of the journalist speak of "newspaper shops."[15] Yet for the most part Kelly seemed more occupied with coming to terms with what was needed to succeed in this new world of marketplace writing than he was in lamenting its existence, and what was needed was the securement of an audience that would buy his products.

This pursuit of readership continues in the early numbers of "The Babler." In no. 3, he provides a revealing confession in which, instead of lamenting the hardships of the journalist's life as most writers similarly circumstanced would have done, he writes of his audience's gracious acceptance of his first efforts. He admits that, when he first "commenced [as a] periodical essayist," he feared he would have neither sufficient time nor sufficient material. He tells us that he

> dreamed of incessant application of pen and ink—but my apprehensions were entirely groundless. I no sooner appeared in print, than a whole army of good persons instantly drew up in my favour; amongst the rest the wife of a city man of fashion, who writes to me. (*Babler,* Harrison 8)

Kelly seems to have learned early on that popular culture survives by flattering its audience, that popular culture, which includes most journalism, is as Herbert Gans points out, user centered. It cannot be successful employing the creator-centered bias of high art but must serve the needs and purposes of its audiences. Then, too, there is the necessity to instruct his audience, and an effective way to manage this is to allow some of the audience to do the teaching themselves by contributing to the series. It is almost as if Kelly saw the virtue of self-propaganda, and his practice of encouraging his readers to contribute, although hardly original with him, foreshadows modern propaganda theory, which emphasizes audience participation as a means of cementing the relationship between an institution and its audience.[16] The theory in brief holds that the more one participates in an organization or institution, the more firmly one becomes tied and committed to that organization. Kelly seems to have understood that the more his readers participated in the very writing of "The Babler," the more loyal to the essay series they would become. The extent to which actual audience contributions were published is beside the point; what matters is that the illusion of participation was established and maintained. Certainly the modern periodical owes at least part of its successful relationship with its audience to the publication of that readership's correspondence.

In later "Babler" essays, Kelly explores the plight of the professional author once again, continuing a general theme that he first introduced in the *Court Magazine*. Living in a writing culture that produced works dealing with what might be called the "author's lament" tradition (as, for example, Johnson's *Account of the Life of Mr. Richard Savage* [1744] and James Ralph's *Case of Authors by Profession* [1758] could be said to illustrate), Kelly understood the possible situations that could enslave a writer in his time and manages in one short narrative, "Babler" no. 46, to represent these situations in the life of a single author who writes to Mr. Babler from his retirement in Derbyshire.[17] This author informs us that he began at the university to write "merely for my own amusement"; and later on, while he was supposed to be studying law, he tells us that "instead of Replies, Rejoinders, or Demurrers, I was . . . engaged in writing some whimses of my own" (*Babler*, Harrison 71). Clearly, this fictional writer began his career not in thralldom to some bookseller or patron but merely because of his, as Kernan might say, romantic self-impulse.[18]

Encouraged by the "compilers of magazines," Kelly's author "enlisted in the army of literary mercenaries" and began a life that ran him "deeper and deeper into debt":

> I was confined to my regular place of work as if I was a shoemaker or a taylor, and very often ordered to do a particular quantity in a particular time. Sometimes, Sir, I have been obliged to write a philosophical essay on Contentment, when my heart was bursting with anguish; and at others, ordered to prepare a poem on Liberty, while the bailiffs were waiting at the door. But the severest mortification of all, was the impertinent freedom with which I was treated by every ragamuffin of the press: the printer would criticise on my performances to my face, and the very devils themselves would talk to me of mistakes, and propose what they were modestly pleased to consider as amendments. (*Babler*, Harrison 71)

Here the author has become the professional Grub-Streeter, the new writer who composes on demand for a wage and who suffers because he lacks professional status. Here too is additional proof that Kelly saw the mechanistic aspects of the new market-oriented writing and lamented the loss of independence, a theme that Lance Bertelsen has noted was important to Kelly's contemporaries in the Nonsense Club.[19]

Finally, after fourteen years of what he ironically calls a "comfortable life," the author finds a kind of anachronistic refuge that adds further irony to his situation: he acquires a patron. He then reverts to the older, court-centered role of the nobleman's dependent. However, this stage of his life leaves our author even more miserable than had his earlier existence at the hands of the booksellers and magazine editors:

> [H]e expected, as an author, that I should support every absurdity he advanced in an argument; and, as a man of genius, that I should always be comical. With this view, he introduced me into all companies; but when he saw I would neither be his parasite nor his buffoon, his friendship very visibly declined: at table I was insulted with the proposal of a wager whenever I presumed to differ in opinion; and then it was instantly recollected, with a loud laugh, that authors were but seldom overburthened with money. (71)

The narrative sounds very much like a variation of the author's lament as it is found in George's story in Goldsmith's *Vicar of Wakefield* and in Mr. Wilson's tale in Fielding's *Joseph Andrews*. However Kelly may appear to condemn the old system of patronage, this narrative ends on a contradictory note, for the author concludes by maintaining that he has sent his story into "The Babler" so that the "real cause of that decline in literature, which has of late been so universally complained of in this kingdom" can be understood: "Alas, what chance have authors to be read / Whose daily writings earn their daily bread?" (72).

It is fitting that in the final "Babler," no. 123, Kelly discusses the "nature of periodical publication" (192) more directly and soberly than he had done in earlier numbers, but he in effect confines himself to the essay series itself and to the problems it presents both for author and audience. The difficulties are summed up in two phrases, which he feels typify the inexperienced journalist's attitude when beginning a series: the writer feels, says Kelly, that he will be "able to go on with an unceasing variety of subjects, and an unabating fervor of inclination" (192). Both feelings are naive, the first compelling the essayist to "enter upon numberless discussions, which require not only a general knowledge of the world, but are often repugnant to his inclination." The second feeling soon passes as the reality of the effort becomes clear and "the mind, with that lassitude which it feels in a constant application to all its other pursuits, flags under the weight of study and fatigue, and anxiously wishes to be disengaged" (192).

So far Kelly has said nothing about the subject that one would not expect to find in a last number of an essay series. Recall that Johnson, in his final essay for the *Rambler,* had complained similarly of the pressures of periodical composition: "He that condemns himself to compose on a stated day, will often bring to his task an attention dissipated, a memory embarrassed, an imagination over-whelmed, a mind distracted with anxieties" ("Rambler No. 208" 318). Then near the end, Kelly writes something surprising, especially if we are expecting more self-pitying analysis, for he claims that under these hard circumstances what keeps writers of such series producing is not the "establishment of their reputations," not the "impatience of restraint," and not even the need to maintain the "instruction of the world" (*Babler*, Harrison 192). Rather, Kelly argues that a writer keeps working in the face of difficulty because he is afraid that were he to cease, his stopping would be attributed to "a want of abilities" (192). So here expressed in the midst of all the rhetoric in "The Babler" about the pain and shame of the Grub-Streeter is the pride of the professional writer, mixed perhaps with another reminder of Kelly's personal insecurity. The pride is stated not in the Olympian tone of Johnson's—"I have seldom descended to the arts by which favour is obtained" ("Rambler No. 208" 316)—but in the direct, almost self-grudging pride of professional competence in the face of great difficulties, difficulties with which other authors do not have to contend:

> There is scarcely a walk of literature which is reckoned so easy, or which in fact is so difficult, as this species of periodical publication. In every other stile [*sic*] of composition, a writer may display his abilities on that particular subject with which he is most intimately acquainted, and may raise a considerable share of character by expatiating on such topics as are most immediately agreeable to his imagination; besides this, he may allow himself what time he thinks proper for the perfection of his works; and is never confined by a want of room, from delivering himself fully upon the minutest point of speculation. (*Babler*, Harrison 192)

Clearly Kelly means to support the dignity of the journalist in this final "Babler," no easy task as Kernan has noted in his discussion of Samuel Derrick, Thomas Floyd, and Samuel Johnson's friend, Savage; these writers, Kernan contends, attempted to maintain something of an aristocratic, courtly tradition of gentle-man-writer for themselves while Johnson created the role of the author for himself. The Kelly of "The Babler" never attempted to pretend he was one of those whom Kernan calls "gentleman-authors"; rather more like Johnson, Kelly sought to participate "fully in the life of the laborer in the print factory" (*Babler*, Harrison 78). Like Johnson, Kelly wishes to obtain some respect for his occupation; such respect can be had, if the evidence from "The Babler" is persuasive, only through an appreciation of the journalist's efforts and conditions of work by his new patron, the audience of readers for which he writes. This desire for respect represents something of a shift from his earlier attitude expressed in the *Court Magazine*, when dignity did not seem to matter so much; it is not clear to me whether this represents a definite shift in professional attitude or whether it is merely the effect of ideological contradiction. Kelly concludes his defense of the periodical writer by noting that

> a reader who does not consider how an essayist is circumstanced, will often have opportunity to animadvert upon his productions with the greatest severity; he will find many subjects handled with little knowledge, and others discussed with less force: his good-nature must therefore mitigate the harshness of his criticism; and he must never pronounce upon the work without considering the situation of the author. (*Babler* no. 123, Harrison 192)

Thus does Kelly end "The Babler" with a discussion of the nature of journalism and the journalist. He concludes on the same note of intimacy and candor with the reader as he began. Kelly's attempt to create a sense of community with the reader through an explanation of how the journalist works stands as one of his most notable achievements in "The Babler."

Because of running commentary on the condition of the journalist in "The Babler," Kelly's reflexivity about the writing processes of the periodical author situates him in the eighteenth-century conversation about the profession of authorship. Knight notes that, in making the coffeehouse central to the *Spectator,* Addison in effect speaks to his audience about itself ("Bibliography" 242), but an equally important aspect of that paper's reflexivity, it seems to me, is its commentary about the life of the writer, particularly the life of the periodical writer. Addison, in focusing on the need of every popular-culture artist to cultivate his or her audience in *Spectator* 124, notes how the journalist "must immediately fall" into his subject and "treat every part of it in a lively manner" or risk having his paper "thrown by as dull and insipid" (Addison 505–8). Yet elsewhere, as Edward Bloom has noted, Addison as a journalist did not seem too concerned with his audience but "looked to those authors who strove for and achieved an importance beyond time and place, who found within themselves the talent of universality which he associated with the classical tradition" ("Joseph Addison" 23). Kelly, on the other hand, in his treatment of the periodical writer and his own time always defended modernity and the modern writer instead of looking to the classical tradition, a tradition that many of his middle-class readers would not have identified with. As we saw in the final "Babler," Kelly does not seek any safe harbor in a classical tradition but rather wants the periodical writer to be accepted and understood in his own time and on his own terms.

In his conception of his profession, Kelly is closer to Johnson than he is to any earlier writer in the periodical tradition, for like Johnson, Kelly views the journalist as something like an intellectual worker. Yet there can be little doubt that Kelly had misgivings about remaining a mere periodical writer; despite his sometimes sympathetic view of the journalist's conflicts and tensions, as seen in the last "Babler," there remains the comic, somewhat ironic tone of his self-reflexivity to the extent that the journalist, as was evident in no. 46, is always ultimately seen as a victim, as a passive creature controlled and insulted by others, including ironically "every ragamuffin of the press" (*Babler,* Harrison 71). Alvin Kernan discusses at length the pressures on the traditional role and mythic self-image of the writer (including particularly the writer working in the Grub Street environment) that the print culture of the eighteenth century placed on authors (82–88). Kernan's work provides a clear understanding of how a young writer like Kelly, caught up in meeting the demands of the Grub Street world, could feel victimized by the conditions of his labor. These conditions led others, like Richard Savage, Christopher Smart, and Thomas Chatterton, to seek refuge in a conception of self, suggests Kernan, that was rooted in an earlier tradition, whereas only Johnson "chose to be openly a modern" (88). Kelly did not embrace any older tradition of the writer but instead, like Johnson, attempted to make the best of the modern world of writing, choosing the role of the professional writer. Of course Kelly was not and is not the hero that tradition has made of Johnson—Kelly had no one to ensure what Kernan calls "mythological monumentalization," the effect of James Boswell's *Life of Samuel Johnson*.[20]

On the other hand, there is in the "Babler" musings on the life of the professional writer a strong desire to escape from the confines of Grub Street. There follows after each situation of the distressed writer that Kelly dramatizes the promise of a way out of the drudgery. In these stories, the fantasy of rescue is always present, rescue from the hackwork and the poverty of journalism. The Grub-Streeter is saved in no. 46 by a timely legacy of one hundred pounds per year, which enables him to retire to the country; while in no. 57, the former writer, Sebastian Spondee, becomes reconciled with his wealthy father, who releases him from the hackwork that had kept him in rags. For Kelly there would be no miraculous rescue of this sort from Grub Street drudgery; rather Kelly set out to extricate himself and to gain security and dignity by succeeding as a dramatist and lawyer. Successful as a playwright, Kelly ironically was never quite able to free himself from journalism.

3

⤜⤛

Kelly in Transition: *Thespis* and
Memoirs of a Magdalen

The substantial body of journalistic work Kelly had produced by 1766
prepared him for another phase in the development of his career as a
professional writer—his career as a playwright. If the anecdote about
the young Kelly's listening to the Dublin players as they talked about their work
in Kelly's father's tavern is to be believed, his interest in drama was early and
firmly established. The attention paid to the theater in every periodical he had
written for since the *Lady's Museum* helped to position him for his first step
toward theatrical fame: the publication on 7 November 1766 of *Thespis,* a satiric poem on the actors and actresses of Drury Lane and the only extended
piece of poetry Kelly ever published. This poem, followed soon after by a second part dealing with Covent Garden, is a bridge between his early journalistic
work and his later career as playwright. My purpose here is twofold: to seek the
connection between the early work—especially "The Babler" and the *Court
Magazine*—and *Thespis* and to suggest how *Thespis* looked forward to Kelly's
career in drama. With regard to this last, the question must be: What did *Thespis*
do for Kelly as he attempted to advance his career as a writer?

No doubt Kelly's theater journalism helped to prepare him for writing *Thespis.*
Decades ago, J. M. Beatty discussed the spate of poems influenced by Charles
Churchill's *Rosciad* (1761 [see "Churchill's Influence"]), but Churchill himself
was probably aware of an already established tradition of poems critical of the
theater or, more specifically, of actors and actresses. There were at least two sources
of general dramatic criticism immediately prior to *Rosciad* and *Thespis;* one was
journalistic criticism, especially after 1756, while the other was situated more
specifically in what might be called the tradition of "actor" poems.[1] The bibliography of this explosion of discourse that comments on acting, actors, and other
theater matters is of substantial length and includes a number of poems that, such
as Garrick's *Fribbleriad* and Edward Thompson's *Meretriciad* (both 1761), suggest
connections to both Churchill and the mock-epic tradition of Pope's *Dunciad.*[2]

More recent comment has focused either on how *The Rosciad* is situated in the evolution of post-Augustan satire (e.g., Lockwood 126–33) or on how the poems may be understood as products of market forces in the new economics of publishing. As Lance Bertelsen puts it, Churchill was "an economic asset even to his enemies. Their attacks—as much as his own poetry—made him a public figure" (85). Bertelsen's point is that both sides in this dispute benefited financially from the public attention caused by their mutual attacks.

Bertelsen's seizing upon the economic force of the *The Rosciad*—and he sees Churchill's other satires in a similar light—suggests that, in the new world of writing for the market, literary productions that themselves generated further compositions that could in turn be marketed were essential for any professional writer's success. Further, those publications that deliberately provoked responses were conscious elements in the writer's construction of his own career; these products are not unlike those that modern public-relations professionals term *spin-offs*. With Churchill, the ultimate purpose of such efforts may have been complicated by his insistence upon literary independence, a goal that he evidently pursued fervently and that lay behind his attack on dependency in critics, especially theater critics.[3] Kelly, however, did not seem to worry about maintaining independence, for as we shall see he cultivated relationships with David Garrick and Sir Robert Ladbroke that were to involve him in traditional client-patron situations, the first in the world of theater, the second in the world of politics. Yet *Thespis* did create its own spin-off: Louis Stamma's *Kellyad* and the anonymous *Anti-Thespis* (both 1767) being just two examples of the marketable goods occasioned by Kelly's poem.

Unlike *The Rosciad*, which takes the form of a trial in which each actor is judged on his or her merits, *Thespis* does not include the trial framework. Rather, Kelly begins with a brief discussion of the difficulties involved in judging acting and then moves quickly to a consideration of each performer: Drury Lane's actors are treated first, its actresses last. Employing the couplet form, Kelly imitates the usual pattern of verse satire by combining praise with blame; in some cases, as with his treatment of Garrick, Mary Ann Yates (known as Mrs. Yates), and Frances Abington (known as Mrs. Abington), there is a great deal more praise than blame. More minute in his criticism of acting style than was Churchill, Kelly includes such bases of judgment as range of voice, facial expressiveness, and appropriateness of role to talent; this last, however, because it involves casting, seems a judgment more justly made of the managers than of the actors.

Thespis plays a somewhat different but related role in Kelly's career compared to that played by Churchill's satire in his. Just as *The Rosciad* stimulated Garrick to secure Churchill's friendship, so evidence suggests that *Thespis* provided Kelly the chance to meet Garrick.[4] Certainly one does not wish to suggest that Kelly's poem was composed for that reason alone—doing so would be to view *Thespis* in a reductive fashion as only a provocative self-advertisement whose flattery of

Garrick was the major motive for its creation in the first place. Kelly after all had been busy writing about the theater world for the *Court* and "The Babler" since 1761, and these experiences naturally gave him the necessary background and justification for such a composition. Churchill, on the other hand, evidently went on a theater-attending binge for a few months only in order to write *The Rosciad*.[5] Still, attracting the attention of the major theatrical figure of his time through flattery while at the same time exhibiting his knowledge of the strengths and weaknesses of other actors and actresses (and thereby demonstrating his own claim to a superior understanding of what is necessary for success on the stage) cannot have been a minor motive for Kelly. In Kelly's self-reflexive meditation on journalism written for the *Court Magazine* and "The Babler" prior to 1766, a central fantasy of his was the escape from the drudgery of journalistic hackwork.

Thespis thus can be seen as a legitimating move, a claim of authority by Kelly that reconfirms his right to speak on theatrical matters. It became a means of access to Garrick and the potential bridge over which he could cross from the humble land of hack journalism to the more fertile fields of theatrical fame. The poem represents a significant step in Kelly's progress toward middle-class respectability, an enactment of that myth of "rising" with which so many of his "Babler" essays were concerned.[6] The publication of *Thespis* brought Kelly the sum of twenty guineas (O'Leary 46) and generated a sufficient number of responses to help make him a more marketable writer than he had been heretofore. A survey of the "Monthly Catalogue" of the *Critical Review* for January 1767, a few weeks after the publication of *Thespis,* demonstrates that the poem generated its own minor discourse explosion, an explosion that included the previously noted *Kellyad* and *Anti-Thespis,* as well as the anonymously authored *Rational Roscius* and *Priam Against Pyrrhus;* later William Kenrick was to weigh in with "On Reading Thespis" and John Brownsmith with *The Rescue: or, Thespian Scourge.*[7]

That Kelly was more marketable is perhaps best demonstrated by the fact that, when the second *Thespis (II)* appeared in February 1767, Kelly's name was on the title page, the first time he had been explicitly connected to any work except for a few poems published with his initials in the *Court Magazine.* Writing here about the actors of Covent Garden, Kelly moderates his satiric tone and, as William Watt notes (57), directs his severest criticism at two of the central critics at the *Monthly Review,* Ralph Griffiths, its editor, and John Langhorne, for their unflattering comments about the original *Thespis (I).* Although criticism of *Thespis II* occurred, it was milder than the strictures that had been directed at the first part; and in general, Kelly must have felt elated that he had attracted even negative attention and had succeeded in publicly praising David Garrick, the man who was to become instrumental in his effort to become a playwright. *Thespis II* singles out Mrs. Mattocks for the palm awarded to Garrick in *Thespis I,* but the praise of her talent does not nearly equal that which is heaped upon Garrick in both books:

Long in the annals of theatric fame,
Has truth graced Garrick with a foremost name;
Long in a wide diversity of parts,
Allow'd his double empire o'er our hearts:
Either in mirth to laugh us to excess,
Or where he weeps, to load us with distress—
Nor is it strange, that even in partial days,
He gains so high an eminence of praise;
When his united requisites are more,
Than ever centred in one mind before:
Say, if we search minutely, from the age
In which old Thespis first began the stage,
And range through all the celebrated climes,
In which it flourish'd, to the present times,
Where shall we find an actor who has prest,
With such extensive force upon the breast,
Fill'd such opposing characters for years,
Unmatch'd, alike, in laughter or in tears?

(Thespis I, lines 81–98)

The theme announced clearly here—that Garrick may be the finest actor of all time—is exceeded later when the panegyric becomes heroic, and other actors are cautioned against attempting to compete with Garrick:

But let my words convictively be prest
On every stage-struck Icarus's breast,
Who, never dreading once to be outdone,
Wings with too bold a pinion on the sun;
And risques, in ill-judged characters, a fall
From some vain flight at excellence in all—
Down from old Thespis to the present hour,
Who, besides one with universal power,
In *every* walk on *every* mind could press,
And soar alike in humour or distress?

(Thespis II, lines 241–50)

Garrick, in *Thespis I* merely the greatest actor who ever lived, now has become a god, and others who would attempt to reach his height are accused of Icarus-like hubris. However motivated by personal ambition Kelly's eulogy of Garrick might have been, it was also sincere, for Kelly's reverential tone toward Garrick remained constant in both his private and his public discourse until the end of his life. Further, although Kelly's praise of Garrick had little to do with the attacks on *Thespis,* Kelly's consistently favorable treatment of the manager after *Thespis* in the *Ledger* and elsewhere would soon draw attacks on him from those foes of Garrick who detested Garrick's reputation as an actor and his power as a theater manager.

Flush with the public attention given him by the *Thespis* poems, Kelly turned to complete a novel he had evidently been working on for some time, probably as early as the summer of 1766.[8] *Memoirs of a Magdalen: or, The History of Louisa Mildmay,* Kelly's only novel, appeared on 31 March 1767—the dedication to the duchess of Northumberland is so dated—after having been advertised as early as 30 October–1 November 1766 in the *London Chronicle* and as early as 10 November in the *Gazetteer,* where the advertisement promised that the novel would be published on "Wednesday next," which was 12 November; why the work was delayed for five months I cannot ascertain, but the 12 November notice gives the number of volumes, as well as the name of the publisher, William Griffin, so the novel was probably well advanced at that time. The appearance of several more notices in the *Gazetteer* throughout the fall of 1766 only adds to the puzzle about the delay. Certainly the attention drawn to Kelly by the publication of the *Thespis* poems would have aided the sales of the novel.

The reviewers had received advance copies of the *Memoirs of a Magdalen,* and the novel was noticed in both the *Gentleman's Magazine* and the *Critical Review* in November. Generally applauded, the novel was called "a pretty imitation" of Samuel Richardson's *Clarissa* by the reviewer in the *Monthly Review* (Nov. 1767) and went through at least two other editions in 1767, one by Griffin and another in Dublin by a conger headed by Peter Wilson and John Exshaw. Two more editions followed by 1800, and two French translations appeared in 1773 and 1800.[9]

This epistolary novel opens by relating how the hero, Sir Robert Harold, has met the heroine, Louisa Mildmay, through the offices of his sister, Lady Haversham. A sentimental rake, Sir Robert believes himself in love with Louisa. During a short prenuptial stay at the Mildmay estate, Sir Robert seduces Louisa; but fearing that she is too amorous to be a faithful wife, he coldly forces her to break off the match, leaving her to inform her parents. After wounding Louisa's brother, Col. Mildmay, in a duel, Sir Robert flees to Europe where he remains for most of the book's remaining action.

Meanwhile, having been sent in disgrace by her unforgiving father to a London relative, Mrs. Darnel, Louisa is reported to have run away with a mysterious gentleman. Actually, we later learn that she has been betrayed by Mrs. Darnel, an accomplice of Harry Hastings, the rake who abducts Louisa. While the whereabouts of Louisa remain unknown, her friend, Harriot Beauclerk, nurses Louisa's wounded brother and falls in love with him. Sir Robert, exiled in Europe, writes to his older friend, Melmoth, lamenting Louisa's fate: his imagination is torn between picturing her a prostitute and hoping that she has somehow escaped infamy.

After eleven months' silence, Louisa writes to Harriot and clears up the mystery of her disappearance: she relates her kidnapping by Sir Harry Hastings, from whose clutches she eventually escaped, aided by two sisters, one a farmer's wife and another a London vendor. Tormented by guilt and emotionally unstable from her imprisonment, Louisa has voluntarily committed herself to the London Magdalen House for repentant prostitutes where she has been staying for three months.

Sir Robert, having heard Louisa's story from Sir Harry Hastings, whom he afterwards wounds in a duel, returns from exile determined to reconcile with Louisa. He writes Melmoth of his intentions, and his friend informs all the others of the happy news. In a final letter of denouement, Lady Haversham narrates the concluding events of the comic ending. The marriages of Sir Robert with Louisa and Harriot with Col. Mildmay occur, and even the two lower-class women, Mrs. Dobson and Mrs. Carter, who aided Louisa in her escape from Sir Harry, are rewarded with money and positions. Sir Harry is permitted to recover from his wounds, but the faithless relative, Mrs. Darnel, drowns in the Thames while attempting to flee to France.

Earlier twentieth-century Kelly scholars have focused on the novel's clumsy narrative and its indebtedness to Richardson's *Clarissa* (W.W.Watt 65–86; O'Leary 236–40). Indeed, *Memoirs of a Magdalen* is filled with various imitations of and allusions to *Clarissa*. When Louisa is abducted by Sir Harry Hastings from Mrs. Darnel's London home, the heroine is even reading Richardson's masterpiece. Sir Robert Harold, a Lovelacian presence initially, rapidly softens into a sentimental figure whose rakishness, never very intense to begin with, is overwhelmed by his sense of remorse at having seduced and then abandoned Louisa. He comes closest to Lovelacian libertinism in his first letter to the Belford-like friend, Charles Melmoth, where he confesses his licentious propensities; the letter is written just before he meets Louisa at Bath for the first time and concerns what he feels will be the time of his life during his stay at Bath:

> [Y]ou may recollect what a propensity I have to be particular with every woman who is fool enough to admit of my familiarity;— therefore, in this precious spot, as there is likelihood enough of employment, you may now and then, probably, receive some accounts sufficiently interesting to keep you from yawning in your great chair after dinner. (1: 2)

This confession of sexual aggressiveness is as close as Sir Robert comes to a rakish posture; and even before his seduction of Louisa, he thinks seriously of marriage: "Matrimony has a frightful sound with it, and yet I am determined some time or other to be married" (1: 18). Even as he relates the details of his seduction of Louisa to Melmoth, Sir Robert sentimentally construes himself, not his women, as victim:

> You have often, my dear Melmoth, called me the most sentimental libertine you ever knew; and once, in a conversation with my sister

Haversham, assured her, notwithstanding all my follies, that I was above laying any unmanly schemes for the seduction of innocence; in this you did me nothing more than justice—You yourself know that, in one half of my amours, the advances were so palpable on the wrong side, that there was no creditable method of getting off, even had I been the most sanctified puritan in the kingdom. (1:42)

In such a confession, Kelly provides Sir Robert with what may seem a justification for his fear of female sexuality, the fear that he later articulates as a reason for abandoning Louisa after the seduction.

The Richardsonian influence on the novel is not limited to the discourse of sensibility and its key concept of delicacy. There are a number of more particular echoes. The London bawd figure of Mrs. Darnel reminds one of Mrs. Sinclair. The months-long imprisonment that Louisa endures in Hampstead at the house of Sir Harry Hastings also obviously owes much to *Clarissa*. Harriot Beauclerk as the faithful friend is a softened version of Anna Howe, and even Mr. Mildmay's social ambition for his son, the colonel, reminds one of the Harlowes' campaign to advance James. Ernest A. Baker, in his *History of the English Novel,* felt that Kelly was rewriting *Clarissa* from a male perspective, suggesting that Kelly's work was a positive response to Richardson. Certainly Kelly could be said to share the Richardsonian agenda of male reformation—or, more specifically, the reformation of the gentleman's code of honor. Kelly's distaste for dueling and heavy drinking in all his conduct literature, his construction of a domesticated, avuncular male in Mr. Babler, and here in his only novel his creation of a sentimental rake in Melmoth all suggest that Kelly's reformist ideology of sensibility had much in common with Richardson's.

Neglected by earlier critics, however, are other concerns raised in this novel that indicate Kelly's rather complex situatedness in what Barker-Benfield has called the "reformation of male manners."[10] These concerns cluster mainly around Kelly's treatment of women, including female community and female sexuality. Kelly's narrative thrust marginalizes male voices as Lady Haversham, Harriot Beauclerk, and Louisa herself come to dominate—indeed, write—the text: these characters' various interactions and interventions—they create many different texts within the larger narrative—become the central sites of the novel. This is not to say that male voices are silent—they clearly are not—but Sir Robert's epistolary exchanges with Charles Melmoth are reactive, and following his seduction of Louisa, he flees the Mildmay home and is ever after moving away from the center of the text. He observes much of the ensuing action from Europe until near the end, when he returns to England for his reconciliation with Louisa; until that time, he remains in large part a passive observer.

Meanwhile, several females become responsible for the central textual activity. Lady Haversham brings Sir Robert and Louisa together, and then once the couple has transgressed, she writes (writes the wrong, one is tempted to say) extensively in order to reconcile the estranged parties, not only Louisa with Sir Robert but also the Mildmays with their daughter. This dominance of female voices (Harriot is also an agent of reconciliation) is accomplished despite the fact that, of the twenty-one letters making up the novel, a dozen are written by men, nine between Sir Robert and Charles Melmoth. Yet the impression remains that female voices create the text. Part of the explanation can be seen in purely empirical terms: for the second volume of the work contains nine letters altogether, of which five are by women, and these five are certainly much longer and carry more of the narrative burden than the ones authored by males. More to the point of the author-authority question is the domination of Lady Haversham as moral agent. Two others, Louisa herself and her best friend, Harriot, also write extensive letters and create texts that are more dynamic, and actually accomplish more of the narrative, than do the male letters. In some sense reminiscent of the Clarissa–Anna Howe correspondence, the women in Kelly's text are not powerless, certainly not to the extent that Janet Todd views the Clarissa–Anna Howe community (84). Rather than passively suffer, these active women remain on the scene, so to speak, while the hero is removed from the site; Col. Mildmay is wounded in the duel with Sir Robert and loses voice as well as mobility. Both young males lose space and hence voice; their silences are filled by the voices of the key female characters constructively working/writing to reestablish harmony.

While the men have distanced themselves from the actual creation of text, the women work and write to reestablish contact and (re)construct community. In my view, this community does not entirely fit the image of the sentimental community of female friends that Janet Todd suggests is one of the key plot elements of the fiction of sentiment.[11] Rather than deeply sentimental, the female community in Kelly's work is practical and involved, as can be seen early on when Lady Haversham states her desire to see her brother married and, to that end, brings him and Louisa together. It is Lady Haversham who, once informed by Mrs. Mildmay of the couple's transgression and subsequent rupture, works to reunite the lovers. Because her activities must be reported to Sir Robert through the medium of Melmoth's letters, Lady Haversham's discourse does not dominate, although her conversation is directly reported by Melmoth. Nevertheless, she does facilitate the exchange of communications between all parties, making certain that her exiled brother receives Mrs. Mildmay's letter on behalf of Louisa and then writing herself directly to Sir Robert in an attempt to persuade him to accept Louisa once again. Her logic cuts through Sir Robert's ungenerous and libertine sentiments concerning Louisa—he had argued to Melmoth, as we have seen, that an amorous woman cannot be trusted even after marriage—and exposes the double standard and contradictions in his attitude toward women:

> In the whole course of your narrative you have but one objection
> to Miss Mildmay, and that is even grounded on a supposition no

less ungenerous than unjust. You men, however, have very contracted notions on these occasions; and generally give up that very vanity, where a lady has shewn any fatal proofs of her regard, which first of all leads you to think of gaining her affections. As long as she keeps you at a distance you think yourselves the only objects whom she can ever honour with her approbation; but if, in the unguarded fulness of heart, she should unfortunately lose sight of her circumspection, and sacrifice her honour through an extravagant tenderness, that moment you sink in your own opinion; that moment you construe what is the consequence of an unbounded partiality for yourselves, into a levity of sentiment, and imagine every body else must be indulged with an equal degree of familiarity. (1: 90)

Men, she seems to say, always misread women. In this and other letters by Lady Haversham—and in many of those by Melmoth—the tone of conduct literature dominates, recalling the moral discourse Kelly had often written for the *Court Magazine* and "The Babler" essay series; and it is language that will appear in the moral set pieces of the sentimental comedies that he will soon compose. Indeed, Sir Robert's ironic claim that the most dangerous time for a woman is between her acceptance of a marriage proposal and the actual marriage is borne out by the novel's events; the sentiment is one of a number of similar maxims that formed Kelly's moral discourse in his early journalism. In this work, Kelly deals exhaustively with the subject of courtship: more than twenty percent of his essays and tales in "The Babler" focus on themes that are, many of them, reinscribed in *Memoirs of a Magdalen*.[12] Indeed, throughout the novel, Kelly's sentimentalism corresponds more to sentiment—to moral thought, that is—than it does to the more modern notion of sentimentalism as excessive emotion. As such, the novel seems to illustrate R. F. Brissenden's contention that the decade of the 1760s was a transitional period in the development of sensibility, with the novels written after that decade exemplifying the more modern notion of sentimentality as unwarranted feeling (105).

In the second volume of the novel, female control of narrative continues. Marginalized females play an important role in Louisa's escape from Sir Harry Hastings's house and in her subsequent voluntary admission into the Magdalen House. Deborah Dobson and her sister, Mrs. Carter, the first a farm wife on the way to the London markets when she encounters the fleeing Louisa and allows her to hide in her vegetable cart, the second a widowed London dealer in butter and eggs who provides Louisa with a comfortable and safe domestic retreat, along with the niece of Mrs. Dobson, form a kind of female community. It possesses the characteristics of the community of women Nina Auerbach describes as a "furtive, unofficial, often underground entity" (1–10); and like others in Auerbach's communities, these women who befriend Louisa are "watchers" (9–10), nursing her through a serious illness that she describes as leaving her mind "totally unhinged" (2: 111).[13] As one of the servants, Mrs. Dobson, is later discovered to be a former employee of Louisa's family, the community in part illustrates what Janet Todd calls the "fantasy of loyal service" (118).

From her refuge in the little community of Mrs. Dobson and her sister, Louisa moves to the much more formal and disciplined community of the Magdalen House, the institution that provides Kelly's novel with its main title, *Memoirs of a Magdalen*. Louisa's stay represents the final episode prior to her reconciliation with her family and her lover, Sir Robert Harold. Before we can look at Kelly's use of this institution, however, some account of its origin and function is necessary.

The establishment of the Magdalen charity, whose function was to rehabilitate repentant prostitutes, was first publicly urged by the indefatigable philanthropist and reformer Jonas Hanway in a pamphlet entitled *Letter to Robert Dingley, Esq., Being a Proposal for the Relief and Employment of Friendless Girls and Repenting Prostitutes,* published early in 1758 and refined in another pamphlet, *A Plan for Establishing a Charity-House, or Charity-Houses, for the Reception of Repenting Prostitutes,* published later in the spring of the same year.[14] Houses of this nature had long been established on the continent.[15] In proposing this charity, Hanway urged that such an institution was needed for Britain's economic survival; his entire focus in the first pamphlet's letter to Dingley is concerned with the relationship between England's ability to make war, the need for more soldiers and sailors (population growth), the desirability of having married military personnel (who would fight more effectively), and the potential for all of this to be realized if only good wives might be constructed from deserted girls and reformed prostitutes.

In his proposals and in later publications that reported on the progress of the institution, Hanway provided a great many details concerning the operation of the Magdalen House itself. Included were many pages of rules and regulations covering the ways in which the young women were to be fed, housed, and clothed. Hanway also provided a specific schedule for managing the women's daily existence: sections on "hours of rest" and "hours of work," for instance, enumerated the rules by which the inhabitants were to conduct themselves. Despite all this readily available material, however, Kelly ignores the actual operation of the Magdalen House in his novel.

Why then did Kelly invoke the charity in the first place if he did not intend to make fuller use of its potential? That the House was surely known to his readership is attested to by the ample coverage of the Magdalen charity in the periodicals of the 1760s, by the very discourse that had constructed it and narrated its success, and even by the publication of at least one previous novel on the subject.[16] Surely Kelly, knowledgeable London journalist, knew enough about the House and its operation to have amplified its presence had he desired to. Further, as a writer experienced in the production of popular-culture materials, Kelly doubtlessly recognized the value of the House as a stimulus to his readership's curiosity: that much is indicated by his use of *Magdalen* in his title.

Perhaps the use of *Magdalen* in the title was a bow to popular-culture sensationalism, raising expectations with the suggestion of lurid possibilities, much as the covers of modern paperbacks do. Yet it is still curious that more foregrounding of the House is not accomplished, particularly in light of the fear of female sexuality, which, one begins to feel, was as much a fear of Kelly's as it was of Sir Robert Harold's. Perhaps, though, if Martin Jay is correct and Michel Foucault has taught us that authorial intentions pale before epistemic directives, Kelly's refusal to exploit the Magdalen House represents the triumph of the episteme of genre, the genre of the sentimental novel. As such, Kelly must reward Louisa, not expose her to discipline and punishment, to rules and regimentation; so he backs away from constructing any narrative that would do more than merely suggest discipline. He places all the vast apparatus of disciplinary technique as represented by the rules referred to above in the background, and he hurries to his generically determined conclusion: the sentimental novel demands a reconciliation and a marriage. Kelly may have shared Richardson's attitude toward the reform of male culture and particularly the reform of male sexuality; but unlike his model, Kelly wanted his novel to be comic, not tragic.

4

From Journalism to the Theater: The *Public Ledger* and David Garrick

lthough Kelly's publication of *Thespis* late in 1766 and of *Memoirs of a Magdalen* early in 1767 placed before the public lengthy works in genres for which Kelly had heretofore not been known, his journalism continued to be a steady source of income, as well as a means of advancing his career. If the journalism helped Kelly to write *Thespis*, then that poem's favorable treatment of Garrick provided Kelly access to the great actor. Yet the editorship Kelly assumed of the *Public Ledger*, probably sometime in the late spring or early summer of 1765, helped him establish himself with Garrick more thoroughly than any flattering poem could have done, for Kelly's control of the *Ledger* allowed him to support Garrick and Drury Lane on a regular basis with favorable reviews of Garrick's productions.

Evidence establishing the beginning of Kelly's editorship of the *Ledger* is problematic, but it is likely that he began to edit the paper no later than July 1765, only five months before his first major editorial position was to end when the *Court Magazine* ceased publication in November 1765.[1] Begun in 1760 by John Newbery, who was to publish the collected *Babler* in 1767, the *Public Ledger* became a major organ of the Court party within three years after Kelly had assumed control and thus attracted the hostility of the Wilkites and other City radicals. At the same time, the paper was involved in the theater world and was accused of steadily asserting itself on behalf of David Garrick.

The major piece of evidence we have for supposing that Kelly's editorship began in or around July 1765 is based on the paper's reprinting, as the *Court Magazine* once did, a number of "Babler" essays directly from—and often with credit to—their source, *Owen's Weekly Chronicle*, where they had begun to appear on 12 February 1763.[2] As Kelly seems to have borrowed consistently only from his own works, and as no other periodical seems to have republished "Babler" essays, it seems reasonable to date his editorship from sometime in 1765, probably from June onward.[3] In the *Ledger* for 3 July, there is a lengthy puff piece for the "Babler" series itself contained within a "story" that claims that some of the essays were reprinted in certain weeks by the thousands and distributed by readers who enjoyed them so much that they wanted to share them with other citizens.[4] Whether this claim has even the slightest basis in fact, it is unlikely that anyone besides Kelly would have provided free publicity for "The Babler." The puff is also remarkable as a vivid example of how writers like Kelly working in the new market-centered rather than older patron-centered literary system needed to sustain a demand for their products. Here self-referencing becomes self-advertising.

Moreover, the puff is contained in a letter addressed to Mr. Babler directly, suggesting that the writer knows that Mr. Babler is also the editor of the *Ledger*. The possibility, if not probability, that the letter writer is Kelly himself does not invalidate this evidence. Finally, beginning on 10 July, a series of "Babler" essays begins in the *Ledger* that are reprinted from *Owen's Weekly Chronicle:* four appear during July in various numbers, and the practice of reprinting continues throughout August and September. Nearly all are noted as having been reprinted from *Owen's*. It seems reasonable that only Kelly would have made such extensive use of the "Babler" material and that, as such, he was editing the *Ledger* at this time.

Evidence of the pro–Court party stance the *Ledger* was to take after John Wilkes's return from exile in the spring of 1768 and the general increase in City radicalism that occurred is slight. Tracing the political stance is difficult because of the absence of extant numbers from the end of 1765 to the beginning of June 1771.[5] Throughout the summer and fall of 1765, Kelly seemed eager to please as many in his reading audience as possible, alternating between, for instance, pro-Pitt and anti-Pitt stances and continually promising readers that it would be his policy not to allow personal abuse of any political shade into the *Ledger's* pages. Such abuse, he wrote in the 23 July number, can only serve "private gratification" without possessing any "public utility."

Indeed, throughout the summer issues, in his deployment of a large number of domestic narratives focusing on manners, Kelly constructs a format that reminds one more of an essay series or a magazine than a newspaper, and even much of the political content is kept at a domestic and personal level by framing the political in the fold of the familiar letter. On one level, this format may suggest that even two-thirds of the way through the century, journalistic genres and modes were still unstable, their boundaries uncertain and shifting. But then again, some of the instability of format might also be due to authorial uncertainty: Kelly had written for newspapers before 1765 but had edited only magazines. It should not be surprising that magazine genres, such as the domestic conduct letter or moral tale, should be imported into his newspaper practices. Indeed, Kelly's editorial voice recalls the homey familiarity of the avuncular Mr. Babler as he answers letters from the paper's readership. These letters, although often with some political focus, sometimes lack large import: in one, a reader wishes to know why sizable forest reserves are needed when no king hunts anymore. Here Kelly establishes an editorial column of sorts, entitled "Observations of Correspondents with Occasional Remarks," which allows him to flatter his audience by noticing them in his column and to personalize politics, thereby rendering abstract and distant subjects more intimate than they might ordinarily have appeared to be.[6]

The few extant issues of the *Ledger* after the early fall of 1765 make it impossible to trace its treatment of theater matters directly and force us to rely on the commentary of neutral and hostile parties to assess the paper's outlook. Nor can we use the last issues of the *Court Magazine* as a basis for testing the truth of what became a frequent charge against Kelly in the future: that he used his position in London journalism to promote Garrick. There were few theater columns in the *Court* during its last months; and at any rate, Garrick was in Europe during the 1764–65 London theater season.

Because the *Court Magazine* for 1765 is inconclusive regarding Kelly's treatment of Garrick, and because the absence of extant copies of the *Public Ledger* after the fall of 1765 prevent one from examining its treatment of Garrick in its theater reviews, ironically knowledge about Kelly's theater journalism—indeed, of his general journalistic practice for the middle years of his career—depends on the reports and attacks of his enemies. Fortunately, the entire run exists of the *Theatrical Monitor,* a periodical whose main purpose seems to have been to attack the general collusion, as it charged, between journalists and theater managers and the specific relationship between Kelly and Garrick. Appearing from early October 1767 until 16 April 1768, the *Monitor* mounted a relentless attack on what it considered the evil politics of the London theater world, aided and abetted by corrupt journalists. Published during most of its brief life by the radical bookseller William Bingley, the *Monitor* developed an analogy between the tyranny of the theater managers and their monopoly and that of the ministers of George III. We must often depend on this journal for information about Kelly's professional life between the publication of *Memoirs of a Magdalen* in the early spring of 1767 and the production of his first play, *False Delicacy*, on 23 January 1768.[7]

In the *Theatrical Monitor* are the first of many public attacks on Kelly from 1767 until the end of his life to which anyone who wishes to study his career must be indebted. As with our reliance on anecdote, mostly of a neutral sort, for knowledge about Kelly's early life, so here we must employ, albeit with whatever skepticism seems appropriate, once again the evidence of anecdote, this time produced by hostile authors. The editor-author of the *Monitor* is not known, but he was someone who knew intimately the London theatrical world, and it is this theatrical establishment and its journalistic propagandists who help to sustain the theater monopoly that "Mr. Monitor," as his correspondents address him, severely criticizes. The journalists are guilty, in Mr. Monitor's view, of prostituting themselves to the theater managers, David Garrick and George Colman the Elder, puffing their productions in return for advertisements and other favors.

Although Mr. Monitor's identity is unknown, we do know the publisher, William Bingley. Bingley, soon to resume publication of the *North Briton* in the spring of 1768, was a staunch Wilkite; he went to jail to protect his news sources; and through his publication of the *North Briton* and later *Bingley's Journal,* he became a leading radical publisher.[8] Just as he later attacked Kelly in his *Journal* for Kelly's defense of the Court party interest, so now Bingley no doubt agreed with Mr. Monitor's criticism of Kelly for Kelly's privileging of Garrick and the theater establishment in general: surely Bingley supported the analogy between the two worlds of politics and theater. He always suspected that the powerful in politics and theater were intent on suppressing competing voices.[9] It may be because Kelly served even in 1767 to embody the analogy between corruption in politics and corruption in the theater that he was singled out for more abuse than either Colman or Garrick: for radicals like Bingley, Kelly's journalistic support of the theater tyranny came to be seen as all of a piece with his support for George III and his policies. Kelly thus functioned as a convenient symbol of all that antiestablishment London detested.

In the first number of the *Theatrical Monitor* (Oct. 1767) appeared a letter supposedly from a writer for the *Public Ledger,* which Kelly was editing, the ultimate purpose of which seems to have been to damn himself, that letter's author, and the *Public Ledger* by making claims that Mr. Monitor interprets negatively. As quoted in the *Monitor,* the *Ledger* writer maintains that just because "the managers have neglected their own interest in declining to advertise with us" does not mean that "we should neglect the regard which is due to our character, and set [the managers] up in a kind of literary pillory to be pelted by every little writer." The *Ledger* spokesman seems to declare that his paper will continue to treat the theater managers fairly even if they refuse to advertise with the newspaper; that neglect will not result, the writer promises, in any hostility toward the theater managers, surely a noble stance to take. However, Mr. Monitor interprets all this not as admirable editorial policy but rather as an attempt to "frighten the managers to a voluntary offering of advertising in that paper." Here the interpretive contest is joined, and the suspicions run high as the *Monitor* writer attempts to control the interpretation and intention of the *Ledger* writer.

The attack on Kelly in this inaugural issue of the *Monitor* is continued in an open letter directed at Kelly that questions his credentials as a theater critic; it accuses him of dwelling in the "mire of Grub Street" and labels him a "hireling." Mr. Monitor indicts Kelly for his partiality to Garrick and Drury Lane and maintains that Kelly's motive is self-seeking: he claims Kelly hopes to become a dramatist and even has a "play at nurse." This open letter further suggests that Kelly would do anything to "be the lick spit of a dirty play-house." That Kelly had indeed been working on what was to become *False Delicacy* was true: he first wrote Garrick on 24 November 1766 to inquire about the possibility of getting a play ready for the 1767–68 season.[10] And in a letter to Garrick dated 27 June 1767, Kelly announced that the play was finally finished: "I have at length got a comedy ready for your perusal." The details of these letters are not of immediate concern; but they reveal Mr. Monitor's knowledge of the theater world and his access to insider information. For the Kelly scholar, corroboration of at least some of Mr. Monitor's information is both painful and reassuring, the last because so much of any attempt to reconstruct Kelly's life must rely so often on hostile sources.

The *Theatrical Monitor* for 16 December 1767 is one of the more interesting numbers because of its extensive detail about immediate theater politics. Attacking Kelly once again, the paper criticizes him for publishing letters in recent issues of the *Ledger* that criticized William Kenrick's play *The Widowed Wife*, which opened at Drury Lane on 5 December of that year. This attack is especially ironic given that Kenrick's play owed a great deal to Kelly's recently published novel, *Memoirs of a Magdalen*. One would suppose that Mr. Monitor knew of this connection and might therefore be inclined to allow Kelly some pique at a play whose very existence stemmed from his novel. But Mr. Monitor praises the Kenrick work so highly (he had also written in favor of Kenrick earlier) that one wonders if Mr. Monitor was not Kenrick himself.[11]

The *Monitor* suddenly interrupted its publication after the 19 December number and did not resume until 30 January 1768 because of Mr. Monitor's serious illness, further indication that this vituperative little paper was a one-writer production. The themes for the remaining numbers—publication ceased after 16 April 1768—were primarily developments of those concerns already noted. Kelly continued to attract Mr. Monitor's wrath: the entire issue of 30 January was devoted to an evaluation of Kelly's first play, *False Delicacy*, produced by Garrick at Drury Lane on 23 January, and demonstrated that Mr. Monitor was not without cause, suggesting that Kelly's partiality to Garrick was due to Kelly's having "a play at nurse."

The ugliest of the concluding attacks on Kelly and Garrick occurs in the 12 March issue when, citing rumors, Mr. Monitor states that, after Kelly's flattery of Garrick led Kelly to submit a play for Garrick's consideration, Garrick at first rejected the piece. However, after having lent Kelly one hundred pounds to complete the work, Garrick then decided to alter the play and bring it to the stage, albeit with little hope of success.[12] There is, however, no way to ascertain the facts: neither Kelly's extant letters nor Garrick's diary for 1767 shed any certain light. If such a loan had been made, neither party saw fit to allude to it, at least not in the surviving documents.

The degree of veracity is a key issue here, for once again I must state that much of what we know of Kelly comes from anecdotes of uncertain origin and from sometimes hostile intermediaries. Certainly some of the charges against both Kelly and Garrick here were leveled elsewhere. The importance of the *Theatri-*

cal Monitor as a source of general information about Kelly's life is clear, for some of what it claims about Kelly can be in part verified by reference to other sources (for example, the letters to Garrick proving that indeed there was a "play at nurse"). In a broader fashion, if we can agree with a key supposition of current cultural theory that what is socially marginal is often symbolically central, then this journal possesses a usefulness beyond its serving as a site of contestable biographical information for Kelly and Garrick. That is, its analogy between the tyranny of the theater managers and that of the Court party suggests that one unknown voice—and later there will be more—in London of 1767–68 saw with some clarity that the different dimensions of power were indeed interconnected, that monologic monopolies in politics, theater, and journalism bore some relationship to each other. To articulate such connections between political culture and cultural (theatrical) politics on the eve of the first of the century's two revolutions is to suggest that Kelly, in the pursuit of literary success, had already situated himself in the midst of some of his culture's central tensions. In fairness to Kelly, it is worth noting that he could not afford to do otherwise. He was, after all, involved in constructing a career for himself as a professional writer and needed to make himself useful to those agents who could aid him in this task.

Clearly, in the pursuit of this career, Kelly was to owe much to David Garrick, and I must return now briefly to 1766, well before the *Monitor* began its attacks on the Kelly–Garrick connection. On 24 November 1766, Kelly wrote Garrick with the idea of writing a comedy. Kelly excuses his intrusion on Garrick by claiming in the letter that his friends "who think much better of me than I can possibly deserve have for sometime advised me to attempt a theatrical piece." He then asks Garrick whether or not he could "give a piece of mine a trial next season if it should be ready in proper time." Toward the end of this first correspondence, Kelly exhibits a tone of deference toward Garrick and of depreciation toward himself that was to mark all of his subsequent communications:

> But that you may naturally think an answer to this question in the affirmative would afford me much satisfaction, yet I beg you will believe that I should be filled with the truest concern if your politeness was to lead you into any promise repugnant in the least to your interest or opposite to your inclination.... [C]onsider this letter then as a mere matter of business; and be assured that the man who now applies will feel no abatement in his high esteem either for your public or private character, because you wisely prefer your own emoluments to his, and decline in the regular way of trade to make a purchase of his commodity. (Garrick Correspondence 24: no. 19)

Essentially, Kelly wanted some sign of hope because understandably he did not wish to spend time in an endeavor that might be doomed from the start, having "a provision besides to make for my family which cannot be trusted to eventual contingencies."

Garrick's response was, despite the story put forth by the *Monitor,* ultimately supportive, and Kelly went on to compose the play that became *False Delicacy.*[13] But my purpose is not now to investigate the genesis of *False Delicacy* but rather to estimate the degree of involvement of Kelly and Garrick in the politics of theater journalism.[14] In their admirable study of David Garrick, George Winchester Stone and George Kahrl consider at length Garrick's association with the periodicals of his day (336–47). In their discussion, Stone and Kahrl assess the validity of contemporary charges that accused Garrick of influencing the press to support his theatrical endeavors; in doing so, they consider three issues: involvement, influence, and censorship. They note that some involvement (i.e., advertising of plays) in newspapers was normal business practice but conclude that Garrick exerted more influence through his pamphlets than he did through newspapers (340–41). Stone and Kahrl also find it "unthinkable" that Garrick could have "influenced or had any censoring hand" in the papers of men like Henry Sampson Woodfall, William Woodfall, Henry Baldwin, Henry Bate, or Francis Newbery, noting that these strong-minded journalists were not "dupes for anyone or any group" (342). Yet one cannot help thinking that such a defense begs the question and does not consider the possibility that a publisher or editor could in fact willingly aid Garrick or anyone else in a mutually advantageous situation.

Stone and Kahrl do not take up the specific question of Kelly and his *Public Ledger,* and as I have already demonstrated in my examination of the *Theatrical Monitor* and of Kelly's earliest correspondence with Garrick, there were not only charges that Kelly and Garrick aided each other but also more than adequate motivation on both men's parts for the exercise of self-interest. Stone and Kahrl claim that "Garrick might well dismiss" (337) the sorts of charges leveled by the *Monitor;* yet they themselves do not explicitly deny these accusations, the major one contending that Kelly consistently favored Garrick and Drury Lane in his theatrical criticism. Yet the absence of *Ledgers* for the years 1766 through the middle of 1771 makes it impossible to settle the question definitively.

Were one thus to try to settle the influence issue solely on the basis of the *Monitor's* charges for the 1767–68 period, one could conclude little with regard to the Kelly–Garrick connection. Yet some evidence exists beyond Mr. Monitor's allegations to suppose that Kelly owed much to Garrick and therefore favored him in the *Ledger.* We have already seen that the charge that Kelly puffed Garrick because Kelly had, in Mr. Monitor's phrase, "a play at nurse" was at least partially true. The examination of these early letters from Kelly to Garrick do help to establish the strong feeling of indebtedness toward Garrick that Kelly retained for the remainder of his life. The indebtedness was not solely due to the aid Garrick gave and was to give Kelly as he attempted to break into the theater world but was also due to the help Garrick provided Kelly in obtaining a pension from the government for the pro-Court stance of the *Ledger* and other journalistic efforts. The pursuit of the Kelly–Garrick connection takes me somewhat ahead of the story of Kelly's career as a playwright, but it is unavoidable, given the importance of the issue.

Some indication of the circumstances of Kelly's political journalism, primarily his role as the editor of the *Ledger* from 1765 to 1772, has already been indicated; it is probable that sometime in the early fall of 1770 Kelly was granted a pension by Frederick Lord North for his political support of the ministry. That support had already cost Kelly dearly, for in March 1770 his second comedy, *A Word to the Wise,* had been damned by a Wilkite mob and was subsequently removed from Drury Lane. In September 1770, however, as Kelly hints to Garrick, much of the pain caused by the damnation of his play seemed about to be soothed by a pension. He writes to Garrick that "this day, Sir, and not before, I have got some certain intimation of Lord N_____'s intention to do handsome things."[15] It is clear from this letter, the full implications of which I take up in chapter 8, that Kelly believed Garrick to have played a key role in obtaining the pension from Lord North:

> Mr. Cooper told me of [the pension] in very obliging terms, adding that what I had done was very much approved and that you were highly my friend. The first part of the intelligence agreeably surprized me, the latter did not in the least; Garrick I have long known, as another term for all the virtues. (Garrick Correspondence 24: no. 21)

The gratitude Kelly felt toward Garrick for both his political pension, said to be two hundred pounds per year, and his early success in the theater makes clear why Kelly might readily support Garrick and Drury Lane. Although the charge by Mr. Monitor that Kelly showed favoritism toward Garrick was made well before Kelly received his pension and before *False Delicacy* was staged, perhaps Mr. Monitor merely perceived the symbiotic nature of the relationship before it had functioned very long. Certainly as time passed, others began to become suspicious of the Kelly–Garrick connection. In *Bingley's Journal* for 29 September and 6 October 1770, there appeared two letters attacking Garrick for, among other things, promoting the plays of Hugh Kelly in return for Kelly's favorable treatment of Drury Lane in the *Ledger.* Although Bingley's feelings toward both Kelly and Garrick were not likely to have been favorable, the two letters are just two more voices added to what was becoming close to a chorus by the fall of 1770. Another of these voices, as Peter Tasch has noted, came from the *Oxford Magazine,* which charged that Garrick kept adverse criticisms of Bickerstaff's *'Tis Well It's No Worse* (produced 24 Nov. 1770) out of the newspapers. While admitting that the charge was not new, Tasch feels that, in this instance, "[T]here might have been some truth to it" (203). Also relevant here is the friendship between Kelly and Bickerstaff and that Kelly always appeared to give Bickerstaff's productions positive reviews.[16]

Kelly and Garrick were also associated with a group of journalists and publishers who in early January 1770 controlled the *London Packet,* at the time undergoing some managerial stress.[17] Evidently the newspaper was not succeeding, and the stockholders met to pledge new funds for its support, as well as to employ a new printer, William Strahan Jr., to replace Henry Baldwin. The new funds that the *Packet* required—each partner had to deposit twenty-five pounds— apparently persuaded several members of the managerial group to resign, Kelly among them. The two meetings (6 and 13 Jan.) at which all this business was conducted were attended by Kelly, but Garrick was absent, his proxy voted by Thomas Becket who was, as Stone and Kahrl note, "Garrick's personal bookseller-publisher-agent" (171). The group controlling the *Packet* placed Garrick and Kelly in business with some of the most influential publishers and printers of journalism of the time, among them Thomas Lowndes, Henry Baldwin, and Henry Sampson Woodfall. It is likely that other groups of similar composition directed other newspapers, and indeed Garrick himself owned shares in four different newspapers at various times (Stone and Kahrl 341).[18] These various interrelationships are discussed more fully in chapter 7, but for now it is enough to say only that, from a modern perspective, these publishing arrangements at times look very much like interlocking directorates.

The most substantial evidence we have after 1772 for believing the charges that Kelly favored Garrick can be found in the Kelly–Garrick correspondence itself. In a letter written 22 April 1773, Kelly praises Garrick for his performance the evening before in the latter's alteration of George Villier's *Chances* and tells his friend that he "wrote a note to Mr. Baldwin of the *St. James's Chronicle* requesting a corner for an account of *The Chances* this evening."[19] Kelly then notes that he has enclosed Henry Baldwin's reply to his request, which was as follows:

> Mr. Baldwin presents his compliments to Mr. Kelly and will think himself obliged for a short and candid account of *The Chances,* under the head of *Theatrical Intelligence.* The want of room obliges him to request it may be short, and he hopes Mr. Kelly will avoid prejudice or gross partiality, though the alteration be the work of a Garrick. (Garrick Correspondence 24: no. 34)

In a defensive tone, Kelly replies to Baldwin, protesting the charge of partiality to Garrick, and says that he was not "capable of literary prostitution." Kelly declines to accept the "honour of a place so condescendingly offered" (Garrick Correspondence 24: no. 36). To Garrick, Kelly simply promises that he will write his account of *The Chances* anyhow and send it either to "the *Morning Chronicle* or to the *Morning Post*" (Garrick Correspondence 24: no. 32).[20]

Later correspondence between Kelly and Garrick yields no further evidence concerning the issue of journalistic influence. Other forms of direct commentary, such as letters to newspapers, no longer echo the charges of favoritism that were uttered by the *Theatrical Monitor* and *Bingley's Journal.* That Kelly was still involved in journalism after 1773 is certain.[21] And his enemies still attacked him for his politics, but the old accusation of his partiality to Garrick does not seem to surface in the press as it once had done. Even when *The School for Wives* was discovered by the anti-Kelly *Middlesex Journal* in the winter of 1774 to have been written by Kelly and not by William Addington, the attacks on Kelly did not revisit the Garrick connection.[22]

It would perhaps be unfair to Garrick to assume that his relationship to Kelly was somehow typical of his associations with other men involved in some fashion with journalism. Other than Arthur Murphy, who had given up journalistic propaganda well before 1767, Kelly was Garrick's only friend who was a playwright, a drama reviewer, and a newspaper editor of some power.[23] Thus only Kelly was consistently in a position, especially from 1765 on, to help Garrick and be helped in turn. Clearly, with regard to material advantage, Kelly received more benefit from this relationship than did Garrick. Garrick not only helped Kelly to become a dramatist but also played some role—for which we have Kelly's own word—in Kelly's obtaining a pension from Lord North. Although other men helped Kelly, as we shall see, no one was more important to him than Garrick in his attempt to rise from Grub Street.

To Kelly's credit, he returned Garrick's aid with a genuine deference and a loyalty that never wavered. It is fair to conclude that Kelly did indeed engage in journalistic activities that benefited Garrick. It seems doubtful, however, that Garrick had to persuade Kelly to any extent. Rather it seems more probable that Kelly anticipated and then undertook those propaganda actions he knew would help his friend and benefactor. Kelly was telling the truth when he remarked to Garrick that "ingratitude is not among the number of my vices" (Garrick Correspondence 24: no. 38).

5

False Delicacy and Its Reception

W hile the *Theatrical Monitor* was busy throughout the fall of 1767 attacking Kelly and Garrick, Kelly was working on the play Mr.
Monitor had said Kelly had "at nurse." The letters from Kelly to
Garrick present an incomplete picture of the genesis of the drama that was to
be called *False Delicacy* but suggest that Garrick aided in its rewriting over the
summer of 1767. Apart from Kelly's address to Garrick in the fall of 1766, there
is ample proof of his interest in trying his hand at playwriting in the structure
of his novel, *Memoirs of a Magdalen*. William Watt pointed out many years ago
that, "in writing the novel, Kelly has the theater constantly in view" and noted
in Kelly's first description of Miss Mildmay that she is compared in height to
"Mrs. Yates of Drury Lane theater" (82).[1] Watt also believed that the epistolary
style is sometimes altered so that the letters often resemble what he calls the "rant
of the theater" (82). And the novel did inspire a comedy, Kenrick's *Widowed
Wife*, produced at Drury Lane on 5 December 1767, only a few weeks before
the debut of *False Delicacy* on 23 January 1768.

But Kelly may have been too busy worrying about his own play to concern
himself with Kenrick's borrowings from *Memoirs of a Magdalen*. According to
William Cooke, *False Delicacy*, after having been rewritten, was presented to Garrick in September:

> Garrick was so much pleased with it on the perusal, that he sent
> him a note expressive of his highest approbation, and among other
> words, we remember, used this expression: "There are thoughts in
> it worthy of an angel." He, however, suggested some slight alterations,
> mostly relative to *stage effect*, and this was all the part Garrick had in
> this comedy. ("Hugh Kelly," Dec. 422)

Watt also summarizes the speculation at the time concerning the amount of help
Garrick provided Kelly; rumors suggested that Garrick had aided Kelly substan-

tially, and it is to put these rumors to rest, one supposes, that Cooke insists that Garrick's role was minimal. Watt suggests that, along with supplying the epilogue and most of the prologue, Garrick probably heightened the part of Cecil, the old bachelor; added the nonsentimental characters, such as Mrs. Harley; and curtailed those scenes that did not advance the plot (91). Watt's view here in minimizing Kelly's talent owes much to the nineteenth-century Goldsmith biographer, John Forster, whose own view of Kelly was sometimes distorted by his partiality toward Goldsmith and his antipathy for sentimental comedy.[2] Nevertheless, that superfluous scenes in the early version or versions of *False Delicacy* existed is attested to by one of Kelly's own letters to Garrick:

> I was just sending the comedy off to you, Sir, when an alteration occurred to me that shortened the first act no less than ten whole sides, and occasioned the pastings which you will find in one or two places of that act; they are, however, legible, and there is no necessity to alter the number of pages after I have told you of the amputation. (Garrick Correspondence 24: no. 17)[3]

The composition, production, and reception of *False Delicacy* generated the first significant amount of discourse about Kelly's private and public life.[4] Then, too, the nineteenth-century biographers of Goldsmith—John Forster and James Prior—refer to Kelly for the first time when *False Delicacy* appeared: Goldsmith's own comedy, *The Good Natur'd Man,* was staged at Covent Garden as a supposed rival to Kelly's play, and the conflict that ensued became the source of the alleged breach in the two authors' friendship.[5] To be sure, accounts concerning Kelly's earlier life existed, as I have already noted in examining the anecdote; and even after the production of *False Delicacy,* the anecdote remained a central source of information about Kelly. But with *False Delicacy,* the anecdotes become more detailed and possess tissues of connection with an empirical historical context, including the lives of other writers, to a degree not seen in earlier biographical discourse about Kelly.

Contemporary accounts note that Kelly, although friends with both Bickerstaff and Goldsmith, had not consulted either friend while writing *False Delicacy,* but near the end of his labors, Kelly, according to Cooke,

> ventured to communicate it to Bickerstaff, who praised it before his face in the highest strains of panegyric; but no sooner turned down the Author's stair-case, than he abused it to a common friend in the grossest terms, and "talked *of his* arrogance in thinking of *comedy* when his highest feather was that of paragraph or Newspaper Essay writing." ("Hugh Kelly," Dec. 422)

Cooke also represented Goldsmith's supposed reaction to Kelly's effort and interpreted Goldsmith's silence to envy of Kelly's success:

Goldsmith kept back and was silent, but, as it afterwards appeared, from the same principle of envy. When asked about Kelly's writing a comedy, he said, "He knew nothing at all about it—he had *heard* there was a *man of that name* about town who wrote in Newspapers, but of his talents for comedy, or even the work he was engaged in, he could not judge." (422)

Thomas Davies, Garrick's biographer, who was less partial to Kelly than Cooke was and who wrote closer to the events at hand, embedded his discussion of Kelly's play in a context more directly related to the theater world itself than to the rivalry among authors. Davies suggested that Kelly's criticism of the actors in *Thespis* still rankled a number of the players, so that Garrick was helpful not just in the composition of the play but also in ensuring the actors' compliance in its staging:

> When the play was ready for rehearsal, [Kelly] consulted Mr. Garrick about distributing the parts: he now, to his great regret, found his error in making so free with those whose assistance was absolutely necessary to him, and without whose consent his play could not be acted. Here too Mr. Garrick befriended him; he prevailed upon Mrs. Dancer to sacrifice her resentment to the interest of the community. To Mrs. Clive, I fancy, he had not the courage to make any application. (2: 136)

Opening on 23 January 1768 at Drury Lane, *False Delicacy* ran for twenty nights and was well received. Despite Davies's assertion that many of the actors were still angry with Kelly, the cast was first-rate and included two actors for whom Kelly had a great deal of admiration: Thomas King, who played Cecil, and Frances Abington, who played Lady Betty Lambton.[6] The complicated plot revolves around three sets of relationships. Lady Betty, a sentimental young widow at whose home the action takes place, has been courted by the respectable Lord Winworth, whose proposal of marriage Lady Betty has turned down before the play begins because she had already suffered through an unpleasant first marriage; she also feels that "a woman of real delicacy should never admit a second impression on her heart." At the same time, Sir Harry Newberg, the only male in the play who could possibly be considered rakish, wishes to marry Miss Rivers whose father, Col. Rivers, has already promised her to Mr. Sidney. Col. Rivers, Lady Betty's brother, steadfastly refuses to hear Sir Harry's suit on the grounds of a "delicate" point of honor: he has promised his daughter to Sidney and refuses to go back on his word even though it is apparent that the daughter does not love Sidney. The third couple consists of Sidney and Miss Marchmont, a poor orphan who has been raised by Lady Betty; she is so delicate (excessively self-deprecatory) to Lady Betty, as Lady Betty is to her, that both women deny their own true feelings for the men they love, so fearful are they of offending each other. Miss Marchmont loves Sidney but has been recently pursued by Lord Winworth, whom Lady Betty still loves even though her delicacy forced her to turn him down. The complications brought about by these entangled relationships and the proper sorting out of the lovers at the end provide the bases for the drama's action.

All of the love interests are in some way controlled and impeded by the various meanings of *delicacy*. The lovers are thwarted by what the chief female center of intelligence in the play, the realist Mrs. Harley, calls in act 2 "this delicacy" that is always "making people miserable" (*Plays* 20). She is aided in her war of comic deflation of the "sentimental folks" (20) by Sir Harry's crusty bachelor cousin, Cecil, a *vir bonus* who constantly mocks current trendiness in both manners and morals. Something of a sentimentalist himself in his insistence upon putting benevolence before self-interest, Cecil nonetheless speaks of morality with a degree of amusing wit, especially when he is rallying his cousin Harry for his coxcomb behavior and for pursuing his self-interest (Harry attempts to elope with Miss Rivers against her real inclination) beyond reasonable limits. Cecil and (especially) Mrs. Harley are aware that all the others in the play are so unselfish that they seem willing to sacrifice their own happiness to oblige one another. And that condition is what Mrs. Harley calls "false delicacy."

Whatever private reservations about the play Kelly's rival dramatists Bickerstaff and Goldsmith may have entertained, there can be no doubt that *False Delicacy* succeeded. Writing from a distance of roughly a decade, Davies admitted that the play

> was acted with much applause, and continued to draw the public to the theater near twenty nights successively. Mr. Garrick supplied the author with prologue and epilogue, which were spoken with great humour by Mr. King and Mrs. Dancer. The critics attacked it as a dull sentimental sermon, but surely not altogether with reason. The plot contains a variety of interesting action; and though many of the sentiments have in them a grave cast, the dialogue in general is gay and sprightly; some of the characters are marked with passion, others distinguished by humour. The piece is interesting, moral, and entertaining, and deserved encouragement. (2: 137)

Cooke, writing at a further remove, could say that

> the success of the comedy was very considerable; and it is but fair to say, it made its way to public approbation entirely from its own intrinsic merit. Some favourable allusions to the superiority of English over foreign education in the second act, caught John Bull's attention, and from that to the dropping of the curtain, it was almost one unremitted scene of applause. ("Hugh Kelly," Jan. 42)

Watt maintains that, after its initial success, *False Delicacy*'s popularity in England declined quickly and, quoting John Genest, claims that there were only three performances of the play during the following two seasons. William Watt was writing before the resources of Stone's *London Stage* were available, but he was essentially correct. In London, there were only four performances in the 1768–69 season, three more in the season of 1769–70, none in either of the next two seasons, and then only three more performances through 1783, including a scheduled one for 20 May 1783 that was canceled at the last minute (G. W. Stone, pt. 5, calendar for 1783). Nor did the play fare much better outside of London. Productions in Bath at the Theatre Royal took place in 1768, 1771, 1772, and in 1783.[7] In Dublin, the play appeared four times during 1770 at the Capel Street Theatre: twice in 1771, once in 1774. In Ireland's provincial theaters, stagings occurred at Cork on 15 August 1768 and at Belfast on 31 October 1768 and 6 December 1771 (see Clark 318 for details). No doubt the play found some acceptance among those who participated in the growing popularity of private theatricals: one such production took place on 25 October 1787 at Blenheim, and surely there were others as well.[8] Even poetasters of the day praised the play: Thomas Underwood's *Poems* (6–7) contains a lyrical tribute to Kelly and his work.

Contemporary interest in *False Delicacy* endured longer outside of Great Britain; in the American colonies and in France, judging by both performances and publication, the play fared reasonably well until near the end of the century. George Seilhamer notes a production, perhaps the first in the colonies, at the Southwark Theater in Philadelphia on 16 December 1768. Presented by the American Company, the play was the "most interesting production of the season," but no details of its performance are provided (1: 242–45). Another production followed at New York's John Street Theater on 14 April 1769. In later years, the play was given in Williamsburg, once again by the American Company, on 14 April 1772, at Philadelphia on 25 January 1773, and at Charleston on 18 April 1774.

The view that eighteenth-century British readers enjoyed reading sentimental plays as much as they did sentimental novels may have been true for French readers as well (see Kaufman 566; and Price 153). French productions of *False Delicacy* have proved difficult to trace, but French translations were frequent in the years immediately following 1768. When the French writer Jeanne Marie Riccoboni wrote to David Garrick sometime in July 1768 to praise Kelly, she had evidently already begun translating the play; she claimed that Kelly "seems to us to be the most *honnête* of creatures; if not an angel, he is a devil; but without being good, can one imagine the character of Cecil" (Boaden 2: 543).[9] Riccoboni then goes on to maintain that the play is suited to French taste and "will please many Frenchmen." Her translation appeared at Paris in 1769, but there had already been one in 1768. Another edition of the 1768 translation followed in 1776, and in 1788 there was yet another translation. In America, too, the play endured as literature, for in 1809 two editions were published, one in New York and the second in Boston.

The critique of delicacy begins with the first scene, when Sidney assures Lord Winworth that Lady Betty has refused him because of "an extraordinary delicacy" (*Plays* 1; act 1), an estimate that is later confirmed when Lady Betty speaks of how a lady of real delicacy does not marry twice. Mrs. Harley then enters, speaks with Sidney who is gloomy about having to marry Miss Rivers, and rallies him on his melancholy and his "funeral-sermon face" (3; act 1) a mild hit at the somber side of sentimentalism. Continuing to confront the melancholic Sidney and the spiritual suffocation that stems from an exaggerated delicacy, Mrs. Harley relates a comic moral tale of the sort Kelly used constantly in his journalism. This tale recounts how Lady Betty's cousin, Lord Hectic, habitually plagues his wife through a persistent fondness. She relates how she had recently visited the Hectics on a warm day only to find Lady Hectic bundled up in bed with a roaring blaze in the fireplace; Lady Hectic was close to expiring from the overly solicitous care of her husband who was afraid she might catch cold after she had been drenched in a rain shower the evening before. Kelly's use of the comic tale as an intervention here is crucial, I believe, in understanding his satiric intentions: the Hectic incident surely demonstrates the same kind of false delicacy in miniature that Claude Rawson has seen as the motivation behind the entire play: "[I]t is the *reductio ad absurdum* of fastidious scruple and misguided tact" (346).

Another indication in act 1 of Kelly's satire of sentimentalism is Cecil's chiding of Lady Betty for her brother's naming his daughter "Theodora" when a traditional name would have done: "And I hate the new fashion of calling our children by pompous appellations.—By and by we shan't have a Ralph or a Roger, a Bridget or an Alice, remaining in the kingdom" (*Plays* 13; act 1). Cecil's complaint about Theodora, which he dismisses as a "charming name for the romance of a circulating library" (13) seems an implicit rejection of the sentimental novel's fondness for romantic instead of realistic character names. Yet the other voice of reason, the satirical Mrs. Harley, disagrees with Cecil; and when he suggests that Miss Rivers should have been called "Deborah" after her grandmother, Mrs. Harley exclaims: "Oh I should hate such an old fashioned name abominably" (17). One might have expected both critics of sentimental discourse to have agreed here; yet the play does not permit interpretations of organic consistency. Indeed, the discussion of names, although a small part of the action, highlights the ambiguity of *False Delicacy* that modern critics have made a part of the play's critical genealogy. Such ambiguity and ambivalence, often manifested in what Kelly's recent editor Larry Carver calls his tendency to "self parody" (Introduction xvii), makes difficult any attempt to seek unequivocal meanings in these dramas.

The claim for complexity can be exaggerated, yet the earlier view of Kelly as a simple sentimental dramatist is challenged in Mark Schorer's 1933 article about Kelly's place in the sentimental tradition. Two years later, William Watt questioned the traditional view of *False Delicacy* "as a model for all that is sickening in sentimental comedy" (130). Using Ernest Bernbaum as typical of this early view, Watt reluctantly admits that the play is "not strictly a dull moral sermon" (131). He goes on to say,

> [T]he characters of the "sense" group . . . spend much of their time ridiculing the various over-refinements and foibles of the others. Thus the same distresses which are apparently calculated to arouse the sympathy of the audience become comic situations if viewed with the attitude of the more sensible characters. So, there is also in False Delicacy a ridicule of manners and an appreciation of comic situation which approach Restoration comedy. (131–32)

When Arthur Sherbo judged in 1957 that "Kelly was not entirely unaware of the absurdities of 'false delicacy'" and further admitted that "there is the temptation to see parody" in some of Kelly's characters' dialogue where the rhetorical sentimentalism is greatest (133), he was suggesting a reading of the play that agreed with Watt's and that later commentators, like Rawson, were to develop more fully.[10] If there exists some direction to the history of critical practice on *False Delicacy,* that direction emphasizes a more complicated and ambiguous play; it ultimately frames Kelly as a more self-conscious author than he has heretofore been considered. That view is in keeping with the image of the self-conscious journalist he had earlier constructed in the *Court Magazine* and "The Babler."

Rawson considers the various definitions of *sensibility* and *delicacy*, two terms Rawson finds nearly synonymous at times, and relates this discourse to Kelly's play. Rawson points out that, in Garrick's epilogue to the play, *modesty* and *delicacy* are nearly interchangeable (341–54).[11] Indeed, in the light of Joseph Donohue's 1970 reading, considered below, where the sentimental characters are perceived as egotists—that is, their false delicacy *is* false modesty—Rawson's conflation is persuasive. His act-by-act analysis of the ramifications of delicacy yields a number of useful observations, such as when he notes that Lady Betty's false delicacy—her refusal to consider a second husband—is also mockingly employed in Jane Austen's *Sense and Sensibility* in the sentimental discourse of Marianne Dashwood (346).

Rawson addresses the tradition that views *False Delicacy* as entirely focused on the "sentimental interest" and argues that Goldsmith's view of sentimental comedy as tearful rather than witty does not apply to Kelly's play, pointing out that, whether or not it is funny, it was nevertheless intended to be so (348). Arguing against construing *False Delicacy* as a sentimental play, Rawson notes that the play's sympathetic characters are not "persons of sensibility"—he refers presumably to Cecil and Mrs. Harley—and further suggests that Kelly was mocking not just a "specific kind of delicacy" but also "the cult of sensibility in general" (349). Admitting nevertheless that sentimentalism encompassed more than

just refined emotion or the lachrymose but also included a broad sense of benevolence, he suggests, rightly I believe, that Kelly embraces benevolence and
then concludes that "hardly any writing of the period, not [Tobias] Smollett's
novels nor the plays of Goldsmith and [Richard] Sheridan, could completely
avoid sympathetic treatment of things which we associate with the cult of sensibility" (350). As noted earlier, even the antisentimental Mrs. Harley confesses
that she likes delicacy. The play, Rawson concludes, is not a satire leveled against
delicacy itself but rather, like *Sense and Sensibility,* it attacks the "excesses of that
quality" (350).

The key point Rawson establishes, compatible with the one that I have made
about Kelly's complex attitude toward journalism—embracing it and yet mocking it—and with Larry Carver's notion of Kelly's penchant for self-parody, is
that "sustained mockery of sensibility may co-exist with a strong sympathy for
it" (Rawson 350, emphasis added). Indeed, the attitude Rawson highlights seems
characteristic of the ambivalence and ambiguity of Kelly's writing career. That
is, in his self-reflexive and self-conscious moments, there exists both acceptance
and rejection of the form or mode at hand, whether that be a supposedly sentimental play or a magazine piece on journalism and journalists. Kelly desires
to attack the form yet embrace it too, and this paradox, as Rawson identifies it,
is that *False Delicacy* "though a satire, . . . is *formally* in the sentimental medium"
(350), a point similar to that which Joseph Donohue makes (114).

Whether this entire ambivalence can be historicized or not is questionable,
but the general situation of satire as both form and tone in the middle and late
century has been significantly dealt with over the years in important works
written by Stuart Tave, Howard Weinbrot, Ronald Paulson, and Thomas Lockwood. Each discusses how in one way or another satire declines, has its formal
structures truncated, has its energies absorbed by other forms, or finds its moral
basis undercut as the century wears on. Without debating these broader developments, I can note that there were other works that, like Rawson's view of
Kelly's play, exhibited a formal structure at odds with a central tone. William
Hayley's poem *The Triumphs of Temper* (1781) is a case in point: his poem is not
tonally a mock epic or even a mock heroic because praise and not blame seems
to be his intention—and yet the poem imitates the structure of Pope's mock
epics in an attempt to employ satiric forms for panegyric purposes.

By 1980 the view of the play as ambiguous gets transformed in Richard
Bevis's *Laughing Tradition,* where Bevis opines that Kelly "includes something for
everyone: a feature of his career as well as of this play" (95). Bevis does not elaborate, but from the context one can assume that, rather than seeing Kelly's ambiguity as a function of unconscious uncertainty on his part, Bevis implies that
Kelly was a market-oriented professional trying to please a varied audience. As
such, the play reveals a deliberate manipulation of cultural attitudes as it tries to
accommodate contradictory or oppositional views. From this perspective, one
can argue (as I have) for Kelly as the consummate rhetorician of popular cul-

ture who needs to play both sides—who must be, in other words, both senti-mental and antisentimental—to do what any popular writer must do: please as varied and as large an audience as possible. This practice is similar to that fol-lowed by Kelly in his journalism on domestic subjects, where, as I noted, he would print essays both supporting and denying, say, a young woman's right to choose a spouse for herself.

Bevis rightly singles out Mrs. Harley for her statement in which she both attacks delicacy and admits its attractions (2.1), and he admits that, "if this is a sentimental comedy, it is remarkably diluted" (*Laughing* 95). He asserts the now familiar judgment of Kelly's ambiguity, noting that, by the end of the play, "[O]ne is left unsure of the playwright's own attitude towards the delicacy of his senti-mentalists." Bevis falls back, then, on the notion of authorial uncertainty, although he seemed initially to have suggested that Kelly's attitude was deliberately con-structed—and not really ambivalent at all—in order to make his product more marketable by addressing both sides of the sentimental-antisentimental issue.

Whatever the long-range critical fortunes of *False Delicacy* were to be, the play's immediate impact on Kelly's life was exhilarating. Once gain, Cooke's bio-graphical sketch in the *European Magazine* provides the greatest amount of in-timate detail of the first night's triumph:

> Kelly's friends anticipated the success of this piece, by ordering an handsome supper at the Globe Tavern on the same night, to receive their little Bayes in all his dramatic splendours. The party consisted of near seventy people, composed of authors, booksellers, and the neighbouring tradesmen, who, from attachment, flattery, or igno-rance, poured out one continued stream of adulation; "it was," in their opinion, "the best first comedy ever produced"—"The Au-thor was a heaven-born genius, and he was destined by his pen to reclaim the former immoralities of the Stage." (Jan. 1794, 42)

Davies provides a broader view of the impact of the play's success on Kelly. Concentrating on its salutary influence on both Kelly's career and his personal-ity, he writes:

> It may be justly said of Kelly, that no man ever profited more by a sudden change of fortune in his favour: prosperity caused an im-mediate and remarkable alteration in his whole conduct; from a low, petulant, absurd, and ill-bred censurer, he was transformed to the humane, affable, good-natured, well-bred man. His conversation in general was lively and agreeable; he had an uncommon stock of ready language; and though not deeply read, what he said was gen-erally worthy of attention. (2: 140)

This fairy-tale assessment of magical transformation needs to be read in the context of Davies's own career, particularly in light of his being driven from the stage by the same sort of "ill-bred" censuring—that of Charles Churchill in his *Rosciad*—of which he accuses Kelly.[12] Davies was referring generally to Kelly's change of fortune; nevertheless, it seems clear that the success of *False Delicacy* was the key event in that achievement of prosperity: the three authors' nights alone yielded more than seven hundred pounds (O'Leary 75).[13] The play also went through five editions in 1768 (Crozier 83; see also Carver, Introduction lvii). A note printed in *Lloyd's Evening Post and British Chronicle* (Feb. 1–3) suggests how popular the play was with reading audiences: "The New Comedy, entitled False Delicacy, was so rapidly bought up, that the Proprietors had sold the whole Impression of Three Thousand before Two o'clock." As the report notes that it was "yesterday morning" (Tues., 2 Feb.), and as the paper was published on Wednesday, 3 February, the demand for Kelly's first play was great indeed; and by Monday, 22 February, it was already in its fourth edition.

If contemporary reports are to be believed, however, there was one important negative effect, already alluded to, of Kelly's success—the falling out with Oliver Goldsmith. Evidently acquainted since 1765, when they were introduced by John Newbery, for whose *Ledger* Goldsmith had written, the two journalists had become friendly enough that Goldsmith, after frequenting Kelly's home, became "struck with the Conveniencies of Matrimony" and thought once of marrying Kelly's sister-in-law. Kelly, who knew that his sister-in-law's temper was not as happy as his wife's, dissuaded Goldsmith from proposing (Cooke, "Hugh Kelly," Nov. 339; Prior 175). The two men, living near each other in the Middle Temple, no doubt remained friendly during the 1765–67 period, and Forster, one of Goldsmith's nineteenth-century biographers, discusses at length their participation in the Wednesday Club at that time. Meeting weekly at the Globe Tavern on Fleet Street, the Club consisted of William Ballantyne; Edward Thompson, naval officer, playwright, and later editor of Kelly's *Works;* William Glover, another Irish Grub-Streeter and friend of Goldsmith; and Thomas King, the comic actor and good friend of Kelly; perhaps Charles Macklin, the actor-playwright with whom Kelly was later to quarrel over Garrick, also attended.[14] As one of the Club's main activities was singing, and as Kelly was said to have a good ear (Oxberry 2: 206), he probably looked forward to the meetings.[15]

It is hardly surprising that Forster and Goldsmith's other nineteenth-century English biographer, Prior, take Goldsmith's side in relating the dispute with Kelly, although Prior is generally more fair-minded in treating Kelly than is Forster. He reports that the quarrel resulted from a meeting, soon after both men's plays had appeared, in the Covent Garden green room:

> Goldsmith stammered out awkward congratulations to Kelly on his recent success, to which the other, prepared for war, promptly replied that he could not thank him because he could not believe him. "From that hour they never spoke to one another:" and Kelly,

reluctant that Goldsmith should be troubled to "do anything more for him," resigned the club. (Forster, bk. 2, 302)

But perhaps Cooke, who knew both men, should be allowed a word on their relationship. In noting the jealousy Goldsmith had for Kelly's success, Cooke says that Goldsmith was "kind, beneficent, and good-natured in the extreme, to all but those whom he thought his competitors in literary fame. . . . Poverty had no terrors for him—but the applause paid a brother poet 'made him poor indeed'" ("Hugh Kelly," Dec. 422). Peter Tasch, noting that Isaac Bickerstaff was also envious of Kelly's success, adds sardonically, "[A]s long as there were two theaters and only two new plays among Goldsmith, Kelly, and Bickerstaff, the three Irishmen could remain friends; but three plays and two theaters was another matter" (127).

And despite the claim that the two dramatists never spoke to one another again, historical circumstances suggest otherwise. As Cooke reported ("Hugh Kelly," Jan. 42), both men were involved in the short-lived *Gentleman's Journal,* only two numbers of which were published (19 and 26 Nov. 1768). But this evidence, as well as the fact that both met at Bickerstaff's house in 1770 to hear parts of Bickerstaff's new play, *'Tis Well It's No Worse* (Tasch 199), must call into question the tradition of perpetual animosity.[16] Still, in 1768 it doubtlessly caused Kelly some pain to have suffered a rupture with Goldsmith. For Kelly's tearful behavior at Goldsmith's funeral in April 1774 suggests that, despite any quarrel, deep feelings for Goldsmith persisted. And as Kelly was soon to learn from his coming journalistic war with the Patriots, a writer who depended on the public for his livelihood could never have too many friends.

6

Confrontation with the Wilkites

lthough the publication of *Thespis, Memoirs of a Magdalen,* and *False Delicacy* placed Kelly in a higher sphere of London literary life than he was accustomed to, he continued to work away in the Grub Street world of journalism. It was this work, after all, that enabled him to produce theater reviews, compose *Thespis* itself, and hence offer something to David Garrick in return for the manager's aid in building a career as a playwright. Tracing Kelly's journalism from 1766 until his departure from the *Public Ledger* sometime in late winter or early spring 1772 is difficult: it simply cannot be done directly because most of the *Ledger's* issues are missing. One must rely once again on occasional facts and anecdotes, the last often produced by anonymous and sometimes hostile sources. Even anecdotes are at times scarce, so that one must often turn to more generalized accounts, written by contemporaries, like Cooke, some years after the events themselves had taken place.

These obstacles to constructing a skeletal record of Kelly's writing career even after he achieved some fame with *False Delicacy* in early 1768 until *A Word to the Wise* in March 1770 are significant. Certainly the events surrounding the production of *False Delicacy* throw some light on Kelly's relationships. Because of the play, we learn of his connection to Garrick; we learn of Bickerstaff's jealousy; and we learn of the supposed dissolution of the friendship with Goldsmith. But by the spring of 1768, the biographical trail once again grows faint. Until it ceased publication on 16 April 1768, the *Theatrical Monitor* continued to attack Kelly for his partiality toward Garrick even after it gave Kelly's first play a positive review. But detailed references to his ongoing professional life—which was still the life of a journalist—are rare. Not until the late spring of 1769 did Kelly come before the public eye once again and begin to leave biographical traces that can be followed to the next main event of his writing life: the damnation of his second comedy by a Wilkite mob.

Kelly was still involved in editing the *Public Ledger,* as he had been for nearly three years. Because copies of the paper for the later years of the 1760s are not available, I cannot tell when Kelly first began to attack the growing Patriotic movement on behalf of George III and his ministers. Possibly he turned the paper against John Wilkes and other City radicals—like William Beckford—soon after Wilkes returned to England from exile in France, which was on 6 February 1768. Soon after, Kelly's old enemy William Bingley gave up publishing the *Theatrical Monitor* and resurrected the *North Briton* to support the radical movement.[1] But contemporary accounts of when Kelly actually entered the propaganda war that haunted him for the remainder of his life are vague about dates. As O'Leary notes (84), Cooke, J. Taylor, Thompson, and Davies all say pretty much the same thing—that Kelly became a political writer in favor of the government—but none provides a specific chronology.

Kelly's earliest political publication was *An Elegy to the Memory of the Right Honourable William, Late Earl of Bath,* which was reprinted in Kelly's *Works.*[2] The poem attacks William Pulteney (1684–1764), the uncle of George Colman the Elder; Pulteney, after having been an important Opposition leader during the Walpole years, accepted a peerage from George II in 1742. Pulteney had been a "Patriot" in the older, pre-Wilkite sense, but upon becoming earl of Bath, he lost much of his political stature. Kelly compares Pulteney's shameful behavior with that of his contemporary, Sir John Barnard (1685–1764), who is praised for being an honest man of principle throughout his long career in the House of Commons.[3] Kelly does not mention Pulteney's personal life, and it is unclear how much he knew of the relationship between Colman and Pulteney, who had married the sister of Colman's mother and had interested himself in his nephew's career by attempting to steer him toward law and away from the seductions of a life in journalism and the theater. Unlike Kelly, who turned to the law after he had begun to write for the theater, Colman first tried to follow the law, possibly to appease his wealthy uncle, but found it a dreary pursuit (Page 45–46).[4] Kelly's poem does not mention Colman, who helped manage Drury Lane in Garrick's absence during the seasons of 1763–64 and 1764–65. As a result of that managerial experience, his own plays, and his connection to the Nonsense Club, Colman possessed no little stature in the literary world. But Colman's staging of Kelly's tragedy, *Clementina,* at Covent Garden in 1771 was still years away. Kelly's chiding of Pulteney for sacrificing principle for a peerage is certainly commonplace enough, but because the circumstances of its composition are unknown, the *Elegy* reveals nothing about Kelly's politics prior to his commitment to the Court party.

In 1766 there appeared a pamphlet, an apologia, praising William Pitt that has been traditionally identified as Kelly's.[5] In Thompson's "Life," this pamphlet is simply called *A Vindication of Mr. Pitt's Administration,* and, as O'Leary notes, it is favorably mentioned by Philip Dormer Stanhope, fourth earl of Chesterfield, in his *Letters to His Son* (O'Leary 88–89).[6] Pitt's political career bore some resemblance to Pulteney's: both were successful and popular while in the Commons but lost esteem after accepting peerages and hence were in their later careers less effective than they had been. The work was composed, says O'Leary, as a response to a pamphlet by Humphrey Cote and John Almon that had attacked Pitt and had supposedly been written at the urging of Richard Temple Grenville, second earl Temple. Almon and Temple were strong Wilkites, and although Almon and Kelly had probably worked together earlier in the decade on the *Gazetteer,* they were far apart politically.[7] Kelly's defense of Pitt in opposition to Almon and Temple may indicate that Kelly began to turn the *Ledger* in an anti-Patriot direction as early as 1766, but I cannot be certain.

In the late winter and early spring of 1768, while the *Theatrical Monitor* was still attacking Kelly for his pro-Garrick writings in the *Ledger,* an event occurred that was later to subject Kelly to abuse from the London radical press at about the same time that this press began to attack him for his pro-Court stance. The event was the arrest and trial of Frederick Calvert. Calvert, the seventh Lord Baltimore, was tried for allegedly imprisoning a Miss Sarah Woodcock during the winter of 1768 for the purpose of seducing her. Tried at Kingston early in May, Baltimore was acquitted, but he earlier faced severe attacks by the press who gloried in this sensational real-life version of *Clarissa.*[8] John Taylor bases his knowledge of Kelly's involvement on a story his father, a good friend of Kelly's, had heard directly from Kelly. It seems that Lord Baltimore, alarmed by the violence of the press attacks, sought Kelly's advice about how to combat the negative stories:

> As the public prints were full of the story, which made a great noise in the metropolis, Lord Baltimore wrote to Kelly, desiring that he would call on him. Mr. Kelly accordingly waited immediately upon his Lordship, who consulted him on the propriety of publishing some answer to the numerous attacks which were made on him through the public press, proposing that Mr. Kelly should take up his cause and publish something in his favour. After entering into his Lordship's feelings, Mr. Kelly advised him to wait the issue of the trial, and then, if public prejudice remained still strong against him, whatever the decision might be, there would be time enough to bring forward a defence or vindication. (J. Taylor 1: 100–101)

Another version is related by the "Memoirs" biographer in the *Town and Country Magazine* (85–86). This writer claims that Kelly had already printed, unrequested by Lord Baltimore, "letters and paragraphs" favorable to his lordship's cause. The differences between the two versions are most significant in the interpretation each writer provides of the episode. Taylor does not interpret this event in any way that can be construed as critical of Kelly: he makes Kelly passive here—it is Lord Baltimore who sought out Kelly. He also constructs a Kelly wise in the ways of journalism, particularly of journalism used as a propaganda tool and as a public-relations weapon. Taylor's focus on Kelly's giving advice frames Kelly as some sort of eighteenth-century media consultant. In contrast, the anonymous "Memoirs" writer depicts Kelly actively soliciting Lord Baltimore's attention by running favorable stories.[9] Indeed, the "Memoirs" author claims that Kelly in general used his editorship at the *Ledger* in his own self-interest:"In this capacity, he had many opportunities of recommending himself to persons of rank and fortune" ("Memoirs," *Town and Country* 86).

Regardless of whether one wishes to see Kelly as actively seeking Lord Baltimore's favor or as only passively involved as a consultant, the anecdote is a critical one, a defining moment, for understanding Kelly at midcareer and for situating him in the conditions of the Grub Street writer in a transitional literary culture.[10] It is a culture in which the old dependence on patronage, the very condition Lance Bertelsen says Churchill scorned, was, if one reads the incident through the lens of the "Memoirs" writer (whose text is ironically itself parasitic upon the Kelly anecdote), still very much alive. But it is also a culture in which the new market-based dynamic was already working itself out, even if sometimes in an uneasy dance with the old. The new is evident in Kelly's independent role as editor of a *public* literary medium and in his public-relations–journalistic knowledge that he offers Lord Baltimore. It is curious that the old client-patron aura hangs on in this decidedly new business climate, as the conclusion of the episode makes clear:

> When Mr. Kelly reached home, he found a very polite letter from Lord Baltimore, written during the few moments he had been absent from the room, and despatched immediately, containing a banknote for one hundred pounds. This delicate act of generosity was characteristic of his lordship. (J. Taylor 1: 101)

An act of generosity, if viewed in the old way, the way of private patron-artist, but an act of payment for services rendered, if viewed in the new way, the way of client-professional. This incident is emblematic of Kelly's writing career, for he was a new man, a popular writer who was dependent on the new market economy of journalism to earn his living; yet he was also caught up in the older patron-client relationship that endured in spite of the new world of commerce. Kelly's relationship to both David Garrick and, as we shall see, to Sir Robert Ladbroke represented that older world, but an older world clearly tinged with the commercial interest of the new.

I must finally agree with the *Town and Country* "Memoirs" author that the occasion was a reenactment of the traditional author-patron relationship, only writ new in the publicly, avowedly commercial medium of the newspaper, the very vehicle that was breaking down—as I discuss when considering the use of the press by the Wilkites against Parliament itself—the traditional boundaries between public and private discourses. For if a Lord Baltimore's private sexual transgressions could be publicized by the new democratic, dialogic discourse of journalism, then surely the political, but heretofore private, transgressions of his brothers in Parliament must soon be opened to the same public scrutiny in newspapers that would soon print the debates in the House of Commons.

The Lord Baltimore event provides a useful transition to the explicitly political phase of Hugh Kelly's career. Indeed, although it is not known when Kelly began to propagandize for the ministers, my guess is that his work began sometime between the Pitt pamphlet and the Lord Baltimore episode. Kelly's defense of Baltimore angered the Wilkite press; it caused one of the earliest radical-press attacks on him. Baltimore's and Kelly's names were linked more than once in the papers: in the *Middlesex Journal* for 10–13 June 1769 appeared an attack on Baltimore, "whose name in some families," says the correspondent, "has been used to frighten children." The story goes on to mock Baltimore's supposed reformation and his plan to build a hospital "for all worn out and disabled debauchees."

One other key event of 1768 must be discussed. On 11 April 1768 (Lacroix 1: 51), Kelly was admitted to the Middle Temple to study law.[11] Contemporary biographers were vague or inaccurate about his career move. Cooke, for instance, says only that "in the year 1769 Kelly, with a laudable view to the security of some professions which might be a more permanent support of this family, entered himself as a Member of the Honourable Society of the Middle Temple" ("Hugh Kelly," Jan. 43); and modern accounts, such as those of W. W. Watt and Lacroix, say little more, mainly summarizing what earlier sources had said.[12] My consideration of Kelly's legal career comes later because he was not admitted to the bar until 21 May 1773.[13] But Cooke's speculation about Kelly's motives are reasonable. In light of Kelly's haunting insecurities about the life of writing, dramatized in the self-reflexive pieces on journalism, it seems sensible to conclude that, ironically, in the midst of the financial success brought by *False Delicacy,* Kelly's doubts about pursuing a literary career even in the more lucrative field of drama forced him to consider a more secure profession. It was as if those earlier radical misgivings still retained their force, and the flights from writing, a theme of those early journalism pieces, are acted out in the commitment to the Middle Temple.

Whether the practice of law brought Kelly that security I consider later. It is enough now to point out that, as David Lemmings shows, in the eighteenth century, "[T]he legal profession was much more open to market forces than any of the other 'great' professions" (176). Lemmings argues that the law was more likely to respond to both social and economic changes than were the other professions and notes the "bar's growing colonization by the middle classes." If one accepts Lemmings's suggestion that the bar was more open than other professions to men of social and economic marginality, then it is not surprising to find Kelly using the law as another way to rise from Grub Street. It is understandable that Kelly joined the ranks of other writers, like Colman and Murphy, in a profession that, like the new world of marketplace literature, was open to talented individuals, regardless of their backgrounds and that, unlike literature, promised more security (175).

While Kelly was beginning his legal studies, the "second" Wilkite movement was gaining momentum, and a series of events occurred in 1768 and early 1769 that drew Kelly further into the political arena from which he never seemed to escape. While Kelly was basking in the success of his play, John Wilkes was slipping back into England from where he had fled in December 1763. Eventually expelled from Parliament and found guilty of a libel against King George, Wilkes had remained in exile, except for brief visits to test the political waters in 1766 and 1767, before finally returning to England for good in February 1768. The war between the Wilkites and the other city radicals and the government of George III that began in the spring of 1768 was to last, with some variation in intensity, until Wilkes was elected lord mayor in the fall of 1775 and finally regained his seat in Parliament. The struggle between Wilkes and the Court was, as John Brewer has shown, as much a literary and theatrical propaganda battle as it was a traditional political and legal struggle.[14]

Brewer spends a good bit of time early on outlining the oligarchic monopoly of political power of the Walpole years (1725–54) when patronage extended into every corner of government. That patronage helped to create the massive political stability of those years at the same time that it excluded many from the political process. When patronage and single-party rule led to a stagnant political atmosphere, new sources became available in midcentury London for the expression of oppositional political views (J. Brewer 7–10). Brewer describes some of these sources as activities and institutions, such as the club, the press, the coffeehouse, and the theater, all of which appear to Lance Bertelsen as the hothouses of a kind of Bakhtinian carnivalesque inversion of traditional politics (227). This emerging oppositional culture, Bertelsen shows, had its roots in the City life of politics, literature, and theater.[15] It was a life personified in the Nonsense Club of the early 1760s, a club whose members were ready to challenge political exclusion and dependency, to contest the oligarchy, even though "the forces of political constraint were at their height" (J. Brewer 7).

This emerging political counterculture began to assert itself fully, I argue, only after Wilkes's return in 1768, whereupon all the old feelings that coalesced around Wilkes in 1763, when, as Bertelsen notes, Wilkes the gadfly had become Wilkes the martyr (197), were able to be exploited by the Wilkite propaganda effort, some of which resembled street theater. Besides the obviously violent riots as discussed by George Rudé, John Brewer, and others throughout the late 1760s and early 1770s, lesser street events, such as parades and processions, menaced those persons not in the Patriotic vanguard; these actions could be said to have acted as media insofar as they conveyed political attitudes in a persuasive, threatening fashion.

Along with live street processions, the radical press also seemed to have considered processions a political literary form, as well as street theater, and printed some of them from time to time. The processionals of the Wilkites are clearly carnivalesque and often amusingly zany, much like the processional elements in the mock-heroic poem. The following comes from the *Middlesex Journal* for 4–6 January 1770 and contains satirical hits at all those whom the Patriots disliked (e.g., Scottish placemen; ministerial propagandists, like Kelly and here especially John Shebbeare; the Court system; the increased presence in London of military forces designed to dampen Patriotic street display; and so forth).

A Procession

1. Drums, fifes and bagpipes, &c. &c.
2. Constables two and two, with their slaves.
3. Justices of W——r, two and two; in the middle of the street, Sir John F——g, alone supported by M——r and K——g, with their judges.
4. A party of the third regiment of the guards with their bayonets fixed.
5. The Addresses carried by the forgers of them, two and two.
6. Scotch Addresses carried by 24 grenadiers of the third regiment, two and two.
7. Ministerial Scribblers, two and two, with their real names chalked in large letters on their backs, and crape hatbands, and black gloves; Sh—— alone, carrying the sixth letter to the people of England.

The political events of March 1770, apart from those directly tied to the riotous damnation of Kelly's *Word to the Wise,* provide an example of an actual street processional that, at least as reported in the paper, must be seen as orchestrated propaganda. On Thursday, 15 March, a few days after the play's failure, Lord Mayor William Beckford, accompanied by various city officials, visited St. James to present King George with their "Remonstrance," essentially a list of Patriot complaints about the conduct of the ministry. The *Middlesex Journal* for 13–15 March describes the event as follows:

> Yesterday at one o'clock, the Right Hon. the Lord Mayor, attended by the Sheriffs Townsend and Sawbridge, the Aldermen Trecothick and Stephenson, the City Officers, about 120 Common-Council-men, and a large body of the Livery of this City went in procession from Guildhall to St. James's, to present the City Remonstance to his Majesty, amidst the acclamation of a vast multitude of spectators assembled on this occasion.

One could argue that this event is merely the formal ritual of government and that the processional occurred as an expected and traditional form. Yet the paper goes on to notice other street activities associated with the Remonstrance that seem, marginalized and unauthorized compared to the processional, to be powerful forms of muscle-flexing propaganda. The *Middlesex Journal* reported that, near the official political scene, "Mrs. Hayley, sister to John Wilkes, Esq., was in a chariot at the bottom of St. James's street, and being known by some of the populace, was complimented with three loud huzzas." And then there was street theater by some less threatening Patriots: "A number of Gentlemen had assembled at the Cardigan-Head tavern Charing Cross, from the windows of which they saluted the Lord Mayor, Aldermen, Sheriffs &c. with French horns and other music." That such street displays were not altogether innocent can be found in the *Middlesex Journal's* editorializing about the risk the king was taking by receiving the Remonstrance rudely (he was said to have laughed at the conclusion of Beckford's presentation of the grievances):

> When the impolitic conduct of a Monarch is supposed to be prin-
> cipally owing to the influence and fallacy of the *creatures* who sur-
> round his person, his subjects, if generous subjects, commiserate him;
> but when his impolicy, unmoved by dutiful intreaty, and unchecked
> by humble complaint, extends even to derision and contempt, a spir-
> ited indignation must be naturally expected to take the place of pity
> and affection. (13–15 March)

The final clause of the article contains a veiled warning: "[A] vast multitude of spectators" could, if provoked, become a raging, powerful mob. Yet the vast multitude also serves to remind us that, as Jacques Ellul has shown, no political propaganda can be really effective unless some form of physical participation is allowed: "[T]he proselyte becomes militant" (29), in Ellul's phrase, only when he has acted physically and thus committed himself publicly, body and mind. Wilkite street action in the form of demonstrations, processionals, marches, and even riots thus bonded the Patriots together and made them a formidable force. When government violence ensued, as it did during the St. George's Fields Massacre on 10 May 1768, martyrs could be created, further solidifying the radical ranks who could feel noble about such sacrifices (Rudé, *Wilkes* 49–50).[16] And all was reinforced when they could afterward read about their collective behavior, as in the reports above, as it was reflected to them by their own media, such as the *Middlesex Journal* and the *London Evening Post*.

The main Wilkite-Patriot propaganda efforts were centered in the print media, which were not just the papers and magazines—the *Middlesex Journal*, the *London Evening Post*, the *North Briton*, the *Parliamentary Spy*, the *Freeholder's Magazine*, and *Bingley's Journal*—but also the occasional poems, pamphlets, and handbills that the Wilkite press cranked out.[17] As Ellul notes, any organization that wishes to make propaganda must do one of two things: it must control the media or have access to it (20), and as the above list of periodicals indicates, the Patriots had developed their own media in which the boundaries between news, propaganda, and popular culture or entertainment were blurred. Both Brewer and Bertelsen understand the role that popular culture, with its dramatizing tendencies, had to play in constructing a popular political culture, at the center of which stood that "Lord of Misrule" (Bertelsen 227), John Wilkes. One of my key purposes here and in the following chapter is to describe this political-culture–popular-culture drama as it unfolded after 1768, extending the cultural analysis that Brewer, Bertelsen, and others contend operated in the early 1760s to post-1768 developments.

I contend that Hugh Kelly played an important, although nearly overlooked, role in this complex cultural struggle from 1768 until 1775.[18] And I focus on his roles as propagandist and as writer of popular culture in this environment. It is a life where, as I have suggested already, theater becomes political and politics becomes theatrical, and journalism drives it all as, through newspapers and magazines, it turns all this conflict into a kind of participatory, democratic popular culture.[19] As such, the propaganda discourses that manifested themselves after 1768 (and here it seems clear that popular culture and propaganda are often indistinguishable) continue that "enormous outpouring of propaganda and commentary" that Bertelsen feels characterizes the early 1760s (196).[20] The period from 1768 to roughly 1775, then, is act 2 of the Wilkes propaganda drama. In the middle of that mazy theater was Hugh Kelly, whose role, though significant, must be glimpsed once again through the lens of hostile commentary and fragmented anecdote. Kelly appears on this scene/site because he was important in the government's propaganda counterattack.

In outlining the conditions that allowed the growth of what John Brewer calls "focussed radicalism," he describes the fragmentation of the political elite as it was weakened by the antiparty politics of the young King George (18). He also discusses the maturation of the press as a contributory force to this fragmentation, a press that could maintain a political campaign on a national scale for several years. Added to these forces is Bertelsen's notion that, with a phenomenon like Charles Churchill and the Nonsense Club, one sees a development of marketable political discourse that fed off itself and produced more discourse in response, all of which became part of a self-perpetuating, profit-making publishing industry: it was a heady blend of poetry, journalism, and theater, all creating a kind of salable popular culture that functioned as political propaganda. Bertelsen writes specifically about the complicated economic activity at the center of which was the theater: "[A] successful play might lead not only to lucrative benefit nights but to play publication and other spin-offs" (71). He refers here to the early 1760s, but the application of his general point about the economic and political aspects of theater can be made for Wilkite activities later in the decade and into the early years of the 1770s, for the world of politics presented the same opportunity for exploitation of the literary market that a successful play did.

I have already noted a number of radical periodicals that formed between 1768 and 1770. John Wheble, a publisher of Wilkite materials, illustrates this entrepreneurial exploitation: not only did Wheble publish the radical newspaper the *Middlesex Journal,* but he also extensively advertised all sorts of other Patriot materials that he published, materials that could be considered spin-offs from the main political theater surrounding all the activities of the star performer.[21] I argue that the entire newspaper was a sociopolitical-socioeconomic advertising machine, a propaganda factory, for Wilkite radicalism that by the early 1770s had developed a remarkable and marketable array of consumer products.[22] It offered ideology for sale, and the flood of publications advertised in this newspaper—pamphlets, poems, letters, and the like—constituted a propaganda discourse of formidable proportions. Wheble took over the printing of the *Middlesex Journal* in June 1770 from William George Edmunds; and in the 7–9 June number, he printed and advertised for himself a pamphlet, *Mr. Horne's Oration . . . to the Freeholders of Middlesex.* From then on, the newspaper became a virtual propaganda organ for the London radicals and for publications that helped to construct that radicalism and were in turn constructed by it.

An examination of the *Middlesex Journal* for the month of January 1771 reveals this propaganda-commercial effort. In the first number, Wheble printed an advertisement for a new periodical weekly called the *Whig,* an avowedly political paper that was to be printed by himself and sold by his brother, William Wheble. In the same number appeared an advertisement for *An Historical Essay on the English Constitution; or, An Impartial Enquiry into the Elective Power of the People,* another obviously political work on a subject, the right of election, dear to the radicals ever since the spring of 1768 when Wilkes had first been denied his seat in Parliament. This work was printed for Edward and Charles Dilly, but a third work, the second edition of *The Letters of Junius,* also advertised in this number of the paper, was once again the venture of Wheble and his brother. In effect, Wheble was making commercial propaganda (the advertisement) for the items of political propaganda that he and other publishers had for sale. These advertisements for political books and journals were accompanied by a constant stream of politically oriented letters to the editor: in this month, the majority of them had to do with the growing conflict between Wilkes and Horne Tooke (born John Horne) as these two leading radicals fought each other in print. Appearing with the letters in the paper's columns were paragraphs dealing with all sorts of city political activity, including notices of society meetings, such as the Society of the Supporters of the Bill of Rights (SSBR), and gossip about city aldermen, especially those Courtier aldermen whom the editor disliked, such as the gossip reported about alderman William Nash's romantic involvement with wealthy widows, the courting of whom, the paper implied, contributed to the growth of Mr. Nash's fortune.

If Ellul is correct in maintaining that any organization that wishes to influence opinion by producing effective propaganda for itself must either control or have access to the media (20–23), then the success of the city radicals during the height of the Wilkite movement owed a great deal to these periodicals, for not only could they carry a daily flow of political information and reportage, but they could also serve in turn as propaganda mechanisms for other pro-radical publications as well. Part of the effort to counter this propaganda machine fell to Hugh Kelly. His efforts in the *Public Ledger* (which formed part of the ministerial propaganda effort) on behalf of George III led to the damning of his second comedy, *A Word to the Wise.*

John Brewer has stressed the importance of the development of organizations in the growth of radicalism in the 1760s and 1770s, noting that the formation of the SSBR (20 Feb. 1769) represented the first "extra-parliamentary organization devoted to a programme of reform" (20–21). The SSBR and the Constitutional Society, formed in protest of the SSBR's policy of aiding Wilkes exclusively but nevertheless a Patriot entity, produced in part the propaganda agenda voiced by the radical periodicals; clearly, because of the funds they raised, these organizations also helped keep the propaganda flowing even when the money was only used to keep printers out of jail or to pay their fines. The journals offered the opportunity to present a broad cultural critique of the older hegemonic culture of early- and mid-eighteenth-century England, which, as Gerald Newman has pointed out, was aristocratic, cosmopolitan, and Francophile. Against this older culture, there developed, in Newman's view, a cultural critique that was middle class, antiaristocratic, nationalistic, and Francophobic.[23] Putting aside the longer-range question of whether or not the middle-class ideology did in fact uproot the older aristocratic ideology, one can say that to a large extent the worldview—what Ellul calls the "myth-system" (31–32)—of these periodicals did often reflect the values Newman outlines. In addition, these periodicals voiced more local manifestations of their audience's ideology, particularly in their biases against the Scots and the Irish and for the grumbling American colonials with whose cause they could identify.

In possession of their own periodicals, then, the Wilkites could fight a propaganda battle with their own weapons. One of their most famous organs was the *North Briton;* originally founded by Churchill and Wilkes in 1762 to oppose the politics of John Stuart, third earl of Bute, the king's favorite, the periodical went too far in attacking the government; and after the publication of what became the famous no. 45 on 23 April 1763, the ministers took legal action against the paper and the author of no. 45, Wilkes himself. This action ultimately led to Wilkes's flight to France on 24 December 1763. When William Bingley decided to resurrect the paper on 10 May 1768, the tensions caused by Wilkes's return to the political arena were running high. Wilkes had been elected MP for Middlesex earlier in the spring and had voluntarily submitted to the courts so that the old 1763 actions still pending against him might be brought to legal conclusion once and for all. But Lord Mansfield (William Murray) refused to pass judgment, and Wilkes languished in prison because the king was adamant that he not be seated in Parliament, which was to meet on 10 May, the very day no. 47, the first of Bingley's new series of the *North Briton,* was to be published. The days passed and still Mansfield refused to pass judgment; Wilkite hostility to him was great, and that resentment fueled the fiftieth number of the *North Briton* (28 May), which attacked Mansfield directly, rebuking him for what it considered cruel treatment of Wilkes and accusing him of blatant favoritism toward the Court position. This journalistic skirmish ultimately led to the imprisonment of William Bingley for his refusal to answer interrogatories concerning nos. 50 and 51 of the *North Briton*.

Bingley was still in prison late in the year when his paper for 24 December 1768 attacked Kelly and the *Public Ledger,* the first time Kelly had been singled out specifically for his political rather than his theatrical bias. The motivation for the attack concerned the occasion of Bingley's brief release from prison earlier in the fall. The *Ledger* seized this opportunity to suggest that Bingley was released because he had finally decided to answer the court's interrogatories, thereby implying that Bingley had cooperated with the ministry. Such a story, if believed, would have seriously compromised Bingley and weakened one of the most outspoken of the Wilkite periodicals. Angered at Kelly's insinuation, Bingley requested that the *Ledger* retract its statement. Evidently, Kelly complied but nevertheless managed to cast further suspicion on Bingley while doing so. The *North Briton,* while attacking Kelly for this trick, suggested in its 24 December issue that the *Ledger* was not popular because of its "direction," an obvious hit at Kelly's editorship. The long battle between Kelly and the Wilkite media had begun.

But the Wilkite press had other reasons to attack Kelly by the end of 1768. One of these reasons stemmed from a trial that had taken place in early August at Guildford. Held before a grand jury, the trial was to determine whether or not certain members of the grenadiers were guilty of murder in the shooting that took place in front of the King's Bench Prison during the May 1768 riots involving the Wilkites. Wilkes had been confined to the prison on the old charges stemming from 1763; various street disturbances in favor of Wilkes occurred between this imprisonment in late April and 10 May, when the riot called the St. George's Fields Massacre took place and provided what George Rudé has called the Wilkites' "first martyrs" (Rudé, *Wilkes*). Among those killed by the grenadiers was the presumably innocent son of a local publican, William Allen; that the soldiers involved were Scotsmen only fueled the flames of the crisis.[24] The soldiers were tried at Guildford on 8 August 1768, and eventually all were acquitted, much to the anger of the radicals who felt that there had been a miscarriage of justice.

The initial issue of the *Middlesex Journal* (4–6 Apr. 1769) contains a direct attack on Kelly's *Public Ledger,* which is said to have "sunk to contempt," no doubt for its anti-Wilkes views. This issue identifies Kelly as the *Ledger's* editor and criticizes his attacks on the Lord Mayor Samuel Turner's character.[25] A more thorough attack occurred in the number for 6–8 April; outlined in a letter to the editor signed only "A. B.," the charges against Kelly are presented as questions, like interrogatories, possibly to provide a legal aura to the document:

I. Did not you (Mr. Hugh Kelly) write the letter signed "five hundred," concerning your "impartiality" in the "cause" of Mr.
Wilkes?

II. Did you not write those most malicious and scandalous attacks
on the Right Hon. the Lord Mayor's character under the signature of "Alcander," by the order of the Duke of Grafton?

III. Do you not at this present time receive a daily stipend from that
minister to defend him from daily attacks on his character?

IV. Are you not to be paid by Lt. C_____ L_____ the sum of
twenty guineas when the election is over, to defend his character against Mr. Wilkes's friends, in the *Public Ledger?*

Because this letter is the first detailed attack on Kelly's politics, some attention
to its particulars is in order.

Behind the first question lies the Wilkites' complaint, directed often at the
Ledger, that the paper's pose of impartiality—its motto was "Open to all but
influenced by none"—was insincere and easily exposed by a careful reading of
letters, such as the one referred to in question one. Question two raises the issue of ad hominem tactics about which the Wilkites were often to criticize Kelly.
With regard to question three, the duke of Grafton, Augustus Henry Fitzroy, did
suffer heavy attacks from the pens of the Wilkites and other critics, of whom
Junius was the most famous; while the fourth question refers to the Court party's
candidate, Col. Henry Lawes Luttrell, given Wilkes's parliamentary seat in April
1769 when Wilkes was refused his seat by the House of Commons. In this and
the final question, the issue of Kelly's status as a paid propagandist is raised; as
noted in the discussion of the Kelly–Garrick connection, Kelly did receive a
pension from Lord North sometime in the late summer or early fall of 1770. To
what extent he was paid, presumably on an irregular basis before 1770, cannot
be ascertained. Yet given his general reputation as a writer for the ministry even
before 1770, and given also the work he did for Lord Baltimore in 1768, the
charge does not appear unwarranted.

Throughout the spring of 1769, Kelly continued to be criticized by the
Wilkite press, principally the *Middlesex Journal.* After the anti-Kelly letter of 18–
20 April, another hostile notice appeared in the issue of 27–30 May, where Kelly
was scorned for writing for the ministry and his paper and its motto ridiculed.
When the *Journal* for 15–17 June announced that Kelly's next play would be
called *A Word to the Wise,* it demonstrated once again that the London culture of
politics, journalism, and the theater did indeed comprise a small and interrelated world. Otherwise, how could Kelly's political enemies have had such intimate knowledge of his next play, still nine months away from production? When
Garrick attempted to stage the play on 3 and 5 March 1770, a Wilkite mob
prevented him from doing so.

The damning of the play created its own paper war of sorts. The newspapers and magazines were filled first with the varied accounts of the riots and later with both pro- and anti-Kelly statements. Typical of the coverage was the following account, published in the *London Magazine* for March 1770. Following the magazine's review of the play itself, the writer claimed that his account of the riot included nothing but the facts and framed his account by acknowledging that Kelly had been unpopular because of his pro-government writing. He then described the beginning of the riot itself:

> The curtain was no sooner raised, than a loud hissing prevented the performers from beginning the play, a considerable time—While, on the other hand, the plaudits of the author's numerous friends, as well as of the unprejudiced, who desired to give him a fair hearing, and afterwards express their censure or approbation, rendered the confusion general. At last the performance commenced; but went on with incessant interruption, except only in the third act, to the conclusion. The performers, totally disconcerted by the tumult, were unable to exercise their abilities, or to remember their parts—Whole speeches, essentially necessary to the conduct of the fable, were left out, and others mutilated for the sake of brevity. In short, the sole consideration was to get the comedy through the five acts in any manner. (119)

When the play was announced for the following Monday, the Wilkites protested, and Kelly, behind the scenes, proposed to withdraw the piece. This gesture only aggravated his partisans, and the riot continued until James Lacy, the only manager in town, announced that the play would be given on Monday, 5 March.

Yet on Sunday, according to the *London Magazine,* Kelly went to Garrick, returned to London because of the crisis, and the two discussed ways of avoiding further troubles. Kelly was not willing to risk further violence merely to pursue his own interests, but Garrick was represented as unwilling to give in to the Wilkite mob for fear that, "if party disputes were once introduced into the theater, our most rational amusements must be quickly at an end" (120). On Monday night, another riot broke out, fueled by the conflict between the Wilkites and Kelly's partisans. Unsuccessful in calming the tumult, Garrick finally read an address by Kelly, who promised to withdraw the play immediately. But his own supporters dissented, and the riot continued for nearly three more hours until Kelly himself addressed the crowd, telling them that he feared for their safety, which address "moderated their rage" (121). A suggestion that *False Delicacy* be given to benefit Kelly on Tuesday evening was accepted; but it was performed with some continuation of the disruptions of Monday evening.

The press printed a variety of reports about and commentary on the riots, and the Wilkite *Middlesex Journal* printed several letters of opinion that seemed designed to justify the condemnation of the play. Pro-radical writers felt that Kelly had received his just deserts because he had recently called the Wilkite mobs the "scum of the earth" (6–8 Mar.).[26] One writer blamed Garrick, warning him against any "inclination to admit political disturbances" into his theater. Yet another anti-Kelly attack in the *Journal* offered the most thorough criticism, clearly demonstrating the radical hostility toward Kelly's politics and his allies, such as Sir Robert Ladbroke and William Beauchamp Proctor, who were associated with Court interests.[27] Addressed to Kelly, the letter began by attacking the "rude behaviour of your polite and worthy friends," who "conducted themselves more like ruffians than civilized Englishmen." This letter, signed "Atticus," continues on to revile Ladbroke and other aldermen and common councilmen of the City who had presumably subscribed to the publication of the play.

Atticus was most angered by Kelly's writing in the *Ledger* on behalf of a "venal ministry," and saved his most severe criticism of Kelly for "trying to vindicate the vilest wretches that ever disgraced literature." He ended this unusually long letter by yoking Kelly's politics with his career as a dramatist, and warned,

> You must expect this treatment, as the consequence of your political conduct and let me assure you, that the public will never forget the affront you have imposed upon them, but for ever persist in rejecting any future dramatic piece, that you may attempt to have performed.

Kelly took the threat seriously: his later plays were brought to the stage either anonymously or under pseudonyms. *Clementina* (1771) was given out as the work of an American clergyman, while *The School for Wives* (1774) was said to be written by Kelly's friend William Addington; Kelly's final two plays, *The Romance of an Hour* (1774) and *The Man of Reason* (1776), were brought to the stage anonymously.

7

Friends, Enemies, and the Damnation of *A Word to the Wise*

After the riots that prevented *A Word to the Wise* from being staged, the attacks on Kelly did not cease immediately, and indeed the warning by Atticus that any future play of Kelly's would be damned affected the production of his plays for the remainder of his career. But the controversy surrounding *A Word*'s damnation also produced positive results. As O'Leary points out:

> However successful his enemies may have felt when the curtain closed on the debacle in the theater on March 6, his friends did not desert Kelly. To recoup his losses in the failure of his play and to give him a public testimony of their esteem, a subscription edition of *A Word to the Wise* was quickly proposed. Within a fortnight it was advertised in the London papers. (144)

The Wilkites ridiculed the subscription drive, as O'Leary notes (146), but failed to stop Kelly's friends from raising a large sum, estimated at about eight hundred pounds. The "List of Subscribers" and the "Dedication" prefacing the edition are of interest in themselves, for they reveal the range of Kelly's friends and political allies who paid the five shillings entitling them to one copy of the play.

The edition, which appeared in the middle of May, was dedicated to Sir Robert Ladbroke, whose importance to Kelly I have already briefly touched upon. A banker, Ladbroke represented the City Company of Grocers for the Bridge Without Ward. It was to Ladbroke's house on Knight-Rider Street, Doctor's Commons, that Kelly moved, probably sometime in late 1769.[1] A great deal of information about Sir Robert Ladbroke can be gleaned from the London newspapers of the time, and as he was the most important patron-friend of Kelly's—Garrick excepted—his own role during the Wilkite years is worth attention. Called the "Father of the City" because of his status as the senior alderman, Ladbroke was a faithful Court party man, usually opposing, firmly but quietly, most of the pro-Wilkite political moves that emanated from the City Council, where the Court of Aldermen was generally more conservative than the Court of Common Council, this last being composed of a large number of small tradesmen as opposed to the aldermen who were usually wealthy merchants and bankers.[2] He led the opposition to the Remonstrance to the king orchestrated by Lord Mayor William Beckford in March 1770.[3] For this stance, as well as others, Ladbroke was sometimes mockingly called "Mother of the City" by the Wilkite press. Those aldermen who voted with Sir Robert were sometimes called "Gossips the Elderwomen." Nevertheless, Ladbroke seemed to have been respected throughout much of London society in the late 1760s and early 1770s. President of Christ's Hospital charity since 1758, his name was associated with many other philanthropic actions in the press.[4]

How many pieces of political propaganda Kelly might have composed for Ladbroke after receiving the pension from Lord North cannot be ascertained. However, Kelly always retained his affection for his patron. When Ladbroke died on 31 October 1773, all the London papers carried respectful and sometimes lengthy obituaries. Kelly was then writing for the *General Evening Post,* and that paper's obituary was laudatory indeed. Published in the 30 October–2 November issue, it ran over four hundred words, making it much longer than the usual obituary. The notice summarized Ladbroke's public career, stressing his representation of London in Parliament and his work for the Christ's Hospital charity. Still more information was provided in the 4–6 November number of the paper.[5]

No one listed as a subscriber to *A Word to the Wise* can be considered as close to Kelly as Ladbroke was, at least not in 1770. Yet the list is a large one, numbering roughly eight hundred seventy-five people, some of whom subscribed for more than one copy. Because a number were political figures of some sort, the list demonstrates how in Kelly's case politics and the theater were intertwined. Some names tell us more about Kelly's personal life than about his public one. There are in this respect a number of Kellys, both in England and in America, who subscribed. A William Kelly of New York, for instance, ordered forty-two copies; and another New Yorker, a Mr. Henry Kelly, also subscribed. The actor Thomas King, whom Kelly probably knew from King's years of acting in Dublin and who was a member of the Wednesday Club, took four copies. Some political allies are easily identifiable—Sir Robert Ladbroke, for instance, ordered twenty copies of the play, his son, four. The pro-Court aldermen also stood out in the list; among them was Thomas Hallifax, sheriff of London for 1768–69, lord mayor in 1777 when Kelly died, and alderman from 1766 to 1789. Hallifax voted against Wilkes for lord mayor in 1772 and generally voted against Wilkite interests. Another was John Kirkman, who ordered four copies and has been described by George Rudé (*Wilkes* 166) as an "occasional courtier"; Kirkman ran for sheriff in 1770 against the Wilkites and lost. Walter Rawlinson, Ladbroke's banking partner and son-in-law, also subscribed; when later elected an alderman (1773) and an MP (1774), he supported Lord North (Valentine 2: 733). Many others on the list, such as Temple S. Luttrell, Alderman John Bird, and Sir Edward Hawkes, were known supporters of George III and his ministers (Valentine 1: 428, 559), but whether they were personally known to Kelly is uncertain.

The subscribers from the literary world Kelly knew personally and included James Boswell, Edward and Charles Dilly, Samuel Foote, William Strahan, John Wheble, and Henry Sampson Woodfall. Strahan, friend of Johnson's and in 1770 printer to the king, was to become a close friend of Kelly's and was later to be one of the pallbearers at Kelly's funeral. Strahan's politics were pro-Court, and when elected MP in 1774, he voted in favor of the ministry. The most surprising name here is John Wheble, the Wilkite who was to take over the printing of the *Middlesex Journal* from William Edmunds in June. Yet Wheble, who took twenty-five copies, was presumably subscribing only to furnish his shop, as were no doubt some of the other booksellers who subscribed, such as the Dillys, who took fifteen copies. As discussed earlier, Wheble capitalized on the commercialization of politics in the 1760s and 1770s, and he no doubt recognized the commercial possibilities of Kelly's play with its political "Address."

Also printed with the subscription edition of *A Word to the Wise* is Kelly's valuable "An Address to the Public," a seventeen-page document, part narrative, part argument. It is at once a narrative of the riot and his role in quelling it; a defense of his political stance, as represented by his work for the *Public Ledger* and for other periodicals; a counterattack on Horne Tooke; and a lament for the politically vulnerable playwright, this last turning out to be another chapter in Kelly's story about the difficulties of professional authorship. In this defense, he denies that the *Ledger* has lacked impartiality yet readily admits that he did himself often write against Wilkes. Claiming that he had "never *expected* or *received* the smallest emolument for his little services" (*Plays,* "Address" vi), Kelly denies he was in the pay of any minister and maintains that his pro-government writings have been written because of his honest convictions; further, Kelly asserts that he has always written to "promote, instead of disturbing, the national tranquility" (vi). In defending himself, he constructs his own conservative myth and argues that

> he used his humble endeavors, rather to extinguish than animate the torch of public discord, and strove, as far as so insignificant an individual could strive, to wrest it from the hand of every political enthusiast, who madly attempted to set his country in flames. (vi–vii)

With words like *discord, enthusiast,* and *madly,* Kelly transports his readers back to the time of *Absalom and Achitophel,* transforming the Wilkites into the "murmuring Jews" of John Dryden's poem while attacking the "rage of party."

The middle section of "Address" merely details the rioting on 3 and 5 March. When he discovered that the Wilkites would also try to prevent the staging on 6 March of *False Delicacy,* he claims that he

> waited upon his friends and begged they would allow him to re-
> linquish his title to these profits since they were so likely to renew
> the disturbances of the theatre. His friends however were for a long
> time inflexible—they pronounced a violation of the compromise,
> no less injurious to the public than insulting to them. (x)

The compromise had to do with the suggestion that *False Delicacy* replace *A Word to the Wise* on 6 March, a compromise that Kelly evidently felt the Wilkites had accepted. Here Kelly tries to make himself appear to be caught between his righteous friends and his implacable enemies. But that slant was taken by the media too, as the report in the *London Magazine* illustrates (see chap. 6).

Kelly reprints in "Address" a Wilkite handbill distributed at the theater on the third night of disturbances, 6 March, when Garrick attempted to play *False Delicacy.* His inclusion of the handbill is a clever move designed to establish the relentlessness of the Wilkite vendetta against him, for the handbill's language ignores Kelly's rights and addresses only what the Wilkites claimed was the oppression of the theater audience:

To the Public

"You cannot be ignorant that one wretch in that infamous banditti, hired by [sic] administration to explain away the rights of an insulted people, is the author of a *Word to the Wise.* As a comic writer, his universal want of abilities has rendered him contemptible. As a politician, his principles are detestable. For these united reasons, you were pleased to forbid the representation of his play Saturday, and prevent it's [sic] performance last night. The author himself begged leave to withdraw it: yet his party are now determined, that you shall support the writer, though you reject the play. This night's representation is for his *benefit.* Shall he with impunity assume a power repugnant to your own?—If the privilege of managers be imposition, the duty of an English audience must be obedience." (*Plays* x–xi)

Here is another connection asserted, similar to that charged in the *Theatrical Monitor,* between the tyranny of theater managers and the tyranny of the Court's ministers. The ironic language of *duty* and *obedience* is naturally meant to inflame the Wilkites, one of whose touchstone political chants was "Wilkes and liberty." Kelly's strategy, on the other hand, seems to have been to make himself appear to be the victim and his supporters reasonable people who, pushed to the wall, could "make no farther concessions":

But Mr. Kelly's friends were now no longer able to suppress their indignation, and being determined to make no farther concessions, they exerted themselves so effectually, that False Delicacy was performed, though with very considerable interruption.—Whole speeches, nay, whole scenes were obliged to be omitted, and such was the rage of undistinguishing prejudice, that it even attacked the personal safety of the female performers. ("Address" xi)

The remainder of Kelly's "Address" presents the historical basis for the Wilkite antipathy toward him. On 30 March 1770, Kelly had been attacked by Horne Tooke at a meeting of Middlesex freeholders held at Mile-End. In his address, Tooke attacked Kelly for his biased reporting of the criminal trial held at Guildford in August 1768, where, as noted in chapter 6, some grenadiers were acquitted of murdering William Allen during the St. George's Fields riot on 10 May 1768. Tooke suggested some collusion between Kelly and the jury's foreman, George Onslow, with whom Tooke himself had become embroiled in a legal dispute soon to be tried.

Kelly effectively defends himself by questioning Tooke's own ethics—he does not refer to the pending Onslow litigation, however—and maintains that, although he differs from Horne Tooke politically, he always

respected Mr. Horne's private character, and did justice to what he considered the well meaning, though mistaken zeal of the spirited freeholder, in the moment of his deepest concern at hearing a minister of peace, preaching discord through his country, and expressing an impatience of dying the vestments of his sacred function, in the blood of his fellow subjects. (xiii)

Kelly's strategy is designed to question with words like *zeal* and *spirited* the emotional balance of his antagonist and to suggest that, as a clergyman preaching "discord," Tooke was violating his sacred duty.

Kelly concludes by discussing the situation of authors with regard to their rights to earn a living and to express political views. Deploring the decline of "dramatic genius," Kelly wonders if any writer would wish to hazard all the obstacles to achieving success as a dramatist if he "has unhappily given one individual an offence. The moment his piece is talked of, a party is possibly formed to damn it" (xvii).

As I suggested in chapter 6, Kelly's name forever remained tainted with political liability, and even a dramatic performance he had nothing to do with, *The Sultan* (by Bickerstaff, 1773), when given out as his work, ran into difficulty. In a letter to Garrick, Frances Abington, the lead in the piece, complained that rumors associating the play with Kelly would bring "popular prejudice against it" (Garrick Correspondence 6: no. 145). Writing in 1773 to Spranger Barry, Arthur Murphy claimed that in 1770 Garrick suggested that he, Murphy, return to political journalism on behalf of the Court party. As Murphy explained to Barry, he had been afraid of doing so: "My reply to Mr. Garrick was that since the year 1763 I had not written one word of politicks, and Zenobia had been acted without any manner of opposition" (Garrick Correspondence 6: no. 145)— unlike poor Kelly's *Word to the Wise,* he might have added, for it is clear from this letter that Murphy feared the Wilkites' power to frustrate his dramatic career. And with good reason.

In the early 1760s, Murphy had suffered the damning of two of his plays because of his support of Lord Bute. As Howard Dunbar noted in his study of Murphy, the followers of Wilkes were responsible for the failure of *No One's Enemy but His Own* when it opened at Covent Garden on 9 January 1764; a similar fate befell Murphy's *What We Must All Come To* (163–65). And Murphy's problems came after he had ceased writing for Bute: as Lance Bertelsen notes (189), Murphy's credibility was destroyed by Wilkes and Churchill; and as a result, his pro-government *Auditor* stopped publishing on 8 February 1763, nearly a full year before his plays were to be driven from the stage, a point that illustrates the Wilkites' refusal to forget past transgressions against them. We are reminded again of the intimate and powerful interrelationships in the entire period from the early 1760s through the mid-1770s—coinciding with the bulk of Kelly's career—between journalism, politics, and the theater.

How intimate that interrelationship was can be illustrated by examining the minutes of the stock company that controlled the *London Packet* in January 1770, only a few weeks before the riots over *A Word to the Wise* took place. Merely listing the names of the shareholders suggests how complicated were the interconnections between politics, journalism, and the theater during Kelly's career. The meetings were primarily held to select a new printer for the *Packet,* William Strahan Jr. being the replacement for Henry Baldwin.[6] Other business had to do with the raising of additional funds—the paper had not been doing well—from each of the twenty shareholders. In addition, new partners were to be solicited; among them Strahan himself, Charles Green Say, and Henry Sampson Woodfall.

Among the current shareholders whose names are listed in the minutes of the first meeting (6 Jan. 1770) were Lockyer Davis, Hugh Kelly, Thomas Becket, Thomas Lowndes, and Richard Baldwin (see Minutes of the Meeting). In the minutes of the second meeting, held 12 January, additional members, some new to the group, were listed: Henry Sampson Woodfall, John Almon, George Colman, Capt. Edward Thompson, Richard and Henry Baldwin, Tom Davies, Caleb Whitefoord, James Macpherson, Christopher Henderson, and David Garrick (represented by Becket).[7] Another member is identified only as "W.W.", whom I take to be William Woodfall based on the fact that he was to become the paper's printer in 1773. In the meeting, they decided to make Francis Gentleman the editor and Mr. Harris the publisher.[8] One week later, the partners agreed to pay twenty-five pounds to support the paper rather than the five guineas stipulated on 6 January.[9] Three partners declined to continue in the stock company, although it is not clear whether they did so because of the increased assessment or for some other reason. Those who declined were Hugh Kelly, Ralph Griffiths, and Lockyer Davis.

I am not concerned here with the immediate business of this group; rather, what is important for my purposes is the collective political, theatrical, and journalistic power and interrelatedness represented by these men. Let us begin alphabetically and consider each in his turn. John Almon, a former colleague of Kelly's on the *Gazetteer* in the early 1760s, had become a leading publisher of Wilkite materials and an avid Patriot. He published the *London Museum* and was involved in the leading Wilkite newspaper, the *London Evening Post*. Becket/Garrick needs little commentary, for we know that Garrick wished to obtain favorable notices of his productions, that he was attacked for currying favor with journalists like Kelly, and that some of his "friends," as Kelly was to refer to them (Garrick Correspondence 24: no. 26), were important people in Lord North's administration.[10] As we have seen, Garrick was to attempt to interest Arthur Murphy in returning to the political propaganda wars on the side of North later in 1770, for although Garrick was friendly to Wilkes, his politics were hardly radical. In the 6–8 June 1771 issue of the *Middlesex Journal*, the editor noted that despite the friendly Wilkes–Garrick relationship, Garrick voted against Wilkes and for William Proctor in the Middlesex MP election and was not a member of the Wilkite SSBR.

The Baldwins, Henry and probably Richard, had always published numerous political items; later Henry was to be fined for publishing a letter by Horne Tooke that the government considered treasonous.[11] Robert published the *London Magazine* for many years and filled it with political and theatrical news. The Woodfall family was even more active in politics and theater journalism than the Baldwins. Henry Sampson Woodfall, famed publisher of the Junius libel on the king in December 1769, ran his *Public Advertiser* with integrity and fought against Wilkite charges that his paper had become pro-Court in 1775 (the charge was leveled by Thomas Northcote, who as "Regulus" attacked both Kelly and Woodfall). In the spring of 1772, Woodfall ran for city office himself; he was a candidate for the position of collector of the land tax on salaries and pensions but was unsuccessful. He, like William Bingley and William Strahan, who also ran for political office, demonstrates yet another interconnection between the worlds of journalism/publishing and politics.[12]

William Woodfall, an ex-actor, was active in theater criticism; his paper, the *Morning Chronicle*, announced itself as a "professedly theatrical paper" (18 Dec. 1776) and printed as much theater material in the early and mid-1770s as Kelly's *General Evening Post*. Others in this list who had political or theatrical connections were Lockyer Davis, nominal printer of the Royal Society of the House of Commons' Votes, and Charles Say, Kelly's old patron. Say's newspapers, the *Gazetteer,* the *Craftsman,* and the *General Evening Post,* were consistently anti-

Wilkes; and the *General Evening Post,* when Kelly was writing for it in the 1772–74 period, consistently supported Garrick.

Perhaps the most political of all this group of publisher-printers, journalists, and theater people who made up the ownership of the *Packet* were the Strahans. William Strahan, even before being elected to Parliament in 1774, where he voted consistently for Lord North, was pointedly referred to in the radical press as the king's Scotch printer. His son, William Strahan Jr., was to vote for the Court candidates, Sir Thomas Hallifax and John Shakespear, in the 1772 mayoral election and, according to the press, had his vote invalidated for reasons not specified. The elder Strahan's newspaper, the *London Chronicle,* was antagonistic toward Wilkes and on 17–20 March 1770 published the advertisement for the highly politicized subscription edition of *A Word to the Wise.* Strahan also owned shares in other papers besides his one-third of the *Chronicle,* which he printed; these included one-twenty-fourth of the *Public Ledger* (purchased from John Newbery on 18 June 1760), which he increased to one-twelfth by 1771, and one-seventeenth of *Lloyd's Evening Post.*[13] By 1773, when Kelly had left the *Ledger* and the paper under William Jackson had become pro-Patriot, Strahan no longer held any interest in it.

Finally, a word needs to be said of Caleb Whitefoord. Best known politically for being secretary to the Shelburne Peace Mission to Paris in 1782, Whitefoord supported the ministry against the Wilkites in the 1770s.[14] His correspondents included Tobias Smollett, James Scott (known for his ministerial journalism under the pseudonyms "Old Slyboots" and "AntiSejanus"), and Henry Woodfall.[15] Scott, in an undated letter from the country, laments that he cannot be back in London fighting the Wilkites but emphasizes that he will not write again without being asked. Smollett, in an 18 May 1770 letter, urges Whitefoord to keep attacking "faction and false patriotism"; while Woodfall writes on 24 January 1775, asking him to defend the Scots against Johnson's asperity in his *Journey to the Western Islands.*[16] Given that Whitefoord corresponded with these pro-Court writers and was a partner with still another ministerial writer, James Macpherson, he appears to have been a staunch anti-Patriot.

Richmond and Marjorie Bond's work on the *St. James's Chronicle* reveals a similar governing structure. This paper began its very long run on 14 March 1761 with Henry Baldwin as its printer; Baldwin organized the original stock company necessary to run the paper. The partners were Baldwin, his brother Richard, Bonnell Thornton, George Colman, David Garrick, Lockyer Davis, Christopher Henderson, Thomas Lowndes, Thomas Davies, Thomas Becket, and Ralph Griffiths. Later Capt. Thompson and Arthur Murphy desired to become stockholders but were denied for unknown reasons (19–21). As the Bonds point out, a number of the shareholders in the *St. James's Chronicle* were also owners of the *London Packet* (23). The Bonds' work tends to confirm my contention that London newspapers operated through what nearly amounted to interlocking directorships.

What then do these long lists of *London Packet* and *St. James's Chronicle* share-holders tell us about the interrelationships of theater, journalism, and politics? First, that to be a partner in a newspaper was almost ipso facto to be included either in political or theatrical networks or in both. One was always already involved. Second, assuming the *Packet's* and *Chronicle's* structure of ownership to be similar to that of other periodicals, it suggests that much of the journalistic discourse produced on both politics and the theater during Kelly's career in the early and mid-1770s was influenced, if not controlled by, an intimate, small group, many of whom, because of their overlapping interests in theater and politics—and in additional journalistic enterprises—could hardly have been expected to be objective or neutral on the issues of the day. Nor, if they expected their peers to aid them, could they have avoided abetting these same peers in some sort of quid pro quo. I do not wish to oversimplify and declare that this group controlled "establishment" discourse that commented on theater and politics in the London of 1770. For clearly there are others—like John Almon, a Wilkite, and like Henry Sampson Woodfall, whose paper really did seem to be "open to all"—to make suspect any such generalization. And then many of these printers ran afoul of the government's zealous prosecution of papers in libel cases through the second Wilkite period (1767–75). Nevertheless, these men composed a group whose interconnections and hence discursive power are amply illustrated by Kelly himself. Kelly was to publish many pro-ministerial letter essays in Henry Sampson Woodfall's *Public Advertiser,* William Woodfall's *Morning Chronicle,* and Charles and Mary Say's *Gazetteer.*[17] Kelly attempted, at least, to publish pro-Garrick theater propaganda in Henry Baldwin's *St. James's Chronicle* and did so in the *General Evening Post* and the *Public Ledger,* papers in which he had a direct hand. He for a time worked with Almon and Charles Say, was good friends with William Strahan, and had his own *Works* edited by Capt. Edward Thompson, himself a playwright and at one time a prospective shareholder in Drury Lane.

A similar though perhaps not as numerous company could be named in the antiestablishment camp, one whose newspapers attacked the tyranny of Garrick (and Colman) as they did the tyranny of the ministers of George III. In this group, already somewhat familiar because of their attacks on Kelly noted earlier, would be those men associated with the *Middlesex Journal,* one of the key radical organs. Among these were Isaac Fell, its publisher when it first appeared in April 1769; William Edmunds, who followed Fell; and the omnipresent John Wheble, who was publishing the paper by 1771.[18] Sometime in 1773, William Griffin, Goldsmith's publisher, took over and published the *Middlesex Journal* until August 1775.[19] Then there was Almon, the arch-Wilkite, and William Bingley, Kelly's old antagonist who published the *Theatrical Monitor* in 1767–68 and *Bingley's Journal,* as well as the continuation of the *North Briton.* Additional radical publishers and writers (including Horne Tooke and Wilkes himself, who both wrote extensively for the papers) included William Jackson (or, while attacking Foote,

"Dr.Viper"), who edited the *Public Ledger* after Kelly and turned it into a radical journal; William Moore, editor of the *Whisperer;* and John Miller, printer of the *London Evening Post,* the most relentless Wilkite paper of all, which never seemed to publish letters critical of the Patriots.

In the pages of the periodicals controlled by these men, the general analogy, earlier noted, between the tyranny of the theater and that of the state was made. Even the 1770 editor of the *London Packet,* Francis Gentleman, was to write that Garrick was responsible for the "polluted sources of all theatrical dulness" (*Theatre* 24) and went on to complain about the theater monopoly, the sycophantic "newspaper friends" of Garrick, and in general conflated the politics of St. James's with those of Drury Lane. Both "kings" are blamed for not protecting real merit:

> And merit, without meanness, as a friend,
> In both may unsuccessfully attend;
> Seek and deserve Protection, but in vain,
> Herein St. James's joins with Drury-Lane.

(24)

Having gotten ahead of myself, I must return to examine *A Word to the Wise* itself. The play revolves around the conflicts of three pairs of mismatched lovers who must realign themselves so that each person weds the right man or woman. Caroline Dormer is mismatched with the good-natured yet narcissistic Sir George Hastings; she would rather marry her father's "assistant in literary researches," the humble Villars. Harriot Montague, an orphan living with the Dormers, is unhappily aligned with Capt. Dormer, Caroline's brother, but prefers Sir George Hastings. For his part, Capt. Dormer has been forced by his father, Sir John Dormer, to woo Harriot but would rather marry Miss Cornelia Willoughby, the daughter of another dependent of his father's, whom he cares for despite his libertine pose. Other characters include the sentimental optimist, Willoughby, who believes, like Candide, that everything happens for the best, and his socially ambitious but foolish younger wife and step-mother to Cornelia; his wife convinces Cornelia to endanger herself by eloping with Capt. Dormer.

Strong elements of sensibility are found in Sir George, who has given up drinking and who is improbably persuaded to risk his life to save Caroline Dormer the embarrassment of telling her father it is her fault that she and Sir George must break off their engagement. Then, too, the play, through language and plot, chastises the rakish Capt. Dormer; he is a sentimental libertine who in act 4 repudiates his past, asks his father's forgiveness, and promises to reform forever. A final sentimental note occurs when the pious Villars tells the company of his being kidnapped from his family in his childhood: the story leads to the discovery that he is the long-lost son of Willoughby, the entire business reminiscent of Joseph Andrews's true history in Fielding's novel. The play concludes with Villars receiving an estate from Sir George and with all the couples rightly aligned.

Because the play was originally damned, almost no contemporary critical commentary exists. In the review of the play in the March number of the *London Magazine,* the author, after a lengthy plot synopsis, discussed the events of the riot, including a narrative of the postperformance attempts by Lacy, Garrick, and Kelly to prevent further disturbances. But lost in the recitation of political tumult was any critical consideration of the work itself. The *Monthly Review* (Aug. 1770, 151) and the *Critical Review* (Sept. 1770, 231) acknowledged the play favorably, but their responses considered the work as a closet drama, not as an acted play.

The play was not presented again in London until after Kelly's death. When performed on 1 May 1777 at the Haymarket and 13 May at Covent Garden, it was well received. Shortly thereafter, a new edition appeared, and on 29 May the benefit production at Covent Garden for Kelly's family was held. For this performance, Samuel Johnson wrote a prologue (he had also been recently asked to write a petition on behalf of Dr. William Dodd, condemned for forging Lord Chesterfield's name on some bonds, and supposedly complained of such work to Murphy: "Why, Sir, when they come to me with a dead stay-maker and a dying parson, what can a man do?" [Piozzi 36].). The benefit netted the Kelly family £108, according to the *London Stage* (G. W. Stone, pt. 5, 87). Its last London performance in the century was at the Haymarket on 21 June 1784.

Well before the London benefit performance, however, *A Word to the Wise* had been doing well in the provinces. It opened the new theater at Leeds on 24 July 1771 and, according to Tate Wilkinson, fared well at Hull, York, and Bath (1: 101, 237). It was a particular favorite at Bath, playing the Theatre Royal throughout the rest of that century and into the nineteenth.[20] At Bath its run of twelve performances may be compared with Colman's *English Merchant* (thirteen times), Goldsmith's *Good Natur'd Man* (five times), and Richard Cumberland's *West Indian* (twenty-three times) and suggests that *A Word to the Wise* held its own against the competition for the rest of the century.

The play seems to have been more popular in America than in Ireland. Seilhamer lists the first American production at Williamsburg in late March 1772 and then again on 2 April. At least one production was put on in Annapolis on 1 September 1772. Worth noting is the appearance in the 23 January 1772 issue of the *Virginia Gazette* of a story demonstrating the readership's familiarity with Kelly's political difficulties, including his newspaper "war" with Lord Mayor Beckford: "We hear that . . . False Delicacy and A Word to the Wise, the productions of the ingenious Mr. Hugh Kelly, whose spirited letter to the Lord Mayor (Beckford) has been read by most people, are in great forwardness" (Seilhamer 1: 291–92).

After at least three successful appearances in Virginia in 1772, the play was put on in Philadelphia by the American Company in the fall of 1772 with the same cast as at Williamsburg and Annapolis (299). *A Word to the Wise* crowned its early American success when it was honored by opening the new theater in

Charleston on 22 December 1773 (330). Performances later in the century occurred on 28 September 1789 at the John Street Theater in New York and again at the Southwark in Philadelphia on 20 January 1791 (Seilhamer 2: 266, 321).

In Ireland the play was only modestly successful. Greene has found only one Dublin performance (at the Capel Street Theatre, 4 Feb. 1774) and four in Belfast between 1779 and 1783.[21] The play was certainly not the success in either Ireland or America that *False Delicacy* had been and *The School for Wives* would be, but at least it was not damned; in fact, if we judge from the *Virginia Gazette* story, Kelly seemed oddly admired rather than condemned for his attack on Beckford.

Not surprisingly, *A Word to the Wise* has not attracted as much modern critical attention as has *False Delicacy* and *The School for Wives*. John Loftis merely notes that *A Word to the Wise* is, though "emphatically 'genteel'" like *School,* "less uniformly good natured than *False Delicacy*" (22). He alludes to the cynical tone of Harriot Montague, whose ironic view of courtship language and marriage seriously qualify the play's sentimentally benevolent tone given it by such characters as Sir John Dormer and Mr. Willoughby. Mark Auburn objects to the play's improbable resolution of the Villars–Miss Dormer love match through the convenient discovery that Villars is Willoughby's long-lost son and to the lack of psychological complexity in Capt. Dormer (15–16).[22] Richard Bevis, disagreeing with Mark Schorer's contention that each of Kelly's plays became less sentimental than the previous one (Schorer 392), feels that *A Word to the Wise* is no less sentimental than *False Delicacy,* arguing that even though Capt. Dormer satirizes sentiment, he turns out to be an "amicable benevolent" himself. Bevis does not think the satire is significant and maintains that the play is sentimental in both plot and expression (95).

Among Kelly scholars, William Watt, as usual, finds it difficult to see any motive in Kelly beyond the sentimental; even though he recognizes that "Kelly is laughing at his bland sentimental comedy" (188), he feels such ridicule—"dressing up his preacher in the garb of harlequin"—is a mistake. Carver, in keeping with his more complex interpretation of Kelly's drama as built upon both "sentiments and a ridicule of sentimental excesses" (Introduction xxxii), finds the play's satiric power in the Capt. Dormer–Miss Montague scene where sentimental language is exposed as excessive and insincere. He particularly points out the "effectiveness of Miss Montague's ruthlessly honest redefinition of the sentimentalist's language of courtship and love that shames and helps reform the embarrassed Capt. Dormer" (xxxiv–vi). O'Leary, focusing on the genuine comedy of the play in its parody of sentimentalism, forms an analysis that in part anticipates Carver's. Noting the ridicule of Capt. Dormer's sentimental speech to Harriot, O'Leary remarks that "[s]cenes such as these which so overtly deride the sentimental graces belie Kelly's reputation as the admiring craftsman of typical sentimental drama" (256).

Yet the reform element in *A Word to the Wise* is significant. There lies behind the characters of Sir George Hastings and Capt. Dormer an interrogation of traditional hard male culture as outlined in Barker-Benfield's *Culture of Sensibility*. As noted earlier, Barker-Benfield discusses at length the attempt to civilize the eighteenth-century male that was central to the movement of sensibility. One of the targets of this reformation was excessive male drinking, something that the reformed Sir George admits to early on in act 1 when he and his friend, Capt. Dormer, argue about their character flaws. Capt. Dormer rallies Sir George on having formerly been such a great figure in the male tavern culture. "Yes," confesses Sir George, "but I soon found out that drink was detestable, and toasting the greatest of all absurdities" (*Plays* 9; act 1). When Capt. Dormer protests that there is hardly a better way to pass an evening, Sir George ironically agrees: "O, an evening spent in this manner must be delectable, especially if a couple of fools should happily quarrel in their cups, and cut one another's throat to prove the superiority of their understanding" (9), a comment that looks forward to the later critique of dueling. Sir George seems an apt example of how, during the course of the century, the new sensitive male was urged to leave off excessive drinking and turn toward a more civilized form of consumer pleasure.[23] Sir George has refashioned himself and now concentrates on his physical appearance, "attentive," as Miss Montague phrases it, "to the niceties of dress" (2; act 1). For this vanity he is laughed at, but it is clear that for Kelly a laughable coxcomb is preferable to a vicious rake, and that is precisely the basis on which Miss Montague makes the distinction between Sir George, whom she will eventually accept, and Capt. Dormer, whom she rejects. Sir George's softer vice places him among the new sentimental males, as Barker-Benfield views them, who reflect in their pleasures the new consumer culture's civilized concern for suppressing violence.

Perhaps the strongest reformist element comes in the attacks on Capt. Dormer's libertinism. Accused of having seduced a number of young women by Willoughby, the sentimental optimist who is father of his next intended victim, Capt. Dormer is beset on all sides for his rakishness, but the main assault comes from his own father. Sir John's first tirade against his son's transgressions comes at the end of act 1 and is repeated in act 5 (84–87) prior to the son's repentance. Early on, he warns his son about his behavior toward women: "[G]allantry, tho' a fashionable crime, is a very detestable one; and the wretch who pilfers from us in the hour of his necessity, is an innocent character, compared to the plunderer who wantonly robs us of happiness and reputation" (16). Capt. Dormer replies that he will not do anything to "bring a reflection upon the honour of my family" (16), but the rakish code word *honor* already suggests that Capt. Dormer may still be what Barker-Benfield calls a "hard male."[24]

Despite Capt. Dormer's confession that he is, like Sir Robert Harold in *Memoirs of a Magdalen*, a sentimental rake, he is preached to throughout the play, if not by his father then by Willoughby and even by his friend, the pious Villars, who is like both fathers a fount of sentimental virtue. Capt. Dormer reforms by the play's end and becomes a new male of sensibility, much to the happiness of his sentimental father whose final rebuke contains strong suggestions of the capitalist-consumer ideology with which sensibility was intertwined.[25] Sir John speaks of his disappointment in his son: "You knew how much my happiness depended upon your reputable rise in the world, and how warmly I expected you wou'd be a credit to your country, as well as an ornament to your family—Your natural advantages were great, and your education has been liberal" (86; act 5).

The final reformist target of the play is the hard male culture's association of honor with dueling.[26] Kelly had often attacked dueling in the past, particularly in the *Court Magazine* and "The Babler."[27] It became a significant reformist theme in his critique of male culture; it was at least as strong as his belief that a parent of sensibility (and here the father-daughter relationship is paramount) will grant his child her or his choice of marriage partner and that a child will express gratitude. However improbable Sir George Hastings's willingness to save Miss Dormer from embarrassment by risking his own life in a duel with her father may seem, there can be no doubt about the seriousness of Kelly's mockery of the entire hard male's code of honor. The code, in Sir George Hastings's view, every day forces men to hazard their lives "in defence of the basest actions" (50; act 3). Later Sir John berates Capt. Dormer for offering to meet Willoughby, an older and less skilled man, in a duel, telling his son that his sword was "to be exerted in the cause of honour, not to be drawn in the support of infamy—I gave it to be us'd in the defence of your country, not to be exercis'd in the violation of her laws" (85; act 5). Sir John had himself been willing to duel Sir George, but the general tendency throughout is to castigate dueling. That Kelly understood the importance of site in his cultural war is attested to by Sir John's desire to hold the duel with Sir George in a tavern, a key symbol of the old male culture.[28] That very club-and-tavern culture, only slightly reformed and transformed, had helped to produce the violence against his play, and ever after Kelly was to bring his new dramas to the stage in ways that would avoid confrontation with the Wilkites and other Patriots.

8

※

Politics after *A Word to the Wise* and the Staging of *Clementina*

F ollowing the damnation of *A Word to the Wise* and its politicized publication by subscription on 17 May 1770, the Wilkite attacks on Kelly occurred more frequently than they had since his involvement of the *Public Ledger* in the contemporary political wars. Yet there were more significant
political activities developing in the spring of 1770 than those fostered by the
controversy surrounding Kelly; there were events that once again served to link
Kelly and the theater to the radical politics of the City. It will be remembered
that in the two letters signed by Atticus published in March numbers of the
Middlesex Journal, the writer abused not just Kelly but also David Garrick and
Sir Robert Ladbroke: Garrick for forcing Kelly's plays onto a hostile audience
and Ladbroke for being supportive of Kelly, "in the chair," as the *Middlesex Journal* put it, taking subscriptions for the publication of *A Word to the Wise.* The
reference to Ladbroke as chairing a committee on Kelly's behalf seems phrased
ironically to invoke the Wilkite SSBR (whose meetings, as reported in the press,
always noted who was "in the chair" for a given meeting), so that Atticus might
indignantly suggest how vast a difference existed between the noble cause of
that Society and the ignoble one of Ladbroke and other Kelly supporters.

Ladbroke was scorned for his leadership of those aldermen opposed to Lord
Mayor William Beckford's Remonstrance to the king, a litany of complaints
presented on 14 March to King George III detailing the radical City's case against
the king's ministers. The 13–15 March *Middlesex Journal* lists the anti-Patriot
aldermen who refused to support Beckford: Ladbroke is among those names,
as were John Kirkman, John Bird, and Thomas Harley, men who either subscribed
to Kelly's play or were otherwise associated with Kelly.[1] Ladbroke, according to
the *Middlesex Journal* for 13–15 March, made the actual motion against the
Remonstrance; the paper accused Ladbroke of reading the motion but maintained that it had been written "at the other end of town," meaning at the Court
of St. James. The political heat must have been raised further when in the same

issue the *Journal* reported that, upon receiving the Remonstrance from Beckford, the king supposedly laughed. Although later doubt was cast on the occurrence of royal mirth, surely Wilkite readers became even more incensed at the Court than they had already been at this news; they were further galled by the paper's reporting that someone "respectable" had given Kelly five hundred guineas to compensate him for the damning of his play.

The spring did not therefore bring any cessation to the vilification of Kelly by the radical press. At the same time, perhaps because it was felt that William Beckford's status needed reaffirmation, the *Middlesex Journal* took pains to inform its readers that, despite the failure of the Remonstrance, the lord mayor was still politically and socially important. That need to bolster Beckford's status may explain why in its 20–22 March issue the paper presented a detailed story of those nobles and members of the House of Commons who had accepted invitations to dine at the Mansion House with Beckford on 22 March:

> We are assured that the following, amongst other Noblemen and Members of the House of Commons, have returned messages that they will dine with the Right Honourable the Lord Mayor this day at the Mansion-house: [there follows a list of forty-eight nobles]. And that they will set out in procession from the Thatch'd House Tavern about four o'clock, and the City Marshals are ordered to meet them at Temple Bar, and conduct them to the Mansion-house. As many of the Nobility and Gentry intend to meet . . . this day to proceed at three o'clock in the afternoon to dine, by invitation of the Lord Mayor of the city of London . . . , many worthy Freeholders of the county of Middlesex intend to mount on horseback, preceded by a band of music, and meet in St. James's-street, to escort the above Nobility, &c. to the city gate, as a testimony of their affection and gratitude to those who so nobly stand forth in support of the liberty and the constitution of their country.

Here is rite and ritual organized and reported, it seems, to remind Patriots that one of *their* champions, the lord mayor, has still retained his dignity and power no matter what slight the Court has recently offered him. Looked at from a propaganda perspective, this story is not so much a report as it is a set of directions for a power display—a street theatrical, in other words—of the radicals' strength presented with the sort of ritualistic framing that will lend it the required status—some nobles are on our side—a legitimating move made out of anxious necessity.

While the *Middlesex Journal* was defending Beckford and his Remonstrance and criticizing the anti-Patriot aldermen, it was stirred by Horne Tooke's 30 March address to the freeholders and began to attack the Court's hiring of propagandists. In its 31 March–3 April issue, the *Journal* claimed that more than ten thousand pounds "are allowed annually by the government for what is called private uses; a great part of which has, it is presumed, for four years past been allotted to ministerial scribblers."[2] Regardless of these figures' accuracy, the report does highlight the awareness in the press of the importance of the professional writer and his new patrons, especially those found in the political marketplace. It is thus not at all surprising that, in the issue for 12–14 April, in a letter addressed publicly to Wilkes by a sympathizer, there is an attack on Wilkes's enemies: the front-page letter singles out Henry Lawes Luttrell, Samuel Johnson, James Scott, and Hugh Kelly as chief nemeses: "[A]fter the impotent attempt . . . of old Sam Johnson, it would be idle to mention the *monkey tricks* of James Scott, or the lifeless effrontery of Hugh Kelly."[3] Except Luttrell, the enemies were all writers, not politicians; Kelly and Scott were the chief ministerial authors, the latter known mainly by his pen names, AntiSejanus and Old Slyboots.

The charge that Kelly's attacks were "lifeless" is perhaps no more to be believed than the comment by Garrick to Murphy that the radicals found Kelly only a "flea bite" (Garrick Correspondence 6: no. 145), for soon the Patriot press was to be outraged by what they considered Kelly's impudent assault on the lord mayor, the context of which is not entirely clear. However, according to Kelly's letter to Beckford published in the *London Magazine* for June 1770 (304–6), Kelly was defending himself against offenses given by Beckford on Monday, 14 May, during a meeting of the Common Council. The *London Magazine*'s report of the council's events of that day reveals that Beckford was himself responding to a letter attacking him that was published in Kelly's *Ledger* a few days earlier. That letter, according to the *London Magazine,* negatively reflected upon Beckford's humanity and his "want of respect for the laws of the land." No mention of any upbraiding of Kelly is made; yet the report obviously lacked full details of the speech, so Kelly's name may very well have been brought up by Beckford. At any rate, it was this incident that Kelly construed as an assault on him and to which he was responding in the letter printed by the *London Magazine* in June; the context provided by that magazine's editor suggests that the letter, dated 25 May, was first printed in a newspaper, but I have been unable to trace its origin. As one of the few examples we have of Kelly engaging in direct political invective aimed at a specific antagonist, the letter is worth examining in detail. One must interpolate in order to reconstruct Beckford's original strike at Kelly; for once, it seems that Kelly had the last word. To be sure, writers counterattacked on Beckford's behalf, but evidently the mayor himself did not choose to respond. As the magazine report of the 14 May meeting is vague, we must depend on Kelly's letter to suggest what the details of Beckford's thrust were.

Kelly first complains that Beckford's hostility was misplaced. The mayor mistakenly assumed that Kelly penned the *Ledger* letter that attacked him on Saturday, 12 May. Kelly uses Beckford's false assumption to counterattack:

> Had your lordship confined yourself entirely to the imaginary delinquency of that letter, I should not have troubled you with this, though I might have thought it strange to hear a lover of liberty

arraigning the freedom of the press; and thought it stranger still to find your lordship offended at a reprehension of your own proceedings, while you were hourly reprehending not only the proceedings of parliament, but even personally taxing your sovereign with more than impropriety. (*London Magazine,* June 1770, 304–6)[4]

Kelly cleverly expands the argument and claims that he is not responding merely to the personal pique of having mistakenly been charged with writing a letter he did not write but is ironically defending liberty of the press against Beckford, who hypocritically wants that freedom for his partisans but not for his opponents and who, although criticizing the king, will not tolerate criticism of himself.

Proceeding, Kelly upbraids the lord mayor for feeling it necessary at the 14 May meeting to mention that the author of the *Ledger,* Kelly, was an Irishman. This act Kelly seizes upon most strongly and makes crucial to his charge against Beckford—that he is "illiberal":

> I now proceed, my Lord, to the illiberality of your national reflection:—it seems, that, as well as undergoing the disgrace of being a poet, I must also suffer the dishonour of being an Irishman; and the sister kingdom, though so eminent for her loyalty, so distinguished for her affection to Great Britain, is at once to be branded with obloquy, because a supposed writer against the Lord Mayor of London is an *Irishman.*—Here, ye sons of that brave, though hardly treated land, here is a proof of Mr. Beckford's *exalted* rectitude. However you have shone in arts or in arms; however as scholars, or heroes, you have gained universal applause, the wreathe must be instantly torn from your brows, and you must relinquish your title to honest reputation, because you are guilty of being *Irishmen.* (306)

After reminding Beckford that he himself was born in Jamaica and that no one detests Jamaicans because one of them may "deserve our universal contempt, or detestation," Kelly goes on to note that Beckford must be aware that "some of the chief ornaments in the present opposition, are natives of the country that you have ungenerously traduced" (306).[5] Not having access to Beckford's original attack means that one cannot determine the justice in Kelly's irritated arraignment. As noted earlier, however, it was true that the radical press expressed a degree of hostility toward the Irish, which although not equal to that directed at the Scots nevertheless strikes a modern reader with some force.

The radicals did not wait long to seize upon Kelly for his criticism of Beckford, one of their heroes. In the 31 May number of the *Public Advertiser,* a letter signed "B. C." takes Kelly to task for having assailed Beckford. The writer claims that Beckford should have known better than to abuse Kelly, noting, "[I]f we tread on the meanest Reptile, it will arouse to revenge itself." He attempts to discredit Kelly's logic by stating that it was "ingenious" that Kelly pretended that

Beckford, in calling him an Irishman, was abusing "a whole nation" but maintains that such a designation of Kelly was only descriptive:

> You might with equal Propriety say, if his Lordship had declared the Author to have been a fat Stay-maker, because those Epithets particularly belong to you, that every fat Man, and every Staymaker in England and Ireland was included and abused by that simple Distinction.

Perhaps the sharpest attack by "B. C." comes near the end of his letter when he ironically notes that Beckford did indeed make a mistake by calling Kelly a poet: "In this Particular," says the writer, "you have certainly been misrepresented."

The writer's final advice highlights Kelly's pride as an author, which trait more than one anonymous political enemy was to claim Kelly possessed: "Know yourself—Do not affect Consequence, and you may escape Contempt and Ridicule; and if you cannot acquire Fame, you may live without Correction." This letter is typical of the assaults against Kelly during the early 1770s: on one hand, there is the continuous resorting to ad hominem argument while, on the other hand, there is only a modest effort made to refute Kelly's arguments. Here the writer's attempt to maintain that calling Kelly an Irishman would be no different from calling him a staymaker is unconvincing in light of the anti-Irish prejudice that was particularly strong among the radical audience of the time.

As for the hit at Kelly's desire for "consequence," perhaps it is fair to say that some radicals did not notice Kelly or would rather not admit that they noticed him. In this respect, it might be recalled that, in one of the two or three mentions of Kelly in Boswell's *Life of Samuel Johnson,* Johnson was said to have forgotten that Kelly was even in the room when Kelly apologized for departing early (2: 48). As O'Leary notes, others repeated this incident as a "measure of Kelly's status among his great contemporaries" (80).

To the radicals, June 1770 may have appeared to be a time of crisis. Not only did Henry Sampson Woodfall go on trial beginning 13 June for printing a Junius letter in his 19 December 1769 *Public Advertiser,* but the death of William Beckford occurred on Thursday, 21 June.[6] Beckford, although never very friendly to Wilkes, nevertheless was revered by the Patriot camp who clearly felt his loss, as attested to by the various encomiums printed in the *Middlesex Journal* and other pro-radical papers in the days and weeks following his death. In the same column in which the *Middlesex Journal* reported Beckford's death (19–21 June), there appeared the following information:

> By the direction of Sir Robert Ladbroke, Hugh Kelly last week ordered a column of the Public Advertiser to be reserved for him, until the Election of Sheriffs, which he has regularly filled up every day with letters under the signature[s] of *Honestus, A Thinking Liveryman, An Indignant Citizen,* &c. abusing the Livery for their late

choice of Sheriffs, whom he calls the *Firebrands of the Community;* and advising the Livery to choose the Aldermen Plumbe and Kirkman, whom he calls the lovers of good government. Aldermen Plumbe and Kirkman are fortunate to have for their champion the avowed advocate for murder: Hugh Kelly having uniformly defended Balse, M'Quirk, Gillam, Murray, M'Leane, M'Laughlin, M'Laughry, and the Kennedys.

Here the writer dredges up Kelly's old sins: his supposed defense of those charged in the St. George's Fields Massacre of 10 May 1768 and in the Brentford election riots of 8 December 1768. Yet the *Advertiser* did indeed publish three letters signed by the very names the *Middlesex Journal* cites: on 19, 20, and 21 June 1770, these letters focused on the upcoming sheriff's election between the Wilkite candidates, William Baker and Joseph Martin, and the Courtiers, Samuel Plumbe and John Kirkman. The intimacy of the world of London journalism is once again demonstrated: since the issue of the *Middlesex Journal* that exposed Kelly's letters was the 19–21 June one and the last of Kelly's letters appeared on 21 June, the editor of the *Middlesex Journal* must have had some inside information that enabled him to identify Kelly's contribution to Woodfall's paper so precisely. As the sentiments and rhetorical strategies remind one strongly of Kelly, I see no reason to doubt the *Middlesex Journal's* accuracy.

In the first letter, Kelly as Honestus attempts to cast the Wilkites and especially those who belong to the SSBR as practicing a kind of tyranny in determining the City's political direction, thus turning the average complacent liveryman, who is Kelly's audience, into a quiescent tool of the radical faction. Invoking the good old days when liverymen were independent—and Kelly here turns the radicals' rhetoric on themselves, for they had always seen themselves as the only independent voices—Kelly argues that today, in contrast, "[W]e now relinquish the Right of determining for ourselves, submit implicitly to the commands of all who think proper to become our Masters." Who are these new masters? They are the "Instruments of Party, the Abettors of Violence, and the Friends of Licentiousness"—the SSBR, whom Kelly later refers to, in a clever piece of diminishing rhetoric, as a "Tavern Club."

On the next day, 20 June, Kelly's second letter attempts to link obedience to the Wilkites as equivalent to slavery and to suggest strongly that to vote for Plumbe and Kirkman—called by this Thinking Liveryman "Gentlemen both of extensive Property and unquestionable Character"—is to "shake off the Yoke of popular Oppression." Throughout this letter in support of the Courtier candidates, Kelly promotes two themes. One states unequivocally that the Patriot party foments civil unrest—"the Disturbers of the public Repose can never be true Friends to their Country." Needed are magistrates who "will endeavour to re-establish your Tranquility." The second thematic thrust suggests that the Patriots are self-interested—"Did they ever court your Acquaintance till they had

Occasion for your Interest? Did they ever seek a Connection with you till that Connection had an evident Likelihood of being beneficial to themselves?" Kelly plays up one of the charges even supporters of the radical cause often brought against Wilkes. Although not mentioning Wilkes by name, Kelly, in harping on the self-interest theme many saw in Wilkes's extravagance (invoking Wilkes's image as a debt-ridden bon vivant given to expensive tastes), attempts to appeal to the more sober voters who may be persuaded that Wilkes jeopardizes what Kelly, in ending the letter, calls "the prosperity of his country."

The final letter of the Courtier propaganda campaign, signed An Indignant Citizen, appeared in the *Advertiser* for Thursday, 21 June, the day Beckford died. Kelly continues his overall strategy of accusing the Patriots of instituting the tyranny that the Wilkites had always attributed to the Court. All the while, he insists that the "universal Dissension" cultivated by the radicals aims to intimidate any citizen who disagrees with the Patriot perspective. Public meetings, Kelly claims, are unsafe because of Patriotic domination: "[W]e have seen that where an Individual ventured to hold up but a dissenting Hand; he has been in actual Danger of his Life." It was certainly true that, as newspaper reports of Wilkite bullying tactics demonstrate, it was hazardous even at formal meetings of the City Council for antiradical views to be aired directly.

During the early summer of 1770, the *Middlesex Journal* temporarily ignored Kelly and the Court party to concentrate on more pressing matters. A new lord mayor to succeed Beckford had to be selected; the two radical candidates were Barlow Trecothick and Brass Crosby, while the Court party entry was Sir Henry Bankes.[7] Beckford's seat in Parliament also had to be filled, and here Thomas Oliver appeared to be the only choice, although illness forced him to withdraw in favor of his brother Richard (*Middlesex Journal* 3–5 July 1770).[8] By the middle of July, all seemed quieter on the London political scene than it had been for months.

By September, the radicals' complaint that Kelly was a paid ministerial writer was about to become true, for as I noted earlier, Kelly received a pension from Lord North sometime early in September. Kelly's letter to Garrick signed and dated in his hand (12 Sept. 1770) constitutes the most compelling evidence we have about Kelly's ties to the Court party's propaganda effort:

Dear Sir,

> Tho at Southhampton Street and Hampton I have been repeatedly disappointed of thanking you personally for your many instances of unmerited kindness, I am pretty confident that my letter will reach you, wherever you are, and that I shall be even more acceptable in this, than in any other way, as it will be the least liable to put your delicacy out of countenance. You never make an awkward figure, but when your own philanthropy is the subject of conversation, and tho you are eternally deserving praise, you cannot bear even a moment to receive it.

This day Sir, and not before I have got some certain intimation of Lord N____'s intention to do handsome things. Mr. Cooper told me of it in very obliging terms, adding that you were highly my friend.[9] The first part of the intelligence agreeably surprized me, the latter did not in the least, Garrick I have long known, as another term for all the virtues, and instead of being amazed at his readiness to serve the unfriended, I should be actually amazed if his generosity had not found that readiness a very considerable satisfaction.

Accept my best acknowledgments my dear Sir for all your goodness to me; if any thing could tender my prospects additionally pleasing it would be for the recollection of their originally resulting from you. My earnest wishes attend for Mrs. Garrick's happiness, as well as the happiness of your whole family, and I beg you will believe me as gratefully as I am

affectionately Dear Sir your most
obliged and most devoted

Hugh Kelly

I would have contrived in spite of the obstacles to have seen you lately but I have been under a severe operation for a disorder of an old standing in the urethra. I believe you recollect the complaint.
(Garrick Correspondence 24: 21)

The outcome of Lord North's "intention" was a pension of two hundred pounds, according to John Taylor, and after Kelly's death in February 1777, Kelly's friend Alderman Thomas Harley took steps to ensure that his widow, in Taylor's phrase, "enjoyed a moiety of this pension till her death" (1: 46). Whether Kelly was to be paid for past efforts, as well as for future endeavors, is not certain.

Now a retainer of the government under Lord North, Kelly was soon to be publicly embarrassed by another indebtedness to David Garrick. As can easily be gleaned from the 12 September letter, Kelly was very grateful to Garrick and had no reluctance in saying so in private. But no doubt a 6 October 1770 letter written by Ferrula and published in *Bingley's Journal* rankled both Kelly and Garrick. Savagely attacking Garrick for his "folly, avarice, and vanity," Ferrula used the case of Kelly as his prime example of how Garrick's vanity could be manipulated by flattery into producing plays that were, in the writer's view, unworthy of acceptance. Recalling Kelly's flattery of Garrick in *Thespis,* Ferrula writes:

The compliments paid you by this gentleman, on the publication of a wretched poem of his, called *Thespis,* published about four years since, induced you to encourage him to a comedy; and told him, he had a vein of humour about him, that he must succeed in. How you could answer such a proceeding to your judgment or conscience, for setting the poor little man on so restiff a hobby-horse, I shall not now enquire, as I would only state the fact. Mr. Kelly, however, took you at your word, and produced *False Delicacy,* a comedy, which, as you were bound to bring out, you instantly sat down with your theatrical pruning knife, and so cut and flashed it, that to use your own words, 'You had rather write a comedy of three acts, than perform such another operation.' However, the poet was to be obliged, so much *labour* for so much *compliment,* and his play was brought out with success.

Inspirited by this first trial, Kelly sat down to a second comedy, taking it for granted he would still meet in you the same *patron* and *corrector;* therefore, in the winter of 1768, he sent you his "Word to the Wise"; and after keeping it some time, you sent him word you should positively bring it out that winter; but most unfortunately for Kelly, some strokes on your public character appeared about this time in the Ledger, which you was informed he had the conduct of, and which, as an impartial editor, he could not avoid inserting; yet it so inflamed you, that though on the Saturday you repeated your promise of putting it into reading immediately, the Monday following you sent it back by your brother George, with the cold apology, 'That you was sorry the season was so far advanced, that you could not oblige him.' Kelly, tho' thunderstruck at this message, on a little recollection saw his error, and very *prudently* accommodated himself to your vanity, by daubing you the whole summer with panegyric. The bait took accordingly, the monster grew kind, and the ensuing winter "The Word to the Wise," like the Prodigal Son, was received with joy and cordiality.

The letter berates Garrick's vanity for several more paragraphs but makes no further mention of Kelly. There is no way to weigh the degree of truth in this anecdote, for as with so many of the anecdotes examined, other evidentiary bases of comparison are lacking. The narrative proceeds with a chronological certainty and a specificity of incident that makes it compelling, even if fictive, but no other contemporary source mentions a breach between Kelly and Garrick, even though other sources are vague about the period between the staging of *False Delicacy* in January 1768 and the damning of *A Word to the Wise* in March 1770. If Ferrula is correct and some delay in the staging of *A Word to the Wise* did occur, that might explain how the 15–17 June 1769 *Middlesex Journal* writer knew the title of the play in the spring of 1769—nearly nine months before the play was actually produced in March 1770: it had already been made ready for the stage sometime during the 1768–69 season. The absence of *Ledgers* for this period, especially for the summer of 1769 when Ferrula claims Kelly assuaged Garrick's injured vanity, prevents further investigation of the matter.[10] Regardless of the degree of truth here, however, Ferrula's charges must have stung Kelly and Garrick. Kelly in particular must have seen 1770 end with relief and must have looked forward with trepidation to early 1771 when *Clementina* was to appear at Covent Garden.

Meanwhile the City radicals were having their own problems. Wilkes and one of his key supporters, Horne Tooke, who had helped to form the SSBR on 20 February 1769 to aid Wilkes in paying off his debts, had been quarreling for some time.[11] In January 1771, the situation worsened. A newspaper war began between the two men as charges and countercharges were traded, primarily over some of Wilkes's older debts, not all of which Tooke felt should be paid for with SSBR funds. Tooke wished to use some SSBR money to help others who had suffered for the cause, one of whom was Bingley, Kelly's old nemesis, imprisoned for nearly two years over freedom of the press issues. In its 22–24 January number, the *Middlesex Journal* reported about a 22 January meeting of the SSBR at which there had been a vote over whether or not to raise funds for others besides Wilkes. Those who wished to support only Wilkes won, and as a consequence, a number of principal subscribers to the Society withdrew and eventually formed the Constitutional Society.

Perhaps the internal strife among the radicals allowed George Colman to produce without incident Kelly's third play and only tragedy, *Clementina*, which opened a run of nine nights at Covent Garden on 23 February 1771. Kelly's authorship was suppressed at first, and a rumor was circulated suggesting that an American clergyman, not yet arrived in England, wrote the play (Cooke, "Hugh Kelly," Jan. 44).[12] In the dedication to Coleman, Kelly wrote that the manager had "distinguished *Clementina* with the most essential attention," a cryptic remark that is perhaps partially explained by the "Advertisement" to the second edition wherein Kelly reported on problems with the cast prior to the opening:

> The chief business of this advertisement . . . is to acknowledge his obligations to the inimitable performance of Mrs. Yates, and to thank Mr. Bensley, Mr. Savigny, and Mr. Wroughton, for their great good-nature in undertaking their respective characters at the short notice of a week, when Mr. Ross unexpectedly returned the part of Anselmo, which had been in his possession above a fortnight, and left it no more than barely possible for the utmost diligence of these Gentlemen, to exhibit a piece, which the public have since been kindly pleased to honour with the most generous approbation. (*Plays*, p. A 2)

Why David Ross declined the part of Anselmo was never explained, although one contemporary source reported that he felt it required a style of acting he could not adopt. In *Thespis II,* Kelly had criticized Ross for being negligent about his performances—"Yet oft through monstrous negligence will strike / His warmest friends with pity or dislike" (lines 61–62)—and although Kelly also praised Ross for his "capacity and skill" (line 91), he complained that the actor was too lazy to reform. According to contemporary reviews, however, the play's modest success did not depend on any of the principal males but rather on Mrs. Yates, whose playing of Clementina allowed the tragedy to survive nine nights. Kelly had praised her highly in *Thespis* for her roles at Drury Lane, mentioning in particular her Belvidera in Thomas Otway's *Venice Preserv'd*. In Kelly's play, as in Otway's, Mrs. Yates was to play a type, the distressed wife, that R. F. Brissenden has shown to be so pervasive in the novels of the time.[13] *Clementina* can be said to resemble *Venice Preserv'd* in more than the theme of the distressed wife and the setting: both plays deal with a political conflict between liberty and tyranny; both present domestic tragedy as in part due to tensions between fathers and daughters; and both depict sexual jealousy as part of the competition among the male characters for the heroine. In the father-daughter relationship, an important thematic in Kelly's conduct journalism, a contradictory ideological position is dramatized. Kelly, on one hand, believes in filial obedience and, on the other, in what Lawrence Stone calls affectional, companionate marriages that require parental indulgence in the choice of spouse.

Before the play opens, Clementina, the daughter of Anselmo, a victorious Venetian general and patriot, has married Rinaldo, the son of her father's worst enemy. Clementina wrongly believes that her husband has been killed in the recent civil war, but actually he has been rescued and will soon return to Venice in act 2 disguised as Granville, the French ambassador, to offer a pact to Venice to protect it from Spanish domination.

At the same time, Anselmo wishes to marry his daughter to Palermo, a brave Venetian officer. Clementina refuses to tell her father that she has already married Rinaldo, whom, again, she believes is dead, on the grounds that Anselmo would revenge himself upon Rinaldo's surviving family; she only tells Anselmo at first that she does not love Palermo. Under parental pressure and driven by filial duty, Clementina relents and consents to marry Palermo before she realizes that Rinaldo lives disguised as Granville. Rinaldo/Granville's offer of friendship from France is spurned by Anselmo, who sees the pact as leading to French domination of Venice. Meanwhile, toward the end of act 2 Rinaldo/Granville discloses himself to Clementina, and they are seen in a loving embrace early in act 3 by the jealous Palermo, who tells all to Anselmo. The general demands that Granville leave Venice immediately and prevents the married couple from reuniting, as they still refuse to inform him of their marriage.

In act 4, Palermo asserts that Clementina, because of her affection for Granville, is not fit to be his wife, while at the same time the grateful citizens of Venice, led by Adorno, offer a throne to Anselmo. The general is angered by the offer, for he is a patriot who loves the republic and thinks a monarchy makes slaves of citizens. Told that Granville has sailed back to Venice to allow Clementina to escape with him to France, Anselmo rushes home and disarms the Rinaldo/Granville forces. Clementina laments her filial disobedience. Despite her confession that she and Rinaldo are married, Anselmo imprisons his son-in-law and refuses to accept the marriage. Granville will still not permit Clementina to reveal his true identity as he continues to fear for his family.

In the final act, Rinaldo/Granville struggles out of his prison cell and challenges Palermo, while at the same time Clementina confesses all to her father in an attempt to save her husband. Anselmo relents but is too late to save his son-in-law, fatally wounded by Palermo. Rinaldo dies, Clementina stabs herself, and Anselmo is left alone to speak the moral that warns against filial disobedience:

> I yield submission to the dreadful stroke,
> And only ask that this unhappy story,
> To future times, may forcibly point out
> The dire affects of filial disobedience.

Contemporary assessments of *Clementina* focused on its political implications. The *Critical Review* of April 1771 felt that some of the play's political sentiments had been introduced gratuitously only to receive "the applause of the galleries, for whose sole gratification they seem to have been introduced" (Review of *Clementina* 311). To support his contention, the reviewer quoted the following lines from act 1, scene 1:

> The people's voice, howe'er it sometimes errs,
> Means always nobly, and is rais'd by virtue;
> Their very faults, illustrious from their motives,
> Demand respect, nay, ask for admiration,
> And soar, at least, half sanctify'd to justice.

Spoken by the patriot Palermo, these lines refer to the Venetians' anger at Rinaldo/Granville's effort to forge a tie between France and Venice; the Venetians see the pact as a disguised attempt to bring Venice under French control. As Watt notes, later in act 4 occurs the most obvious political sentiment: the people, represented by Adorno, praise Anselmo as the "great preserver" of Venice and offer to crown him king (W. W. Watt 214). Denying any interest in personal glory, Anselmo rejects the honor, which he views as sapping the "bulwark of the popular freedom" (*Clementina* 4.3). The *London Chronicle* (9–12 Mar.) reported that this scene "met with the highest applause from the audience," but whether Watt is correct in thinking that "Kelly was actually catering to the wild enthusiasm of the very Wilkites whom he had professed to despise" (214–15) is another matter I take up shortly.

Certainly other contemporary reactions assumed that Kelly played a Wilkite card. Francis Gentleman (who wrote *The Theater: A Poetical Dissection* under the pseudonym "Nicholas Nipclose") reacted to *Clementina* as follows:

> Kelly between the sister muses steers,
> Too grave for laughter, and too light for tears;
> If Clementina claims thee for her sire,

To pastry-cooks consign her, or the fire;
Nor dare to play the double dealer's part,
In sentiments so foreign from thy heart.

(29)

In a footnote, Gentlemen writes, "Several impotent attempts at patriotic strokes were made in this impotent tragedy; which, if derived from the Ledger essayist, must be double dealing with a witness." Imitating the Wilkite newspaper warnings, Gentleman even advises Kelly to "forego the city's father" (a reference to Kelly's political writing under the direction of Ladbroke) if he wishes to achieve literary fame.

General response to the play was mixed, but the major reviews were negative. The *Critical Review* attacked the play savagely: "Of all the dramatic performances which of late years have met with any degree of success, this is by far the meanest, whether we consider its fable, characters, or language" (311). John Hawkesworth in the March 1771 *Monthly Review* also decried the play's language: "Love is made to court one hero with *ripe roses,* and another is said to drag a *chain of being,* a lady is compassed *round* with *surrounding* virgins" (Review of *Clementina* 254).[14] Hawkesworth complains about insufficient motivation—Clementina's refusal to marry Palermo, for instance—but then he and the writer for the *Critical Review* were basically examining the play as literature, not as theater. Surely theater audiences would not worry as much as professional critics about infelicities of metaphor.

Not all contemporary reaction was as hostile as these two reviews. In a regular feature called the "British Theatre," the *London Magazine* for March 1771 assessed the play using the traditional heuristic of fable, manners, character, sentiment, diction, and representation. The writer praised the story as "at once natural and interesting" and was not troubled by Anselmo's attempt to persuade his daughter to marry against her inclination. "Anselmo's motives," he claimed, "for urging an union so apparently repugnant to his daughter's inclination, are noble" (148); the writer allows, however, that some may feel as Richardson's Clarissa did in a similar situation.

The play ran for nine nights beginning on Saturday, 23 February, and ending on 9 March. According to G. W. Stone, the play did not appear again during the century. It had a somewhat longer history in Ireland, appearing in Dublin five times by 1776 and three times in Belfast from 1771 until 1774. It was put on in Lishburn in 1775 and then at Cork in 1780.[15] In America, Philadelphia was the only city that saw a production of *Clementina;* according to Seilhamer, the New American Company, primarily made up of members of the Kenna family, played the tragedy for the first time at the Northern Liberties Theater on 8 April 1791 (2: 300, 304–5), and T. C. Pollock notes productions in the city by the company later that month and then again on 16 March 1792 (164). Watt feels that these latter-day productions in America "may well have been prompted by Irish patriotism" (W.W.Watt 220), but the initial production was due to Mrs. Kenna, who, according to Seilhamer, felt herself the rival of Mrs.Yates and wanted therefore to play all of her roles (2: 304).

After 1792, *Clementina* seems to have completely disappeared from the stage; nor is there much mention of it in modern critical literature on eighteenth-century drama. "A poor dull pseudo-classic production, in spite of its Italian scene" is all Allardyce Nicoll can manage to say. He concludes that regardless of the "high price which Kelly received for the copyright and the esteem in which some contemporaries held the drama we cannot in any wise credit it among the even moderately successful tragedies of its class" (79–80).

Modern studies of Kelly's work say little about the play. O'Leary dismisses it in a short paragraph, concluding of Kelly that, "whatever his gift for comedy, his tragedy was one more victim of the left-handed eighteenth-century tradition that held tragedy greater than comedy and impelled every stageworthy author to try his hand at the hallowed genre" (162). Watt notes that Kelly was really only writing a tragic version of his typical sentimental comic plot and specifically mentions the heroine's conflict between her desire to marry the man she loves and an equally strong inclination to maintain her filial duty (W.W.Watt 209–10). He also writes that the plot follows closely that of Elizabeth Griffith's *School for Rakes* (1769). I cannot agree that the play is just a version of Griffith's play, which features a repentant rake and a sister-brother whose comic conflict often reminds one of the combat in Fielding's *Tom Jones* between Squire Western and Mrs. Western.

Clementina is of most interest as a vehicle for political sentiment; but instead of viewing the introduction of republican sentiments as hypocritical, however, I think it more productive to recall once again Kelly's need as a popular writer to cater to his audience. It is with this imperative in mind that Leo Hughes discusses both Colman's epilogue to *Clementina* and Johnson's prologue to the opening of Drury Lane in 1747:

> Hard is his lot, that here by Fortune plac'd,
> Must watch the wild Vicissitudes of Taste;
> With ev'ry Meteor of Caprice must play,
> And chase the new-blown Bubbles of the Day.
> Ah! let not Censure term our Fate our Choice,
> The Stage but echoes back the publick Voice,
> The Drama's laws the Drama's Patrons give,
> For we that live to please, must please to live.
>
> (Johnson qtd. in Hughes 87–88)

Besides once again reminding us of the state-theater parallel, Colman's epilogue to *Clementina* focuses, as Johnson's prologue did, on the need for the popular dramatist to heed his audience:

Thrice happy Britain, where with equal hand,
Three well-pois'd states unite to rule the land!
Thus in the theater, as well the state,
Three ranks must join to make us bless'd and great.
Kings, Lords, and Commons, o'er the nation sit;
Pit, box, and gallery, rule the realms of wit.

                              (Colman qtd. in Hughes 78)

But the politics of the play itself are not as simple a matter as Kelly's contemporaries and Watt seemed to feel. A close examination of the play's political action yields, I believe, a more complex situation, one that acknowledges a key difference between the republican hero of Venice, Anselmo, and the political hero of London, Wilkes.

In the crucial fourth act, Anselmo is offered the throne of the Venetian republic by a citizenry labeled by their hero as "giddy men" who have forgotten their "duty to the state." The speech Anselmo delivers to this entirely too enthusiastic populace dramatizes him as anything but a John Wilkes figure, eager for power, money, and fame:

Long, my brave friends, against the Spanish tyrant,
Have the exalted citizens of Venice
Fought the great cause of justice and mankind:
And will you now, triumphant over force,
From downright gratitude embrace a chain?
What has your glorious fortitude effected,
If in the full fraught transport of your souls,
You lift the man you fondly call deliverer,
To sov'reign rule, and crown him for your master?
In such a case your blessing is your bane,
And Spain, a foe less deadly than Anselmo.

Anselmo clearly refuses the kind of public adoration that Wilkes cultivated; he rejects the worship of what some in the press of the early 1770s called the "mobocracy" when they referred to the street mobs who blindly followed Wilkes. Anselmo is clearly a patriot in the best sense, for he disdains being made the source of a personality cult and refuses what he calls "despotic power" even when his countrymen wish to burden him and themselves with such a bestowal.

Far from being an endorsement of Wilkes and the Wilkites, *Clementina* suggests that a true patriot resists deification at the hands of a mob—those "giddy men"—and will instead remind them that "the man is half a traitor to the state, / who only serves it for a sordid motive" (4.2). This last seems a contemporary reference to the very self-interest that Wilkes had been accused of pursuing by the Rev. Tooke and others in the weeks before the play appeared. The reference seems particularly apt at a time when Wilkes and his followers in the SSBR had

100

declined to share the Society's funds with other endangered radicals, such as William Bingley. *Clementina,* then, as we have seen with Kelly's earlier plays, can be construed as deliberately ambiguous and ambivalent, as playing up, as the comedies do, both sides of a question. There is, once the local historical context of the tragedy is known, enough evidence to make available both pro- and anti-Wilkes interpretations.

From a financial point of view, *Clementina* suffered no such ambiguity. All contemporary reports suggest that Kelly did very well indeed. Cooke, in his *European Magazine* biography, claims that Kelly received two hundred pounds for the copy from the Dillys on "no other stipulation than that of its running nine nights" ("Hugh Kelly," Jan. 1794, 44). He suggests that such a large sum was risked only because Kelly had developed a high reputation since the success of *False Delicacy*. But if the Dillys had hoped to reap as much success from *Clementina* as had Richard Baldwin and others involved in the publishing of *False Delicacy,* then they were disappointed. Instead of the four editions that *False Delicacy* went through in less than a year, the tragedy had but two.[16] There were two more in Ireland, one in Belfast and another in Dublin. Nevertheless, if Arthur Simons Collins is correct, Kelly received fifty pounds more than the usual sum for the publishing rights (267). Nor should we forget that the nine-night run was certainly a respectable one, long enough for the play to be considered a modest success and to give Kelly three author's nights, so that perhaps his total income from *Clementina* was close to four hundred pounds.[17] Kelly had by February 1771, then, written half of the plays he was to write; and although his income was a substantial one, especially now that he was receiving the two hundred pounds a year from the ministry, nearly two years would pass before his income would again receive a substantial boost from a new play, *The School for Wives,* which was to be produced at Drury Lane on 11 December 1773. Meanwhile, Kelly's career as a journalist would continue to involve him in the political turmoil of London, and his career as a barrister would begin.

9

❧

Politics before and after *Clementina* and Departure from the *Public Ledger*

homas O'Leary claims that, for the two-year period following the staging of *Clementina*, he found no trace of Kelly's activities until the appearance of *The School for Wives*, except for the exchange of letters between Kelly and David Garrick and Kelly and Henry Baldwin in late April 1773 over a controversial Kelly review of Garrick's revival of *The Chances* (164). Even W. W. Watt, who tracked down many periodical attacks on Kelly, has little to say about this two-year period from *Clementina* (Feb.–Mar. 1771) until Kelly's review of Goldsmith's *She Stoops to Conquer* in March 1773 (230). He mentions Kelly's conflict with Wilkite Capt. Miles Button Allen in late 1772, but his chronology for this newspaper confrontation is erroneous: Watt places the quarrel in late 1772, but it actually occurred in January of that year and was followed by a fistfight in Vauxhall Gardens on 25 June 1772, some months after Kelly had left the *Ledger*. Although a reconstruction of Kelly's activities from March 1771 to March 1773 is difficult, a careful survey of the newspapers yields enough material to build a narrative of his professional life. Once again, the primary source of such events must often be various hostile notices.

I begin early in 1771, prior to *Clementina's* staging, when Kelly published political pieces so angering the Wilkites that they needed little urging to condemn the play. One piece sometime in January attacked Serjeant John Glynn.[1] As Joel Gold has noted, Glynn was the most formidable of the London radical lawyers and had been an MP for Middlesex since December 1768. In January 1771, however, if not before, reports suggested that, while managing Glynn's campaign funds for this election, Horne Tooke used some of the moneys for other purposes, or at least so charged the Wilkites. Kelly, writing under the pen names "Lycomedes" and "Simon Simple," entered the quarrel with an attack on Glynn. His motive for such a sortie is obvious: to exacerbate the Wilkes–Tooke split.

Assailing Kelly for his "impudence" in falling upon Glynn, a letter signed "Sir Paddy O'Connaught" appeared in the *Public Advertiser* for 29 January 1771. Calling "Sir Hugh Wormwood" a "damned impudent fellow," the writer juxtaposes Serjeant Glynn's learnedness with Kelly's "degree" from "Brazen Face College, Dublin," where he received the "D.I.F." ("Damned Impudent Fellow"). O'Connaught concludes that Kelly's "impudence" has changed him from a "harmless Psalm-saying Journeyman Stay-maker to conceit himself to be a great Lawyer, a great Poet, and a great Statesman, and to look down upon all above him as a Set of Reptiles," the "Reptiles" referring to the leading radicals. The old charge of vanity is raised, and the equally tired reference to Kelly's early work as a staymaker is aired; new is the reference to the "great Lawyer," for although Kelly was admitted to the Middle Temple on 11 April 1768, this comment was the first by the radicals on Kelly's pursuit of a legal career.

After *Clementina*'s staging on 23 February, the radical bloodhounds soon sniffed out Kelly; when they did, the attacks were sudden and vicious. The Wilkite *London Evening Post* printed a letter signed "Detector" (26–28 Feb.) that exposed what the writer felt was a campaign of misinformation by several newspapers and directed by Kelly himself to hide his authorship: "The town has been with great care and dexterity prepared for giving a kind reception to the new tragedy called *Clementina*," wrote Detector, who then quoted the planted newspaper reports designed to make the population think the play was written by anyone but Kelly: "'We have been assured, that the new tragedy . . . has suffered a severe purgation in the licensing-office, on account of the strong sentiment of patriotism and spirit of liberty which it contains.'" By the end, however, Detector loses his patience and exhibits anger at Kelly's subterfuge. He finishes his letter in a tantrum of invective:

> Now let it be known, that this *American Divine,* as *remarkable* for *modesty* as *genius,* and said to be out of England, is actually the indecent writer of these puffs in his own favour; and, notwithstanding his patriotic sentiments, and strong flame of liberty, is no other than Wormwood, Lycomedes, the hackney puff-maker to impostors, the toad-eater of playhouse patentees, the volunteer sycophant of corrupt ministers, the constant reviler of all patriots, the advocate for murderers, and the resolute champion of those who most violate the laws, and seek to undermine the constitution of this kingdom, and who has not so much *False Delicacy* in him, as not to be ready to say *A Word to the Foolish as well as the Wise,* when it can in any way be made to answer his purpose, by either contriving or propagating imposition or falsehood.

Like many political letters that appeared in late-eighteenth-century newspapers, this one requires in nearly every line some historical contextualizing equal to that one might devote to a political poem filled with historical allusion. Even a 1771 reader would need to have paid close attention to the current political dialogue to understand the intertextual meanings of Wormwood and Lycomedes; a reader would have to know something of Kelly's journalistic support of Garrick and of his defense of the government in the trials for murder that followed the St. George's Field Massacre of May 1768 and the riot fomented by the bullies Edward McQuirk and Lawrence Balfe at the Middlesex election of December 1768. The writer assumes, then, a great deal of local political knowledge in his readers, expecting each reader to be able to interpret the gaps and allusions. The point I wish to make is that no citizen who was a careless reader of eighteenth-century newspapers could successfully negotiate these letters. The drama of politics as captured in the newspapers demanded careful, competent reading.

Yet Wilkites seem to have made no attempt to interfere with *Clementina*'s performances. Perhaps they felt that it was too late, given that it had been playing nearly a week. Then again, possibly many of them had already been so taken in by its pro-Patriot rhetoric that they were angry at themselves for having been duped. They may also have felt that any attack might backfire. They may have recalled that *A Word to the Wise*'s damnation only led to a great financial boon to Kelly through a lucrative subscription edition. Whatever the reason, *Clementina* was allowed its nine nights' run, but once that was concluded, the *London Evening Post* ran on the front page of its 12–14 March edition a scathing denunciation of the play. The paper's ire may be understandable because it was the most pro-Wilkite of all newspapers, so much so that it frequently printed attacks on its fellow radical paper, the *Middlesex Journal,* for its pro-Tooke stance.[2]

The attack, running a full two columns and signed by "Ticklepitcher, Junior," criticized the tragedy on nearly every imaginable basis—its diction, versification, and plot were all angrily condemned. The writer could hardly believe "that Clementina should force its way to public representation, under the management of so intelligent a gentleman as Mr. Colman." Deciding that Colman would never have accepted the play on literary grounds, he ascribes Colman's acceptance of *Clementina* solely to ministerial influence: "which position, once admitted, incontrovertibly fixes Mr. Kelly for its author."

Some of the fervor of the anti-Kelly tirades possibly reflected the generalized frustration in the London radical community early in 1771. The condition had more than one cause. First and most important was the ongoing quarrel between Wilkes and Tooke that, carried on through letters in the newspapers, not only divided the radical camp but also effectively presented an opportunity for the Court party to gain a significant victory in the fall when William Nash, a pro-ministerial alderman, was to be elected lord mayor for 1772. Second, as the Wilkes–Tooke conflict continued, the radical printers were also subjected to ministerial legal actions to punish what the government considered their abuses, mainly the printing of the debates in the House of Commons, which had traditionally been forbidden. A number of newspaper printers were ordered to appear before the Commons, but the main culprits were John Wheble of the *Middlesex Journal* and John Miller of the *London Evening Post,* who went into hiding instead of appearing. When Wheble was eventually arrested and brought before Wilkes at the Guildhall, Wilkes released the printer on the grounds that no one could arrest London citizens but an officer of the City. The freedom of the press issue thus expanded into a contest of legal jurisdiction between the City and the House of Commons. The Commons ignored Wilkes but had arrested and placed in the Tower two other London officials who had defied them in the printers' incident, Mayor Brass Crosby and Alderman Richard Oliver. By the time these two were finally released on 8 May, they had achieved something close to heroic stature among the city radicals and a number of city councils throughout the kingdom (Rudé, *Wilkes* 164). The printers were left unpunished, and the papers continued to print the Commons debates. Ironically, as throughout the Wilkite years, the disputes created their own commodity culture, for publications were spawned dealing with the freedom of the press and the issues raised by the various trials.

But after early May 1771, the Wilkes–Tooke letters resumed and the radicals were back to fighting each other. The split seemed to be embodied in, as much as anything, the radical societies; the SSBR continued to support Wilkes financially, while the Constitutional Society appeared willing to raise funds for all radicals in legal difficulty.[3] Even the radical papers seemed to be involved in the intramural quarrels and thus had little time to abuse the ministerial journalists: the *Middlesex Journal* attacked what it termed the *Post*'s slanderous stories, while the *Post* bitterly complained that Parson Tooke controlled the *Middlesex Journal*. Meanwhile, the *Public Advertiser,* printed by Henry Sampson Woodfall, who opened the pages of his paper to all sides, found room in its letters section for attacks on Hugh Kelly. Once again it is to a hostile letter that we owe our knowledge of Kelly's political journalism during the late spring and early summer of 1771.

Printed in the Monday, 3 June number of the *Advertiser* was a letter signed "Candidus" that exposed Kelly as the real writer of a series of letters that had been appearing in the *Public Ledger* under the name "John Hampden." Angry at the irony of Kelly's borrowing a pen name from among the parliamentary heroes who fought against Charles I, Candidus takes the usual route of radical attack on Kelly by ridiculing both his past occupation of staymaker and his supposed vanity in considering himself equal to the task of criticizing City radicals who are more wealthy and socially prestigious than he is:

> Whoever has attended to the various Letters wrote under different Signatures, but known to be the Product of H__h K___y, would naturally be led to suppose, by the Freedom of his addressing the greatest and most distinguished Characters of the Age, such as the Marquis of Rockingham, Lord Chatham, Lord Temple &c. that he

was at least of equal if not superior Quality to the abovementioned Lords. We have known a Journeyman Staymaker declare himself to be superior to a Chief Magistrate of this City, one who was not only highly distinguished by his Affluence, but was well known to be equal in Honour, Integrity, and true Independence to any Man in the Kingdom.

Candidus's last reference is to Kelly's May 1770 attack on Lord Mayor Beckford. Curiously, the radicals who strove for more democracy in Parliament and did not like being called the "scum of the earth" often ridiculed Kelly for his humble status. Of more importance, however, is Candidus's quoting a Hampden/Kelly letter that shows Kelly attempting to exploit the conflict between Wilkes and Tooke by discrediting both of them: "The quarrel between Mr. Wilkes and Mr. Horne [Tooke], is, in my Opinion, highly reproachful, shameful, and disgraceful to them both: It is evident, from their Letters, that they knew too many bad Things of one another." Kelly brings other city radicals, like Townsend and Sawbridge, into his argument and further attempts to split the radicals by claiming that these men did not owe their popularity to Wilkes but rather that Wilkes owed much to their political efforts in the City.

From this attack and similar ones by Candidus until the end of July, we learn that Kelly was still editing the *Ledger* and taking an active role against the Patriots and their supporters. We also learn that Kelly did not confine his assaults, if Candidus is correct, to middle-class London radicals but also leveled them at Oppositional peers, such as Lord Temple and Lord Chatham (William Pitt). At least five letters signed by Candidus appeared in the *Public Advertiser* in June and July attacking Kelly, primarily for the content of his John Hampden letters, which were apparently coming out at about the same time in the *Ledger*.[4]

The *Ledger* itself, for which there are a few numbers extant for 1771, provides evidence of Kelly's continuing campaign against the radicals. Only six numbers of the paper are extant from the fall, and at least three of these contain strong attacks on Wilkes. One views him as un-English at his core, a Frenchified dandy; that charge probably touched sensitive Patriot nerves, given their generally excessive cultivation of Englishness.[5] Another (2 Oct.) criticizes Wilkes's role as sheriff; while a third (22 Nov.) even contains a mock vision of Wilkes's funeral, attended by all the London mob and street riffraff. Because Kelly left so little in the way of manuscript and archival materials, it is not likely that we will ever be able to estimate with certainty all of the various causes that contributed to Kelly's attacks on Wilkes. To an extent, Wilkes was the natural enemy of Kelly, whose commitment to the reformist culture of sensibility combined with his Courtier politics to view Wilkes as the archseducer, part Achitophel and part Rochesterian or Lovelacian devil. He was the rake who had become a political figure and who now was attempting to seduce the London masses instead of young maidens; Wilkes's particular blend of politics and Eros, a gentlemanly seducer and crowd-pleasing tyrant, must have embodied for Kelly all that was evil.

Sometime in January 1772, probably under the name "Meanwell," Kelly published in the *Ledger* a letter or series of letters attacking the Wilkite street bully Capt. Miles Button Allen. According to Watt, who quotes a stanza from a poem published in the 18–20 March 1773 number of the *St. James's Chronicle,* it was this attack that precipitated Kelly's departure from the *Ledger:*

> At the Ledger he work'd; till a Bankrupt he prov'd,
> > When Allen, like Goose, he did roast;
> And therefore his Shop he has lately remov'd
> > To the *General Evening Post.*
>
> (qtd. in W. W. Watt 327)

The reasons behind Kelly's abuse of Allen are not clear, if in fact he did precipitate the quarrel; nor is it clear why, of all the Wilkites Kelly had assailed in his years as editor of the *Ledger,* it was this particular assault that would somehow cause his departure from a paper he had run for approximately seven years. It is true that William Faden was to lease the paper in 1773 for three years; Kelly may have known of Faden's intentions and as a result felt his position with the paper in danger.[6] Or he may have received a better offer from the Say family, who still controlled the *General Evening Post* although its printer was Samuel Bladon. Later I take up the evidence suggesting that Kelly's labors for the *General Evening Post* began early in 1772, but first I look at Capt. Allen's political career, if haranguing the livery and physically threatening citizens constitute a career, to understand why Kelly, despite protests to the contrary, may have wished to abuse him. I then move to the summer of 1772 when an actual physical confrontation between Kelly and Allen took place. This fight created its own paper war, which in turn provides some evidence about Kelly's earlier departure from the *Ledger.* Once again, newspaper accounts serve as the major source of knowledge about these few months of Kelly's public life.

Capt. Miles Button Allen before becoming the object of Kelly's ire played an ambiguous role in the Wilkite activities of the late 1760s and early 1770s. He seems to have first drawn attention to himself by a challenge to Courtier MP Sir William Meredith; for this challenge, he was promptly arrested and imprisoned in Newgate before being released in May 1769.[7] One Wilkes biographer, Horace Bleackley, writes that on the morning of the election between Henry Lawes Luttrell and John Wilkes the mob paused long enough on their march to the Brentford polling place to cheer Allen, then in Newgate and described by Bleackley as "one of their more irrational fellows" (222).[8] The irrationality of Allen was seen even by his fellows; the accounts of his many addresses to the livery at the Guildhall suggest some found him a tedious bore, while others considered him something of a comical hothead.[9] Later in the decade, even formerly friendly audiences occasionally grew tired of Allen's tirades: in the 23–

25 June 1774 number of the *Middlesex Journal,* a story reports that Allen was forced off the hustings while attempting to "speechify" and was "soon silenced."

It remains unclear why Kelly should have condescended to abuse Allen—something that, in the paper war following the 25 June fight, he directly denied doing—who was only a sergeant in the Wilkite army. The few surviving numbers of the *Ledger* for January 1772 make it impossible to locate the original attack, and the radical press did not mention the incident. Only after the two men had assaulted each other on 25 June does one learn anything at all of this January activity. On Thursday evening, 25 June 1772, Allen met Kelly at Vauxhall Gardens; words were exchanged; and a brief fistfight ensued. Admitting that he struck the first blow after being provoked and that had others not intervened he would have suffered badly at Allen's hands, Kelly in his explanatory letter published in the 27–29 June number of the *Morning Chronicle* claims only that he published letters by others critical of Allen but denied attacking him directly in January 1772 until Allen attacked him. Kelly admits that he responded with a refutation of Allen's charges—"I gave him the lye direct under my hand," wrote Kelly. As I have pointed out elsewhere ("Hugh Kelly, William Jackson" 523–27), every reference to Kelly's editorship was in the past tense in this summer paper war: Kelly himself clearly states "when I *was* editor of the *Public Ledger*" in the *Chronicle* letter (emphasis added). He nowhere suggests that he is currently working on the *Ledger,* and Allen calls him the "late Editor" of the *Ledger.* This evidence, combined with that offered by the poem in the *St. James's Chronicle* suggesting that Kelly left the *Ledger* after "roast[ing]" Allen, makes me think that Kelly did leave the paper sometime early in the winter of 1772.[10]

Other evidence exists to suggest that Kelly left the *Ledger* early in 1772. William Jackson, later known as Dr. Viper for his attacks on Foote, has been traditionally associated with the *Ledger* (Bataille, "Hugh Kelly, William Jackson" 525), and although it is unlikely that Jackson was involved much before Kelly's departure, there may have been a period of transition when both men worked for the paper. For in the 18–21 January 1772 number of the *Middlesex Journal,* Wilkes complains of being attacked in the papers by Robert Holloway, James Stephens, and William Jackson, and Jackson has not been linked with any paper at this time except the *Ledger.* In addition, by March 1772, the *Ledger's* "Theatrical Review" feature claimed for the first time to be written without "managerial influence," perhaps in response to the old charge that under Kelly the paper had always favored Garrick. And Capt. Allen claimed in his letter to the *Morning Chronicle* (30 June–2 July 1772) that a friend had published in the 11 February 1772 *Ledger* a warning to Kelly; Allen reprints that warning in the *Chronicle,* and it seems doubtful that Kelly, had he still been editor, would have allowed its publication, so personally insulting is it in tone.

Examining the *General Evening Post* for the winter and spring months of 1772, one finds support for the external evidence that Kelly was writing for that paper. The internal evidence that Kelly wrote for the *Post* in 1773 and afterwards is compelling, and I discuss it later. The evidence for early 1772, although not conclusive, is reasonably strong and consists of a number of tendencies and specific items that, taken together, suggest his hand. First, there is a continuous praise of Garrick by the several dramatic critics who appear in the paper; this treatment may be contrasted to the sometimes harsh treatment Garrick received in the post-Kelly *Ledger:* in its 13 November 1772 number, the paper prints an apology from its publisher, Francis Newbery, for an 18 June 1772 attack on Garrick in connection with the Bickerstaff scandal that became a newspaper sensation during the summer of 1772.[11] The *General Evening Post* praises Garrick for his acting (11–14 Jan.) and for his alteration of older tragedies. In general, the paper's sustained interest in the theater also suggests Kelly's hand. Only the *Morning Chronicle,* edited by William Woodfall, a theater critic and former actor, came close to matching the volume of the *Post*'s theater news. The paper also consistently promoted themes—the quality of the current moral comedy (16–18 Jan.) was one—that Kelly had always supported and generally agreed with the direction of the modern theater, another Kelly thematic in "The Babler" and the *Court Magazine.* There appear pseudonyms, such as "Crito," "Honestus," and "Senex," that Kelly had used before, again especially in the earlier journalism. The criticism of actors and actresses often reminds one of Kelly's practice in *Thespis;* in Crito's 13–15 February piece, for instance, the criticism focuses on the inability of many actresses to memorize epilogues. By May, the constant parade of insider information about people Kelly knew well—theater people, like Garrick and Foote, and political people, like Ladbroke—exceeded the coverage of other newspapers and suggests that Kelly wrote for the *General Evening Post.* Even the Kellys' social life is mentioned: Elizabeth Kelly's costume for a masquerade is described on one occasion.[12]

When the Kelly–Allen "rencontre," as Kelly phrased it, took place on 25 June, the *General Evening Post* printed a long explanation of the affair in a light favorable to Kelly; it actually sounds as if Kelly wrote it. The piece ends with raising the issue of Capt. Allen's military trial at Belisle during the Seven Years' War, which ended with his dismissal from the army (4–7 July). In the next issue, however, the paper printed a piece by "Veritas" that calls into question Kelly's version of events, particularly challenging Kelly's account of his own bravery. Veritas implies that Kelly was prudent rather than courageous and did not choose to duel with Allen. He closes by bringing up the "much-injured *Miss Woodcock,*" an allusion to the Lord Baltimore rape trial of 1768 when Kelly may have defended Baltimore. In a backhanded tribute, Veritas admits Kelly's writing prowess: "As to the malignity of his pen, however to be despised, no person can dispute his infernal capacity."

In admitting to the pages of the *General Evening Post* a letter critical of himself, Kelly only practices a pattern of occasional blame in a general context of praise that his enemies had often said dictated Kelly's treatment of Garrick: that is, he generally favored "Roscius" (Garrick) but occasionally allowed a critical commentary to be inserted in the *Ledger* to give some credibility to the paper's motto: "Open to all but influenced by none." He also allowed one or two items in defense of Wilkes into the 1771–72 extant numbers of the *Ledger;* it is thus not surprising that the Veritas assault was given space in the *General Evening Post*.

The amount of coverage the papers provided the incident was exceeded during the summer only by the quarrel between Garrick and Kenrick over *Love in the Suds*. The various charges and countercharges between Kelly and Allen and their partisans appeared in July. Among those papers involved were the *Middlesex Journal,* now supposedly under new management but still possessing a strong anti-Kelly bias; the *Morning Chronicle,* published by William Woodfall and the source of several anti-Kelly pieces to appear in the last few weeks of the year; the *Public Advertiser,* the paper willing to carry on the affair longer than the other papers and edited by Henry Sampson Woodfall; the *London Packet,* in which Kelly had had a recent financial interest; and the *General Evening Post.*[13]

Meanwhile, after printing the Veritas letter, Kelly's *Post* kept silent about the Allen–Kelly affair; but throughout the summer of 1772, the paper defended Garrick, especially against newspaper attacks by disappointed authors, and praised Kelly's favorite actors, Frances Abington and Thomas King.[14] The paper criticized Allen, but focused its attack on Allen's abuse of Courtier Lord Mayor Nash (14–16 July) rather than on his altercation with Kelly. The August issues contained brief notes on Sir Robert Ladbroke and his family, even editorializing about the new house Sir Robert had constructed for his banking business. The theater pieces, signed by familiar Kelly pseudonyms, like Senex, dealt with topics of abiding interest to Kelly. Senex wrote in the 22–25 August issue about the persistence of managers using inappropriate performers for certain characters when their houses possessed more suitable actors and actresses. Kelly here engaged in a knowledgeable examination of current casting practices, and the focus on the criticism of acting is reminiscent of his *Thespis,* except that he has learned to moderate direct complaints about performers. He probably published under the name "Lorenzo" (19–22 Sept.) a piece praising the London actors and actresses and defending their profession: Court politicians were not the only beneficiaries of Kelly's increased sophistication in public relations.

August also saw the resurgence of the Allen–Kelly quarrel. In its 11–13 August number, the *Middlesex Journal* reprinted an attack on Kelly that originally had appeared in the *London Packet;* addressed to Allen, the writer maintained that the captain was wasting his time because Kelly would not fight and had in all his political writings only "obeyed the mandate of his superiors; and upon their bounty he has to depend for the maintenance of a large family." Kelly's reply came out in the *Public Advertiser* for 4 September. From this letter, we learn that Kelly was doing well enough to be able to spend the summer season in Chelsea, where he was when Allen was supposedly hunting him sometime after the 25 June incident. That Kelly knew how to fight with a pen, if not a sword, and was willing to do so can be seen in the following excerpt from this letter in which Kelly wonders how Allen can possibly expect to be free from newspaper attacks:

> Yet let me ask, what political Sanctity there is about this Varlet, that he should be exempted from the Animadversions of the Press, at the Moment he himself squirts his little Insolence through this Vehicle on the first Members of the whole Community. As far as Crimes can raise him from Insignificance, he is a public Man; as public as his Friend Mac Quirk; and will he then pretend, while yelping in the Pack of Mongrel Sedition at King, Lords, and Commons himself, that any body who can stoop to the Drudgery, has not a Right to rake into the Kennel of his Character?

One can understand Wilkite rage at Kelly's invective: he was good at it, more than a match for amateurs like Allen, here reduced in one phrase ("squirts his little Insolence") to the status of a Yahoo.

There is something more serious here too, and it goes to the heart of the general complaint many in the second half of the century made against newspapers: that they made public what was heretofore private; not only politics themselves but the lives of political figures too. Kelly announces a principle of political journalism; that is, if one enters into the public realm and engages in political debate, then one must be prepared to have one's private character scrutinized and judged—and also abused. Vincent Carretta has argued that one big difference between the political satire in Pope's time and that of the early 1760s was the increased level of personal abuse (229). Although Carretta refers narrowly to political satire in more formal modes, certainly this invective is noticeable in political journalism. Some resisted this power of print, of public exposure through journalism, and did not like the private character of anyone or any institution written about; yet not even the House of Commons could forbid any longer the public airing of what after all concerned the public. With the newspaper, Kelly seems to say, there is no place to hide, not if one wishes to take part in what ought to be public debate: there is no "political Sanctity." And no sanctuary, either. Kelly himself was probably as much vilified in the press of the late 1760s and early 1770s as any political-literary figure, but he knew that was the new game and never complained. Foucault may have been right about the increasing power of the central state to observe its citizens, but because of the rise of journalism, in all its forms, such surveillance obviously worked both ways.[15]

More important issues pushed the Allen–Kelly quarrel once more into the background as the London press prepared for the next election of the lord mayor at the end of September. In its 28 September issue, the *Public Advertiser* printed a letter addressed to the livery and signed "Aristides" that the *Middlesex Journal* for 29 September–1 October identified as Kelly's. As with his January 1771 strategy to divide the radicals further when he attacked Tooke's management of

Serjeant Glynn's campaign for Middlesex MP, so here Kelly attempted to exploit the friction between James Townsend, the non-Wilkite radical mayoral candidate, and Wilkes himself. Both were running against the ministerial candidates, John Shakespear and Thomas Hallifax, but Townsend had been at odds with Wilkes for some time, and Kelly realized the only way that a Court candidate could gain one of the two top positions in the Guildhall election would be to divide the radicals enough so that Wilkites would not vote for Townsend and Townsend partisans would ignore Wilkes.[16] This circumstance had occurred previously when William Nash, a Courtier, became lord mayor. Kelly pursued that strategy beginning in the second paragraph of his 28 September letter:

> Mr. Wilkes and Mr. Townsend are now nominated by the Patriots of London as Men upon whose Election to the Mayoralty our Happiness is again essentially to depend; yet what is the Character which these wonderful Men publicly give of each other? Doesn't Mr. Townsend call Mr. Wilkes a most unprincipled Impostor? And didn't Mr. Wilkes last Year thank the Livery in Print for spurning the "brutal Tyrant," Townsend, from that very Seat of Chief Magistracy which he himself now hopes to gain by an avowed Association with that Gentleman? . . .

> Is the Liberty of being their Slaves the exalted Freedom for which we are contending? And will you, Patriots of London, still go on to worship those despicable Idols, which the most inconsiderable Towns at the Extremity of the Kingdom have sense enough to view with Contempt? . . . The Kingdom at large, Gentlemen, pities your Weakness tho' it laughs at your Folly.

Turning the tables on the Patriots, who had always called themselves the "popular" party, by placing their situation in the larger national perspective was a clever but unsuccessful strategy. The vote gave Townsend and Wilkes a comfortable margin of victory over Hallifax and Shakespear, and the aldermen selected Townsend over Wilkes to be mayor; the Court candidates, however, asked for a scrutiny of the polls, which action Kelly supported, accusing the Patriots of having altered the poll's records. The Patriots felt that only a few honest mistakes had been made and claimed that Kelly, a "literary prostitute," had been hired to embarrass them by calling for a scrutiny. The 23 December letter to the *Morning Chronicle* addresses all this while accusing Wilkes of aiding the ministerial aldermen because he was piqued at not becoming mayor:

> The scrutineers on the part of the ministerial Aldermen . . . hired that literary prostitute, H-gh K-lly, to write something for them, that might give an air of plausibility to their conduct; and by way of materials for the work, informed him that there were some few lit-

eral mistakes in the poll-books . . . which Mr. K–lly was to make the most of he could. Mr. K–y undertook the job and made the poor scrutineers set their names to as ridiculous a piece of bombast, as ever appeared in a sentimental comedy.

The letter goes on to criticize Wilkes for aiding the ministerial position and Kelly's argument for his own purposes.

Between the election and the aftermath of the scrutiny in late December, Kelly was often mentioned in the radical press. A notice in the *Middlesex Journal* for 10–13 October, for instance, satirizes him for his involvement in the Goldsmiths' Hall scrutiny.[17] As 1772 drew to a close, Hugh Kelly remained vitally involved in London journalism and politics. He was perhaps more of a force to be reckoned with than ever before, for during the year more than one Wilkite had grudgingly acknowledged the skills of his pen. Despite the Patriots' victory in the mayoral election, the editor of *Bingley's Journal* felt it wise to watch Kelly's every move. How else can one explain the note in this paper's 24–31 October number simply reporting that "Aldermen Harley and Hallifax dined with Hugh Kelly on Saturday last, at his house in Gough-Square." An enemy of the people demanded constant surveillance.

10

The *General Evening Post,* Kelly as Barrister, and *The School for Wives*

William Watt felt that "Hugh Kelly was not in an enviable position in 1773. He had a growing family to support, and he could no longer depend on the steady income of his position on the *Public Ledger*" (238–39).[1] I would argue, on the other hand, that Kelly was facing perhaps his *annus mirabilis,* that 1773 was to be the apex of his career; during the year, he was not only called to the bar to begin what must be considered a legal career of reasonable though brief success but was also to see produced before the year's end *The School for Wives,* arguably his best and certainly his most popular play. His economic situation at the start of 1773 could not have been as bleak as Watt felt because Kelly was laboring for the *General Evening Post* in what the internal evidence suggests was a steady fashion; the salary for this journalistic work must have compensated for the loss of the *Ledger's* editorship. He was, moreover, still collecting his two-hundred-pound pension from Lord North. Finally, as the accounts of his attendance at masquerades attests, even his social life seemed pleasantly full.

The evidence of his continuing to write for the *General Evening Post* is strong.[2] I begin with the paper's review (4–6 Feb.) of Garrick's production of *The Merchant of Venice.* It is devoted almost entirely to an analysis of the weaknesses of the trial scene. The critique focuses on the trial's legal aspects, examining it from a lawyer's viewpoint. The reviewer praises the actors, especially Thomas King, whom the writer calls a better Shylock than Charles Macklin, famous for that role. He also lauds Mrs. Abington in her role as Portia: "Portia never had a better representative than Mrs. Abington." I have already noted Kelly's partiality for King and Abington, but the key indicator of Kelly's authorship is undoubtedly the legal analysis itself. To be called to the bar on 22 May, Kelly was understandably examining the play from the perspective of his new professional knowledge.

In an earlier issue (2–4 Feb.) was a review under the "Dramatic Strictures" column of Murphy's *All in the Wrong,* which the writer confesses having seen in its original production in the summer of 1761.[3] While praising the acting of Abington and King, the writer recalls the earlier cast. Kelly in 1761, it will be recalled, was beginning to edit the *Court Magazine,* where he also published his first dramatic criticism in a column called the "Green Room"; it was the start of work that enabled him to compose *Thespis* in 1766.

In the early months of 1773, Kelly also pursued an active social life, which he felt necessary to publicize in the *General Evening Post.* In its 18–20 February issue, the paper printed a long report, probably by Kelly himself, of a masquerade at the Pantheon in which are mentioned George Colman, Capt. Edward Thompson, and Mr. and Mrs. Kelly: "Mr. Kelly, in a dress similar to that worn by Mr. Reddish in *Almida.*[4] Mrs. Kelly, in a fancy dress." This masquerade was one of several Kelly was reported as attending, and just a month after the Pantheon masquerade, in his 23 April letter to Garrick about the *Chances* puff, he requested a favor of Garrick that suggests that attending masquerades was something he and his wife did frequently: "There is a masquerade my dear Sir this evening, and I should be much obliged to you if you'd give my servant an order for the Nun's dress worn by Miss Jemmy in the *Provoked Husband.*"[5] Drury Lane, it seems, provided Mr. and Mrs. Kelly's costumes.

Kelly's theater journalism demonstrates in its detail that he was in some way involved in quarrels, even if only as a close observer rather than as a participant, among players, writers, and managers. Cecil Price remarks that the theater became so popular in the 1770s that journalism featured more criticism than ever before, although at times this discourse was more a matter of gossip and puffs than it was critical analysis (136).[6] Kelly's work for the *General Evening Post* supports Price's contention, as Kelly's own intimacy with the theater provided him with that "insider" perspective necessary to obtain details of theater people's lives in the first place. In the 4–6 March issue, for example, an obvious insider view is presented of the most recent conflict between Garrick and Murphy over the latter's feeling that Garrick had not treated him fairly through the years. Kelly takes up Murphy's specific charge that *Alzuma* had deserved to be performed at Drury Lane in 1770 (it had just been put on by Colman in Feb. 1773) but that Garrick, fearful that Murphy's past political journalism might have encouraged the Wilkites to riot against *Alzuma* (as they had done against *A Word to the Wise*), had unnecessarily put off the performance.[7]

Kelly seems always to have been on good terms with Murphy, but direct commentary on one another's works and lives is minimal. There is some suggestion in his *Life of Garrick* that Murphy may have resented Kelly's access to Roscius after the success of *False Delicacy,* but his comments about Kelly reveal little.[8] The two men actually had a great deal in common: both were Irish and had gone to London as young men to seek their fortunes. Both began as journalists before becoming dramatists and had taken on the City radicals, for which activities they suffered severely Murphy having found a harsh reception for both *No One's Enemy but His Own* and *What We Must All Come To* (Covent Garden, 9 Jan. 1764), Kelly having to disguise his authorship of his plays from 1770 on.[9] Both wrote theatrical journalism, as well as political material, and each established a legal career. That little record exists of even the most casual contact, professional or social, is one of the puzzles of Kelly's private life. Certainly each man's relationship with Garrick was dramatically different, Kelly respectful and grateful, Murphy somewhat suspicious and antagonistic. Indeed, Murphy was a proud man and may have disapproved of Kelly's dependency.

Before the month was out, Kelly's theatrical politics were in greater evidence than they had been in his defense of Garrick. Soon after the Murphy piece, the *General Evening Post* printed a lengthy account of Foote's *Piety in Pattens* (6–9 Mar.), but the reviewer, almost surely Kelly, did not once raise the issue of sentimentalism. In stark contrast, the *Middlesex Journal's* reviewer praised Foote's work highly and particularly mentioned, as Kelly did not, the satire on sentimental comedy. "In the comedy," writes the reviewer, "are some very fair and laughable ridicule on the stale, hash-meat truths, which modern writers are so eternally cramming their pieces with." That sentimental comedy was still alive and well, nevertheless, is suggested by the disgusted reviewer's admission that the audience "did not entirely conceive . . . that it was a burlesque of a very insipid species of dramatic writing, now too prevalent and too successful" (13–16 Feb. 1773). Kelly's review, on the other hand, is entirely free of judgment; throughout, its tone is cool; it is almost as if he were determined to ignore the barbs Foote aimed at his form of comedy.

In this number of the *General Evening Post,* a reader complained that the regular dramatic criticism occurring in the *Post's* column "Dramatic Strictures" was one-sided; he argued that the column found fault with every play produced at Covent Garden but that when the same drama was offered at Drury Lane it was praised. Annoyed by this display of theater politics, the writer concluded by calling the author of the "Strictures" the "Trumpeter in Ordinary to Drury-Lane." But there was no defensive response from the newspaper. Here then Kelly appears secure as journalist and dramatist: he could afford to let Foote's satiric slashes at sentimental comedy go unanswered.[10] He could also confidently admit attacks against his theater politics that claimed he favored Garrick over Colman.

Such cool detachment ended when Goldsmith's *She Stoops to Conquer* appeared at Covent Garden on 15 March 1773; soon after, on 16–18 March, the *General Evening Post* published a lengthy commentary—"review" would be inaccurate—about the play and the critical issues it raised. Signed "Catcall," whom I take to be Kelly, the piece was nearly an entire column long and discussed the general subject of sentimental comedy, defending it against those like Goldsmith who favored "laughing" comedy.[11] Kelly objected to mere laughter on the grounds that comedy's "peculiar province" was to "blend a little of *utile* with the *dulce,* and to mix instruction with risibility," a position he had always maintained.[12] Kelly proceeded to attack *She Stoops to Conquer* on the grounds that common sense and nature were violated in the play:

> ['T]is probability with [the admirers of the play] for a well-bred young fellow to mistake a gentleman's house for an inn, and an exquisite joke for a son to drive his mother a round of thirty miles through execrable roads, till at last he fairly souses her in a horse-pond. If this is comedy, Mr. Editor, and if whatever makes us laugh most upon the stage, is of course to be the best comic production, Mr. Messink, the machinist at Drury-lane house, is the foremost comic poet of the age; for his pantomimes would force a grin from a puritan, and are an inexhaustible mine of the *comical* to the spectators.[13]

Goldsmith's success, coming so soon after Kelly's kind of comedy had endured an attack from *Piety in Pattens,* clearly stung Kelly and threw him into the defensive posture revealed here. In the final paragraph, Kelly's conscience began to bother him:

> But what a Zoilus, Mr. Editor, what an envious son of Grub-street, must I not be, to animadvert in this manner upon a piece which has been received with the loudest acclamations? Alas, Sir, I only follow Doctor Goldsmith's example, who designs the play in question as a satire upon many productions which have been honoured with the universal applause of that very public, whose praise has now rendered him so amazingly important.

This tit-for-tat strategy seems understandable in a journalist who has worked hard and long in the dirty, no-holds-barred milieu of Grub Street, and it is no mere stylistic cliché that Kelly employs that very word, *Grub Street,* in his honest confession of jealousy. At another level, the incident perhaps reminded Kelly once again that he had always wished to escape the Grub Street milieu.

In an attempt—a marketing strategy, perhaps—to rally the audience for his kind of comedy, Goldsmith had published his pointed "Essay on the Theatre: or, A Comparison between Laughing and Sentimental Comedy," in the *Westminster Magazine* (1 Jan. 1773; see Goldsmith 3: 209–13).[14] Goldsmith's neoclassic, Tory, generic distinctions were naive even in 1773. His notions of genre purity and class-ridden absolutes—he felt with Aristotle that only the "lower Part of Mankind" (210) should be exhibited in comedy—were quaintly elegiac in an age that thronged to John Gay's *Beggar's Opera,* that had recently in the 1760s seen a number of little "high men" as prime ministers under George III rise and fall as quickly as the Thames's tides, and that was currently destabilized by the Wilkite street carnival at home and the American tensions abroad.

Goldsmith's restricted notion of comic genre would rule out Kelly's kind of mixed comedy, what Robert Hume has persuasively labeled "serious comedy" ("Multifarious Forms" 18–20), as well as the comedy of many others, like Colman and Cumberland, who also featured characters, some of them London merchants, primarily of the middle or even upper middle classes, in such plays as *The English Merchant* (1767), *The West Indian* (1771), and *The Man of Business* (1774).[15] Kelly had personal reasons for avoiding a laughing comedy that would severely satirize the foibles of the very social group—the urban middle classes—to whom he had addressed himself since "The Babler" essays' conduct literature, with whom he himself identified, and upon whom his success as a writer depended. But even had he been tempted, he had before him the example of his friend Bickerstaff's *Love in the City* (1767), which satirized the London middle classes and fared poorly as a result.[16] Apparently, Samuel Foote got away with satire directed at the merchant classes (Chatten 105, 120–21) in such plays as *The Bankrupt* (1773) and *A Trip to Calais* (1775), but others did not seem eager to try. In his "Essay on the Theatre," Goldsmith prints an anecdote about a friend who was unmoved by a sentimental drama and exclaims that, "'as the Hero is but a Tradesman, it is indifferent to me whether he be turned out of his Counting-house on Fish-street Hill, since he will still have enough left to open shop in St. Giles's'" (213). One can only wonder how violent the consequences would have been had such a sentiment been expressed on the stage.

Part of the reason that dramatists had to tread carefully when dealing with the urban merchant classes can be found in Bertelsen's notion that the new reading and presumably theatergoing audiences who were constituting themselves around Wilkite political issues could not be insulted (260–61). Indeed, as John Loftis notes, the Georgian dramatists tended to treat the merchant and business classes much more favorably than the Restoration playwrights ever did (35). Loftis comments that these dramatists generally avoided deeper social and political issues (31) and suggests two reasons for this avoidance: one, the audience, at least the affluent part, did not want to hear of the suffering of the lower ranks; and, two, the licenser through censorship could keep out political controversy (32). But it may be that in the theater-politics-journalism triad lurk additional reasons. The first, implied in Bertelsen's discussion, is that those urban merchant segments of the audience did not wish to be criticized any more than did the affluent, and any professional writer who dared to attack their political values, even in a nondramatic mode, such as a newspaper letter, would pay a high price, as the example of Kelly and his *A Word to the Wise* demonstrates. Further, because of the discourse explosion of political journalism in the 1760s and 1770s, there was less need for Georgian dramatists to be political, at least in an overt way. The drama did not have to become a political vehicle when there were more than enough pamphlets, newspapers, and magazines to fill the need for committed political discourse. And one needs to remember that during the 1760s and 1770s a number of dramatists as journalists contributed to this political discourse: Kelly, Colman, Kenrick, and Murphy all did so. Thus, dramatists with political interests to pursue had ample outlets in journalism for such interests.

Not long after the events surrounding *She Stoops to Conquer,* Hugh Kelly began another career. On Saturday, 22 May 1773, Kelly was called to the bar. Little has been recorded of Kelly's law work even by his friends who left biographical sketches of him. John Taylor, a young man when Kelly began to practice law, has only the following incident to relate in his *Records of My Life*:

> Mr. Kelly, as I have said, was, perhaps too lofty, pompous, and flow-
> ery in his language, but good-natured, affable and gentlemanly in
> his deportment, even to an excess of elaborate courtesy. An unlucky
> instance of his loftiness of language occurred, as well as I can recol-
> lect, on the trial of the notorious Barrington, who had picked a lady's
> pocket. The prosecutrix seemed to be inclined to give her evidence
> with tenderness, and the culprit might probably have escaped pun-
> ishment, but unfortunately Mr. Kelly pressed her a little too much,
> and seemed to convert her lenity into self-defence, when he ad-
> dressed her in the following words: "Pray, madam, how could you,
> in the immensity of the crowd, determine the identity of the man?"
>
> This question was wholly unintelligible to the simple woman,
> and he was obliged to reduce his question into merely "How do
> you know he was the man?" "Because," said she, "I caught his hand
> in my pocket." (1: 98–99)

Kelly's contemporaries left general judgments of his legal career rather than specific anecdotes. The "Memoirs" writer for the *Westminster Magazine* concluded that Kelly had been successful as a lawyer and "was rising into reputation as a barrister, when Death untimely snatched him from the scene" (118); while the "Memoirs" author in *Town and Country* was equally positive in his assessment: "His application to the law entitled him to be called to the bar, and as a Coun-sellor, he made a very respectable figure" (85–86). Cooke, whose *European Maga-zine* biography of Kelly is extensive and who was himself a lawyer, devoted sev-eral lengthy paragraphs to Kelly's legal career, generally judging his success to be somewhat less than other contemporaries had estimated it. As much of what Cooke says about Kelly's legal work deals with the final phase of his life, after the failure of *The Man of Reason* in 1776, I wish to delay a full consideration of Cooke's discussion, but Cooke felt strongly that Kelly's taking up the law rela-tively late in life was not the most prudent move he ever made ("Hugh Kelly," Jan. 45–46). Cooke mentioned the large number of barristers who, although properly educated (and perhaps he meant to suggest that Kelly was not so edu-cated, lacking as he did a university degree), were nevertheless "obliged to wait four, five, six, nay sometimes ten years before any accident drew them forward to anything like a profitable practice" (46); and he contended, rightly, that Kelly did not have, given his family's needs, that luxury of time necessary to the establishment of a law career.

Cooke, however, wrote of Kelly as he was in 1776, and yet he actually began the practice of law well before giving up his work as a dramatist. Cooke is thus incorrect in implying that Kelly did not seriously take up the law until after the failure of his last play. As we shall see, Kelly became involved in an important case soon after his admission to the bar; in fact, his participation came well before his fourth play, *The School for Wives,* was produced in December 1773. But before I examine that case, I must first mention yet another opinion of Kelly's law career offered by a contemporary, that of Sir John Hawkins. A Middlesex justice, Hawkins in his *Life of Johnson* claimed that Kelly "practiced at the quarter-sessions under me" but had "little success" (518). Apart from the fact that Hawkins was often egregiously wrong on other matters relating to Kelly (he said Kelly died in 1769, for instance), the Middlesex Sessions were held at Hicks's Hall in Clerkenwell, while Cooke claimed that Kelly practiced at the Westminster Quarter Sessions under Sir John Fielding at Westminster Hall. Obviously, he may have handled cases in both halls, but newspaper accounts suggest that Kelly worked most often at Westminster. In his study of Hawkins, *A Proof of Eminence,* Bertram Davis notes that a degree of "animosity between the two Quarter Sessions was an almost inevitable result of their overlapping jurisdictions" (240); and that animosity, combined with a rivalry between Hawkins and Fielding, must be considered when assessing Hawkins's opinion of Kelly's success.[17]

A little over two months after being called to the bar, Kelly became involved in what the *General Evening Post* called "one of the most important cases which has been for many years agitated in the Courts of this Kingdom" (31 July–3 Aug. 1773). The writer, presumably Kelly himself, must be allowed some exaggeration of the case's importance, given that it was probably his first significant piece of legal business. The facts of the case (which came before the lord chancellor at Lincoln's Inn Hall), as set out in the *General Evening Post* report, are as follows.[18] When an Irish peer, the third Viscount Boyne, Frederick Hamilton, was still a minor in 1737, he married Elizabeth Hadley, a poor young woman who was also a minor. Because of the financial standing of the young Lord Boyne, according to law the marriage could be voided. An attempt to void it was made by Lord Boyne's guardian in 1738, but the case was initially decided against him, and after appeals the entire situation remained inconclusive. Meanwhile, in 1746 Lord Boyne married another woman, a Miss Mooney, by whom he had several children. She lived as Lord Boyne's acknowledged wife; and during that time, Mrs. Hadley offered no legal protest.

After Lord Boyne's death in 1772, the original suit by the guardian was resurrected, but still no conclusive judgment was rendered. The eldest son of Lord Boyne ultimately petitioned the Court of Chancery in England for a Commission of Review, the first step in having the case determined. The son won the right to a commission, and Kelly was one of the advocates who argued on behalf of the eldest son, who wished to inherit the title. At issue was not merely a right of succession but also the disposition of the estate and the very legitimacy of a family. Obviously, given his inexperience, Kelly could not have played an important role in the case. That he was even a part of the proceedings suggests that his legal peers saw in him potential talent. It also demonstrates that Kelly began his legal career soon after being called to the bar and did not confine his practice to either Westminster or Hicks Hall. Finally, the legalistic language of the report argues strongly that, despite his new career, Kelly had not yet forsaken journalism.

In the fall, Kelly was busy working for John Roberts in his contest with Lord Mayor Frederick Bull for the Ladbroke seat in the House of Commons, as the 25–27 November issue of the *Middlesex Journal* had reported. In its next number, the paper defended its announcement of Kelly's efforts on behalf of Roberts: the "paragraph in this paper of last Saturday, relative to Hugh Kelly's being employed in the interest of Mr. Roberts, is an absolute fact, notwithstanding it was contradicted in the Morning Post of yesterday." The *Morning Chronicle* of 30 November leveled its own blows at Kelly: "Whether that wretched prostitute Hugh Kelly is employed by Mr. Roberts, is not the question; but it is an absolute fact, that he has sent an address for the gentleman to the public papers, and the denial of it in a morning paper of yesterday, is an impudent lye." The opposition writers' need to expose every piece of political propaganda Kelly penned must once again call into question Garrick's 1770 judgment that Kelly was just a "flea bite" to the radicals. This relentless pursuit of Kelly after 1770 suggests that his bite was formidable.

In the midst of these political episodes and only a few days before *The School for Wives* was to appear, the following report, introduced as the "Extract of a letter from Dublin, Nov. 30," was printed in the *Morning Chronicle* for 1 December:

> We were all agog here for several days lately, in consequence of a paragraph that appeared in some of the London papers, purporting that Hugh Kelly, Esq; barrister at law, and author of False Delicacy, was set out for Dublin, in order to make some enquiry here relating to the cause of Lord Boyne, now pending before the court of Delegates in London; but that gentleman not having appeared as yet, puzzles folks here what to conclude. On his side, knew he but all, he has reason to regret not coming; as very great civilities were intended to be shewn to him here by all ranks of people; and that our university intended to complement him with the honorary degree of Doctor of Law, as they had conferred a like favour on Mr. Cumberland, the author of the West Indian.—If the paragraph of Mr. Kelly's coming hither was meant by enemies as a joke,

we can see no humour in it, or if calculated, by any of his friends, to cover some literary or political expedition, we are too far removed from the scene of action to be able to penetrate into the reason of such a measure.

This report itself was possibly a joke, as the paragraph it referred to seems non-existent. Certainly as an Irishman and the youngest member of the legal team working on the Boyne case, it would have been reasonable for Kelly to travel to Dublin in search of information relevant to the case, but as I can find no paragraph announcing Kelly's trip to Dublin in the papers for the fall of 1773, the editor of the *Morning Chronicle,* William Woodfall, may have been involved in this elaborate mocking of Kelly's pride in his status, his old one as dramatist and his new one as lawyer. The last sentence, mentioning a possible joke, seems to provide a clue for my interpretation of this "Dublin letter" itself as a hit at Kelly's vanity.

While Kelly was preparing to stage *The School for Wives* and attempting to stave off Patriot election victories, he lost the friend who was, after Garrick, the most important patron he ever had. On 31 October, Sir Robert Ladbroke died. The *General Evening Post* for 30 October–2 November printed an extensive obituary, considerably longer than those printed in other papers (more than four hundred words), not surprising given that Kelly knew the family well. The paper provided an extensive account of Sir Robert's career, which began in 1740 when he was first elected alderman and included his election as lord mayor in 1747, as well as his representation of London in Parliament since 1754.[19] Recall that Kelly had been living in one of Ladbroke's houses in Doctor's Commons as early as April 1770 and had publicly proclaimed his indebtedness to Ladbroke in the 1770 dedication of *A Word to the Wise.* The radical newspapers appeared to have been accurate in their charges that Ladbroke sometimes directed Kelly's ministerial propaganda, and probably Ladbroke provided aid, financial and otherwise, when Kelly required it. Kelly could only have felt Ladbroke's loss keenly and must have wondered if he would ever gain another political friend of equal importance.

After the unhappy fall, the success of *The School for Wives* was, doubtless, pleasing. Produced by Garrick on 11 December 1773, the play became a solid hit and was performed twenty-four times during 1773–74, the long run making it the most successful play of the season. The immediate reception was generally positive, and the papers speculated about the author's identity, some attributing the play, as Kelly had evidently hoped, to William Addington, others naming Sheridan as the writer (W. W. Watt 241; O'Leary 165–66; Gottlieb 5, notes 3 and 4). Following the initial reception, John Taylor visited the Kelly home in Gough Square to congratulate the family. Only Mrs. Kelly was at home, and she exclaimed to Taylor: "Yes, we have stolen a march upon the patriots" (1: 100).

Kelly had labored to make the play acceptable to Garrick, who rejected the original offering during the summer of 1773. On 24 July, Kelly had written to Garrick after the latter had turned down the initial draft, evidently feeling that the play needed far too much rewriting. Undaunted by Garrick's poor opinion, Kelly wrote optimistically as follows:

> I am very sorry you should think the labour of altering the play so herculean. "False Delicacy", you know, was in a much more deplorable state at this period of the year 1767, and neither of us lost credit or money by it. Far be the wish of my heart of injuring your interest in the smallest degree, and I can have no desire of injuring my own. I therefore only beg that, if I produce you a play, of which you yourself entertain an opinion, you will give me a turn this winter, as the potboiling reasons, I have before mentioned, make it *essentially* necessary. I have the advantage of your remarks upon what has been already offered, and am certain of working out something, which I trust will neither wholly disgrace Drury-lane, nor give you reason to be ashamed of the indulgence hitherto shown to,
>
> Dear Sir, your most faithful and most obliged,
>
> *Hugh Kelly*
>
> P.S. I am at present at no other literary work whatever. (Garrick Correspondence 24: no. 25)

The suggestion of financial distress aside, it would be interesting to know what Kelly felt counted as "other literary work" because he certainly was involved in the *General Evening Post* and in the fall, if not before, was to write extensively on behalf of the ministerial candidates. He was also beginning his legal career and surely had to strain mightily to shape what became *The School for Wives* into a viable product. Then again, the success of the play perhaps owed, as *False Delicacy* did, something to Garrick's hand, which was the opinion of Horace Walpole, who was with Garrick and some other company the evening the play opened.[20] Yet secrecy was maintained, as Mrs. Kelly's remark to John Taylor suggested, and neither Kelly nor Garrick was mentioned as a possible author when the reviews appeared.

The play centers on a married libertine, Mr. Belville, who eventually—after some comic escapades with two younger women, Miss Leeson and Miss Walsingham—returns, a reformed rake, to his patient wife. A subplot involves another libertine, Gen. Savage, who has lived for years with a termagant mistress, Mrs. Tempest, yet secretly fancies, like Belville, the spirited Miss Walsingham. But Miss Walsingham, in love with Capt. Savage, the general's son, keeps both older rakes at bay with her wit and intelligence. In the meantime, the long-suffering Mrs. Belville is aided in her attempts to regain her husband by her aunt, a would-be sentimental dramatist, Lady Rachel Mildew. In this comic melange also appear three characters relevant to what might be called Kelly's Irish theme: Miss Leeson, who falsely believes that Belville is an Irish theater manager eager to put her on the Dublin stage; her brother, Mr. Leeson, an impoverished lawyer who, after discovering Belville's designs on his sister, challenges him to a duel; and Connolly, Leeson's faithful, pragmatic Irish servant. Through Connolly's good sense and loyalty, Kelly attempts to rescue the image of the Irish from traditional stage stereotyping. Another character of note, Torrington, is employed to counter the negative image of the lawyer: it is Torrington who generously provides Leeson with an estate at the end so that he may marry Miss Moreland, Mrs. Belville's sister.

Belville as the center of the action is discovered by his wife and Lady Rachel visiting Miss Leeson. Embarrassed and repentant, he promises to reform; yet after receiving a letter of assignation, purportedly from Miss Walsingham but really the work of Lady Rachel, he plans to meet her at a masquerade. After luckily disarming Leeson in a duel, Belville, once again made guilty by his wife's anxiety over the duel, vows to change his behavior forever. He meets the woman he thinks is Miss Walsingham at the masquerade and tells her of his reformation, whereupon she unmasks to reveal herself to be his wife. After the comic confusion created by the competition between father and son, Gen. and Capt. Savage, for Miss Walsingham is cleared up, the play ends happily with Belville coming forward to reject the notion that the only business of comedy is to make people laugh. The conclusion thus reinforces Kelly's view of comedy's function to provide both instruction and pleasure.

Most of the newspaper reviews of *School* were positive, and even those with a negative tone, such as the *Morning Chronicle* and the *London Evening Post,* contained some favorable commentary. The laudatory notices appeared in the *Lloyd's Evening Post,* the *London Chronicle,* and the *St. James's Chronicle.* Kelly's own *General Evening Post* naturally supplied a favorable review but not excessively so, in keeping with Kelly's usual practice of restrained self-praise. The *Post* reviewer stated that the play "contains many fine sentiments, some strokes of wit, and several reflections on popular subjects, that met with applause, but a perusal of the plot will show our readers, that many of the characters are borrowed from other plays" (11–14 Dec.). This extremely long review, combined with exact quotations from the unpublished play, suggests that Kelly authored the piece himself. His perpetual enemy, the *Middlesex Journal,* provided a plot synopsis along with a very positive review, calling the incidents "judiciously contrived and well arranged," the plot "sufficiently interesting," and the stage business "exceedingly well managed" (11–14 Dec.). Even Kelly did not become as enthusiastic about *School* as did the *Middlesex Journal's* reviewer, who concluded by declaring, "Upon the whole, we cannot help pronouncing this Comedy possessed of every requisite merit," adding that the author will "do honour to the British stage." It is no wonder that when the paper discovered the true author of *School* its rage knew no limits; but at the moment, Mrs. Kelly's feeling that she and her husband had "stolen a march upon the patriots" had become more deliciously ironic than she could have hoped.

The play's reception by the magazines was more complicated and less positive, although here again even the negative view found in the *London Magazine* (Dec. 1773) was qualified by its conceding that "The School for Wives will undoubtedly procure honour and emolument for its author." But the magazine's writer found fault with the plot and the sentiments, declaring that the former had "little real merit" and that the latter were "all placid." The writer, without elaborating, also criticized the absence of "original characters" and "natural situations." He concluded by stating that, although the play will succeed on the stage, it will not "prove the most satisfactory . . . to the nice, the critical, and the dispassionate closet readers" (577–79).

By any commercial standard, *The School for Wives* was a clear success as its twenty-four performances and five editions in its first season demonstrate. The play continued to be moderately popular with London theater audiences, as well as those in Ireland and America, until at least the end of the century. G. W. Stone, in *London Stage,* notes twenty-seven performances from 1774–75 through the 1799–1800 season. The piece seemed to enjoy something of a minor revival in the late 1790s because from 1793 through the end of the century it was given eight times.[21] In Bath, the play ran with some frequency until at least 1805 (Hare 233–49), while in Ireland it was presented in the smaller cities, such as Limerick, Belfast, and Derry, ten times between 1774 and 1795 (see Clark 318).

Evidence that theater patrons often were careful readers of the plays they attended is provided by an anecdote given by the playwright John O'Keeffe in his autobiography. Discussing the first performance of *School* at Cork, O'Keeffe says that the bailiff incident was hissed (1: 234–35).[22] As William Watt explains, the audience was merely reacting to new, unfamiliar material and resented what they thought was improvisation. They cried out, "Keep to the words of your author," and only after the actors had shown their prompt book to the audience did the objectors allow the play to continue. Finally, the play occasioned a rivalry between the two Dublin theaters from late January through March 1774. Thomas Ryder, the manager of Smock Alley, announced in late January that he would present the play but could not get it ready as quickly as William Dawson, the manager of the smaller Capel Street Theatre, could do. Dawson brought out his version some ten days before Ryder. As Watt notes, the rivalry was heightened because both managers played the role of the Irish character, Connolly (269–70).[23]

In America *School's* prompt staging may have been prevented by the colonial tensions, although one edition was published prior to the outbreak of hostilities.[24] Yet no performances of the play have been recorded before 8 May 1788 when it was produced at the New York John Street Theater by the old American Company. As William Watt comments, it was a "gala occasion . . . , an all-

Kelly program, for Kelly's farce, *The Romance of an Hour,* served as the afterpiece"
(270). The play remained moderately popular in New York until at least 1797,
for seven performances at the John Street Theater have been recorded. In Philadelphia, according to Seilhamer, the first performance was offered on 12 November 1788.[25] Four more presentations were given by 1795, including one at
the University of Pennsylvania on 3 June 1790. During the 1790s, a number of
other performances were put on in Baltimore, Boston, and Charleston. In the
first Charleston production, the play was announced as *The School for Wives; or,
The Faithful Irishman,* an obvious emphasis having been placed on the character
of Connolly. Charleston also saw the last recorded American performance on
14 March 1800 (W. W. Watt 271). Altogether *The School for Wives* held its own
through the end of the century, playing fourteen times in the former colonies.
To be sure, it did not match the popularity of Cumberland's *West Indian* (thirty-
eight performances) or Garrick and Colman's *Clandestine Marriage* (twenty-five
performances), but it was certainly the most popular of Kelly's pieces on the
American stage.

That the play's plot features a rake, Mr. Belville, finally brought to his sentimental knees by his long-suffering and virtuous wife demonstrates that Kelly's
campaign of male reform continued. Gen. Savage, played by Kelly's old friend
Thomas King, is another rakish male chastened in part by his comic, shrewish
mistress, Mrs. Tempest. But as the Tempest character suggests, there are elements
of more traditional comedy here, and the contrast between Miss Walsingham
and Mrs. Belville makes that clear. Walsingham, especially in her pointed repar-
tee with Belville, reminds us of the witty woman of Restoration comedy. But
as Janet Todd points out, the Walsingham kind of female is replaced in sentimental literature by a "genteel feeling lady who could raise domesticity to the
female equivalent of a profession" (20), a description precisely suiting the long-
suffering Mrs. Belville. The Walsingham character suggests that, while continuing his reform agenda, Kelly also combined elements of the old comedy with
elements of the new.

This blending of comedy types and what that blending says about the evolution of Kelly's artistic vision is one of the three subjects modern critics have
discussed. The other two are the nature of Kelly's attitude toward sensibility and
the relationship of the play to both its modern and its eighteenth-century theater context. John Loftis has remarked on what he considers to be Kelly's en-
larged social vision, focusing on Kelly's "sympathetic portrayal of character types
who had traditionally been objects of ridicule: the Irish and the lawyers" (23).
Loftis also credits Kelly with a broader moral concern insofar as he "confronts
the fact of depravity" (23) in Belville; behind Loftis's remark lies the fact that
Kelly had always been accused of a facile optimism. Earlier Mark Schorer had
similarly pointed to *School* as presenting characters that are "successfully comic"
(392) and had approved of Kelly's defense of lawyers and Irishmen even as he
complained that his defense is not strong enough. Schorer finds Connolly to be

"dull, lacking any of the spirit of good humor that make such low characters as Tony Lumpkin and Croaker amusing" (399). But Schorer generally admits that the play is more "truly comic" (399) than any of Kelly's other efforts. Still another modern commentator, Diane Corvasce, feels that, in *School,* "the handling of the usual materials gives evidence of Kelly's growing competence handling the elevated sentiment, the comic character and the humorous scene" (164). To illustrate these last two, Corvasce points to the character of Lady Rachel Mildew, the would-be sentimental dramatist, whom Kelly satirizes. Calling the creation of Lady Rachel a "skillful innovation," Corvasce finds the dramatist an "ingenuous satire on all that is sentimental" (167).

Indeed, the entire question of Kelly's stance toward sentimentalism appears once again in the treatment of *School* by modern critics. Claude Rawson, although not referring to *School* specifically, asserts that Kelly demonstrated that "sustained mockery of sensibility may co-exist with support of it" (36), a sentiment clearly supported by Corvasce and by Larry Carver, who finds "criticism of sentimental comedy itself a central theme" of the play. Carver's useful view of how Kelly manages this criticism is worth quoting at length:

> [T]he criticism elicited through Lady Rachel is not simply or always directed at sentimental absurdities. Some of it is pseudo-parody that . . . allows Kelly to protect himself and also to satisfy his bourgeois audience's demand for some, but not too much, morality. For example, Mrs. Belville, when she learns that her husband is to be in a duel, really does break down in tears. The whole scene is extremely sentimental, but not because of the tears or because virtue has entered a high state of distress. Lady Rachel's comments mitigate the effects of the tears and prevent pathos. Lady Rachel finally has a moment in which life lives up to her art; as she says of the tearful Mrs. Belville, "Now I am extremely glad to see her so, for if she wasn't greatly distress'd it wou'd be monstrously unnatural." But the scene is sentimental because Mrs. Belville goes on to deliver a moral essay on the disastrous effects of dueling on the family and on society in general. (Introduction xxxix)

As Carver demonstrates, Kelly plays both sides of the street, having his tears and satirizing them too. But this Kelly is not much different from the early Kelly of the *Court Magazine* and "The Babler" in which he could in the same self-reflexive piece of journalism *about* journalism mock his practice while practicing it at the same time. Whether this move always constitutes self-protection, as Carver suggests, I cannot determine, but Carver's picture of Kelly is more attractive and persuasive than the view that suggests he did not know what he was doing.

Related to this simultaneous embrace and rejection of sentimentalism is Richard Bevis's discovery that Kelly's studied ambivalence gets expressed, as I have noted, in the differences between the acted version of *School* and the printed text. Bevis points to the ending of the play, where in the printed text Kelly's didacticism and self-consciousness are explicit:

> BELVILLE: I sha'n't, therefore part with one of you 'till we have had a hearty laugh at our adventures.

> MISS WALSINGHAM: They have been very whimsical, indeed; yet, if represented on the stage, I hope they would be found not only entertaining, but instructive.

> LADY RACHEL: Instructive! Why, the modern critics say that the only business of Comedy is to make people laugh.

> BELVILLE: That is degrading the dignity of letters exceedingly, as well as lessening the utility of the stage. A good comedy is a capital effort of genius and should, therefore, be directed to the noblest purposes.

> MISS WALSINGHAM: Very true; and unless we learn something while we chuckle, the carpenter who nails a pantomime together will be entitled to more applause than the best comic poet in the Kingdom. (qtd. in Bevis, *Laughing* 37–38)[26]

As Bevis asserts, the theater audience never heard this statement of Kelly's comic creed, for the last three speeches were added for the printed version alone (37–38). Bevis rightly contends that Kelly's decision was dictated by his recognition that he had to please different audiences, something that suggests that, as I have argued all along, Kelly was an accomplished professional who knew that he needed to provide his audience with what they wanted rather than with what he wished them to digest.

Kelly developed this talent early in his career when, in the *Court Magazine* and "The Babler" essay series, he had to flatter his audience by speaking to their needs. What this practice sometimes led to when Kelly catered to audiences with different desires (the theater audience versus the reading public, for instance, or daughters versus fathers in conflicts over courtship advice in the periodicals) was the charge of ambiguity or ambivalence.[27] Yet if my view is reasonable, *ambivalence* is probably the wrong term. He merely presents two sometimes opposing stances in his didactic journalism, in one situation upholding a daughter's right to choose her own husband and in another insisting upon filial obedience. It may be a misnomer to label these conflicting attitudes *ambivalent* or *contradictory,* for Kelly deliberately preaches both stances simply because each appeals to different segments of his audience. Kelly could hope that playing up one side of a question was not noticed by readers of the other side, just as an editor of a modern woman's magazine hopes that the feminist piece does not excessively annoy her traditional women readers who will eventually see their values articulated too. Commentators who fail to appreciate the necessity of flattering both sides of an issue are usually operating from the premise of high culture that holds that artistic expression, even didactic expression, must be organically consistent and voice the author's vision. This creator-centered view of the writer is a construct of a romanticism/idealism that Kelly would have found foreign. For he was, as noted earlier in employing Herbert Gans's terms, an audience-centered writer, not a creator-centered artist.

So although I find much of Bevis's commentary on *The School for Wives,* as well as his more general summation of Kelly's drama, persuasive, I must diverge from his conclusion that Kelly was a "shrewd fence-sitter with a mixed style" (*Laughing* 96), a style that ultimately did not work. Following Arthur Sherbo, Bevis concludes that such a style ended up in contradiction: a funny sentimental play simply does not work (96).[28] But apart from the fact that, as Carver has shown, *sentimental* was a highly complex and unstable term undergoing change even in Kelly's time and that for Kelly the meaning of *sentiment* as a kind of moral thought was far more operative than our modern sense of it as connected to exaggerated emotion (Introduction xxxi–xxxii), such judgmental formulations as those proposed by Bevis and by Sherbo tend to suggest that Kelly was conflicted or did not realize what he was doing. I argue the contrary: that he knew very well what he was doing, which, to employ Bevis's fence-sitting image, was to walk on both sides of the fence at different times—and deliberately so. Kelly's problem was that in a play, unlike in editing a magazine or in writing an essay series, playing on both sides would be readily apparent to audiences; the ploy could not be disguised as well in drama as it could be in "The Babler," where the serial nature of the literary activity was, unlike that of a play, temporally and spatially segmented to minimize any effect that the taking of contradictory positions might have. Kelly's practice, then, cannot be merely summed up as contradictory; it is no more contradictory than commercial theater itself, which Robert Hume has rightly described as both "conservative and faddish" ("English Drama" 89).

11

The Aftermath of *The School for Wives* and *The Romance of an Hour*

ich in dramatic successes at its beginning and end, 1774 was to be a
complicated year for Hugh Kelly, who from the middle of the year
on returned to the political journalism from which he never seemed
to escape. The year began with *The School for Wives* successfully performed week
after week in London, so that by spring the play reigned as the most popular
piece of the season. It enjoyed even greater success in Dublin, where it was produced by two competing companies. No political activity appears until late June,
when his journalism thrust Kelly once again into the cauldron of political life
as he sought to defend King George's colonial policies. The year ended happily
with Kelly's final stage success, the two-act afterpiece, *The Romance of an Hour,*
produced at Covent Garden on 2 December and well received even by his enemy, the *Middlesex Journal.* Before late June, we only catch glimpses of Kelly as
he attended a play or, more dramatically, mourned at Goldsmith's funeral. As usual,
we find him abused by the radical press, yet these attacks seem much reduced
from previous years. But after late June, writing under the pseudonym "Numa,"
Kelly was almost continuously employed until the fall of 1775 in pro-Court propaganda in support of George III's American policies. He would not be not identified as the Numa writer for many months.

As the year began, however, Kelly's *School,* if not always Kelly himself, was
continually in the news. In its 4–6 January 1774 issue, the *General Evening Post*
printed both the prologue and the epilogue to the play; and on 5 January, the
Morning Chronicle published a letter from a "Templar in the Boxes" that provided
a critique of the acting: Thomas King and Frances Abington are praised, but
Samuel Reddish, who played Belville, is said to have misunderstood act 2. The
same paper reprinted (6 Jan.) most of the section of act 4 concerned with dueling, including the most sentimental scene in the play, where Mrs. Belville is
shown weeping over Belville's impending duel with Leeson. On 7 January, a

reader complained that his copy of the play did not correlate with the acted version and argued that the printed version was the superior one. The letter lends support to Richard Bevis's contention, noted earlier, that the acted version of a comedy and the printed version were often quite different (*Laughing* 34).[1] But this protest may also suggest that some who both saw and read a given play did not always prefer the acted version, perhaps because the closet reader desired the very sentimental elements that Bevis rightly notes were underplayed in the acted version.[2]

On 4 April 1774, Oliver Goldsmith died. That Kelly felt his loss deeply, despite the supposed coolness between the two authors since the rivalry of *False Delicacy* and *The Good Natur'd Man* is attested to by his behavior at Goldsmith's funeral. Forster describes the funeral as follows:

> Reynolds's [Sir Joshua's] nephew, Palmer (afterwards Dean of Cashel), attended as chief mourner: and was accompanied by Mr. Day, afterwards Sir John Day, and judge advocate-general at Bengal; by his relative and namesake heretofore mentioned, Robert Day, who became the Irish Judge; and by Mr. Hawes, and his friend Mr. Etherington. These were unexpectedly joined on the morning of the funeral by Hugh Kelly, who in the presence of that great sorrow had only remembered happier and more friendly days, and was seen still standing weeping at the grave as the others moved away. (bk. 2, 463)

No tableau as sentimental as Forster's appears in any of Kelly's plays; yet neither Forster nor Prior, the most important of Goldsmith's nineteenth-century biographers, questioned Kelly's sincerity, as some contemporaries did. Prior, not always kind to Kelly, defended him, convinced that Kelly's tribute was genuine and maintained that the charges that Kelly attacked Goldsmith in the years following 1768 were never proved. Prior reprinted an attack on Kelly's mourning of Goldsmith but does not note the source:

> Hence K—— who years, without honor or shame,
> Had been sticking his bodkin in Oliver's fame,
> Who thought, like the Tartar, by this to inherit
> His genius, his learning, simplicity, spirit;
> Now sets every feature to weep o'er his fate,
> and acts as a mourner to blubber in state.
>
> (2: 175)

Most contemporary accounts of Kelly's participation in Goldsmith's funeral were kinder and did not impugn his sincerity. In the *Morning Chronicle* for Thursday, 6 February 1777, shortly after Kelly's own death, an anecdote claimed that, when Kelly heard of Goldsmith's illness, he called every day "at his chambers to enquire how he did, and requested as a favor that he might be one of the mourn-ers, as it would give him an inward satisfaction to pay the last tribute of respect and friendship to so valuable a man." I have previously noted two incidents where Kelly and Goldsmith met professionally and socially after their quarrel of 1768: those incidents, combined with this evidence, suggest that Kelly's feelings to-ward Goldsmith, even if once hostile, had changed. Perhaps Prior was right that the quarrel was abetted by others for their own amusement (2: 175).

By late spring of 1774, Kelly was back in the public eye, for on 3 June a let-ter by Maj. William Addington to Kelly, in which the major confessed that Kelly wrote *The School for Wives,* appeared in the *Morning Chronicle*:

To HUGH KELLY Esq. Dear Sir,

As the theatrical season will be closed tonight, I take this first op-portunity to throw off the mask. I most sincerely, then, congratu-late you on the success of your School for Wives, and here at the same time I announce to the world, that you are the real author of that well-received comedy. Should any one enquire, why as such I have appeared, or why I should in this manner declare myself;—to the first I make answer, "A Word to the Wise," as the most compre-hensive reply I can hit on:—to the other I shall only thus briefly observe, I think it now time to have the public convinced, that I no more can submit even to the imputation of depriving another's bosom of the pleasing satisfaction of merited applause, than I can plunder his purse of the reward of his labors. I am,

Dear Sir,

Your sincere friend and servant,

WILLIAM ADDINGTON

The editor William Woodfall's reaction to Addington's confession was mild: he merely observed in the *Morning Chronicle* that had the play failed, Addington's name would have suffered. He lamented the intrusion of politics into the the-ater. Faction was responsible, he wrote, for "obliging a man of letters to please them, and reap the harvest arising from having pleased them by stratagem" (7 June). Not so understanding was Kelly's old enemy, the *Middlesex Journal*. Its editor had already attacked the play's Dublin success in March, but after Addington's letter of 3 June, the *Middlesex Journal* showed Kelly no mercy.[3] The radical pa-per began its assault by inserting a paragraph (4–7 June) in which a foreign dig-nitary at St. James's Court during the king's birthday celebration noticed a fencing master in attendance. Upon inquiring of his English friend if such people were usually admitted, he was told yes, and the friend then pointed out Hugh Kelly, who is viewed as socially inferior to even a fencing master.

Before the controversy surrounding *School's* authorship had dissipated, Kelly was already writing on behalf of the ministers, pitting himself against the Lon-don Patriots and their press. But the conflict would not this time be over London politics. Indeed, during the early months of 1774, the London press slowly shifted its emphasis from local Wilkite politics to the overseas arena and the conflicts with the American colonies. I cannot detail these changes exhaustively, but it seems clear to modern readers of the London press in early 1774 that the discourse devoted to the colonies was beginning to exceed that concerned with the London radicals. To be sure, the Worcester parliamentary contest between Thomas Bates Rous and the Wilkite Sir Watkin Lewes that Kelly had been involved in during 1773 was still an issue, and the *Middlesex Journal,* a defender of Horne Tooke against Wilkes, was not happy with the latter's political behavior, complaining in June that Wilkes had not stood strongly enough against the Quebec Bill, a piece of legislation radicals opposed because of its favoritism toward Catholicism and its tolerance of French civil law.[4] Yet even here the *Middlesex Journal's* focus is on North America, and that focus had been increasing throughout the winter and spring of 1774. Indeed, one of the conflicts in the newspapers in the spring concerned Benjamin Franklin and Alexander Wedderburn over Franklin's exposure of ministerial agents in Massachusetts who were unsympathetic to the colonists.[5] Perhaps by June the Court was losing interest in London politics, for ministerial writers did not mount a serious propaganda campaign against the Wilkite candidates for sheriff of the city and the county of Middlesex. The election attracted little attention, and the Patriot candidates, John Williams and George Grieve, were elected without fanfare in the last week of June.

However, in this last week, the Court opened up a new propaganda campaign as Kelly, using the pseudonym Numa, began a series of letters in defense of the Parliament's North American policies. The subject of these letters was the Quebec Bill. Passed by Parliament on 22 June, the bill provided a stable government for Canada and respected its French traditions by tolerating the Roman Catholic Church and by retaining French civil law. The Wilkites felt too much had been granted to Catholicism and criticized the retention of French political structure. On Thursday, 28 June, Kelly's first Numa letter appeared in support of the bill against these Patriot objections. Kelly's authorship of these letters, which continued for well over a year, was not to be confirmed until he wrote on 7 September 1775 to David Garrick. In this letter, primarily concerned with his final play, *The Man of Reason,* Kelly informed Garrick that

> Numa is mine, and many other signatures are mine also. Your friends are satisfied with my assiduity at least, whatever they may think of my works; and let the writer be ever so indifferent to their opinions, they are frequently very flattering to the attachment of the man. (Garrick Correspondence 24: no. 26)

Assiduous Kelly was, for between 28 June and the end of 1774 alone, he published a dozen Numa pieces. More important, the letter suggests that Garrick and Kelly were still politically linked, as they had been since at least 1769: it is

Garrick's "friends" who are to judge the efficacy of Kelly's efforts. The only surviving letter of Kelly's after 1770 to mention his political journalism, the piece demonstrates that Kelly fairly earned his two-hundred-pound pension. It proves that he never quite escaped the drudgery of a Grub Street journalist.

In his first letter, Kelly argued, as a sentimental dramatist might, that the Quebec Bill showed justice, humanity, and benevolence to a conquered people. Yet the king's compassion toward the Canadians is twisted, wrote Kelly, by the inversions of the "Popular Pen," which seems determined to view the bill as "either a despotic inroad upon our religious Rights, or a total subversion of the civil Constitution." Exposing the false alarms of the Patriot press that had tried to paint the bill as affirming Catholicism as the "established Worship of Canada," Kelly effectively accused the Patriots of lacking tolerance, thus dramatizing the hypocrisy of their own shrill claims of persecution by an intolerant ministry and Parliament. Kelly also questioned the motives of the Patriots who at first supported the bill. Only after the Patriots saw it supported by the ministry did they discovered its dangers. Only then did Henry Fox, Edmund Burke, and Lord Chatham of the Opposition doubt the bill. The bill, far from establishing Catholicism, merely tolerated it, pragmatic in a country primarily Catholic, Kelly argued, but also agreeable to the "dictates of Benevolence." Kelly's pen was brought to bear on this issue largely because it was this bill that once again rallied the London Patriots, cool to the colonial cause since the Boston Tea Party in December 1773, to support the Americans. This renewed support was in part based on the Patriots' feeling that the bill was a prelude to further ministerial despotism aimed at all of North America.[6]

During the remainder of the year, at least eleven additional Numa letters appeared in the *Public Advertiser,* all concerned in some way with American issues. The letters fall into two groups: one from late June through 30 July contains seven letters concentrating on a defense of the Quebec Bill. The second group, comprising four letters, was published in December 1774 and defends the ministry's general American policies while criticizing the Patriots' support of the colonies. Only one letter appeared between August and December—on 10 October, a letter was published that defended the Quebec Bill once again. Kelly's silence may not have been due to work on his fifth play, *The Romance of an Hour,* because it was submitted to the licenser in late September 1774. Yet Kelly may have curtailed his journalism in the fall, not wanting to risk discovery of his authorship of the letters so close to the staging of his comedy. Concern about a possible Wilkite damnation may have troubled him.

Kelly undoubtedly received satisfaction at escaping the wrath of the Wilkites when his afterpiece, *The Romance of an Hour,* was successfully produced by Thomas Harris at Covent Garden. Appearing on 2 December 1774, the play was first greeted coolly by the *Middlesex Journal* on 1–3 December. The reviewer, after providing a plot synopsis, concluded that "[t]he piece was preceded by an excellent Prologue, and followed by as admirable an Epilogue, which indeed, like the trappings of embroidery, serve but to render the deformation of the wearer more glaring.—Surely Roscius has been meddling here." In its next number, the paper's reviewer, after observing the play's second performance, noted that the play "has been much shortened since the first night's representation, was received with the warmest applause; and when the managers have made a little more use of the pruning knife, we apprehend will become a favourite Farce" (3–6 Dec. 1774).

The plot centers around the plight of Zelida, a young woman from India, who at the death of her father has been left in the care of Col. Ormsby. As Ormsby cannot leave India when Zelida sails for England, he entrusts her to his friend Brownlow. During the trip, Zelida and Brownlow fall in love, although the latter conceals his feelings, knowing that Zelida is intended for Col. Ormsby. As the play opens, Zelida has been living under the protection of Brownlow's sister, Lady Diana Strangeways, and her husband, Sir Hector Strangeways, a middle-aged naval officer and libertine. Sir Hector's propensities for nautical jargon and his general roughness of manner make him and his equally nautical son, Orson, objects of laughter.

Upon learning that Ormsby will soon arrive in London to marry her, Zelida, loving only Brownlow, decides to return to India with her faithful Hindu servant, the noble Bussora. Zelida's honest feelings and Bussora's candid criticisms of British morality highlight their discussion of Zelida's plight prior to their departure from the Strangeways's home. As the first step of their return to India, they take up temporary residence with a sister of Adm. Strangeways's purser, Pillage, himself just arrived in London to get Sir Hector's help in securing his promotion. When Ormsby arrives, he is shocked to find Zelida gone and begins to suspect Brownlow's interference. Brownlow protests, claiming he had asked Zelida to marry Col. Ormsby as originally planned by her deceased father. Ormsby, however, remains suspicious and challenges Brownlow.

Pillage conducts Sir Hector to his sister's house to meet Zelida. Unaware of her identity, Pillage wishes only to provide the lecherous admiral with an attractive woman, hoping that Sir Hector will support his promotion. Zelida and Sir Hector immediately recognize each other, and Sir Hector urges Zelida to hasten to Brownlow's lodgings to stop the duel between Brownlow and Ormsby. Zelida rushes to Brownlow's; the duel is prevented; and the self-sacrificing young woman declares herself ready to marry Ormsby to preserve Brownlow. Her faithful Bussora intervenes to declare that his mistress loves Brownlow, not Ormsby. The latter, convinced that Brownlow did nothing underhanded to force Zelida's feelings, gives her up to Brownlow. He, in turn, confesses his love for Zelida after having attempted to persuade her of his love for another to preserve her for Ormsby.

The play was generally well received, most reviewers evidently contented, as the *Middlesex Journal*'s reviewer was, with the shortened version of the second performance on 3 December. Perhaps the most negative note was sounded by the *London Packet:* "In the hash which the fat-dramatic dish cook of Gough Square . . . set down before the town, and recommended as a well relished supper, we taste some of the substantial joints of Goldsmith's bill of fare" (5–7 Dec.), accusing Kelly of borrowing the inspiration for his nautical character from Hardcastle and Tony Lumpkin of *She Stoops to Conquer*. Other reviewers were less harsh, and although admitting that the play had little originality in its "plot, character, or dialogue" (*St. James's Chronicle* 23 Dec.), these analyses stressed the positive. The *St. James's Chronicle* claimed that naval characters, such as Sir Hector, will always please a British audience who will recognize their origin in Smollett's Commodore Bowling; while the *Critical Review,* acknowledging the plot's indebtedness to Jean-François Marmontel's story "The Proof of Friendship," nevertheless concluded that *Romance* "may be considered as an original composition" (Review of *Romance of an Hour* 480) that will "not diminish the reputation that Mr. Kelly has already acquired." In the *Monthly Review* (Jan. 1775), George Colman attacked the play for its borrowings from Marmontel, even though Kelly had admitted his indebtedness.[7] Colman noted the sentimentality of the play, especially the character of Bussora, whom he found "a simple gentoo in the garb of a methodist preacher" (91).

Comparing the Larpent Collection copy submitted by Thomas Harris to the licenser on 24 September 1774 with the printed edition (Kelly, *Plays*) reveals that, as the *Middlesex Journal* suggested, a pruning knife had been needed. In a number of scenes, the printed version is shorter, sometimes significantly so, than the Larpent version. More interestingly, the printed version is less sentimental than the Larpent copy, suggesting once again that Bevis's view that the printed version of a sentimental play was likely to be more sentimental than the acted version was not always true (*Laughing* 32–38). In one case, an entire scene disappears in the printed version; in the Larpent copy, prior to the scene where the two lovers of Zelida, Brownlow and Ormsby, are about to duel, the madcap son of Sir Hector, Orson Strangeways, intervenes and offers to fight in his uncle Brownlow's stead. The incident disappears from the printed version. Another substantial section of the Larpent version, an attempt by Lady Strangeways to repair her relationship with her husband, Sir Hector, is entirely missing from the printed version. This attempted reconciliation in which both husband and wife admit their faults and talk about how to revive their lost affection is as sentimental a scene as any in the play. Other cuts represent attempts to cull wordiness and generally do improve the crispness of the dialogue, but none is as substantial as the two omissions just noted.

The *Middlesex Journal's* prediction that *The Romance of an Hour* would become a favorite farce was not borne out. In the first season, the play was presented ten times, the last performance occurring on 19 April 1775. It appeared twice the next season and then disappeared until it was presented at the Haymarket with *The School for Wives* on 16 November 1784. By the end of the century, it had been performed in London only fifteen times. It fared indifferently in the provincial theaters, put on by Henderson's company at Bath in January 1775 and at Cork on 31 July 1775. It then was given sporadically for the next decade or so.[8]

In America, the play was presented before *The School for Wives* appeared, as William Watt notes (289), and had a fairly successful career before 1800. The initial American performance, 27 December 1782, was by Lindsay and Wall's Company in Baltimore; it then was presented by the old American Company at John Street Theater on 8 May 1788 as the afterpiece to *The School for Wives* (289; Odell 1: 267).[9] *Romance* was given four additional times in the 1790s, the last at the John Street on 30 May 1799 (W. W. Watt 290; Odell 2: 58).

Modern commentary on *The Romance of an Hour* has been limited: it was generally ignored by Frederick Boas, George Nettleton, Ashley Thorndike, and other historians from the early part of the twentieth century. Bevis's *Laughing Tradition*, on the other hand, fully considers the afterpiece as a form and situates *Romance* in that tradition. He identifies three modes of the afterpiece in the century: the sentimental, the comic, and a class that combined elements of the first two. Bevis claims that the sentimental mode occurred only five times between 1737 and 1777 and points out that Kelly and Capt. Edward Thompson, a Kelly biographer, were responsible for two of these occurrences. Bevis dislikes *Romance*, claiming that it

> bears out Sherbo's observation that if a treatment of sentimental themes is brief it lacks emotive power. The dialogue is uniformly dismal, and the "humor" disastrous. Its main gesture is towards humanitarianism: an honest Indian servant resolves a foolish quarrel between English gentlemen. (*Laughing* 104)

As Bevis generally feels that the true comic spirit of the eighteenth-century British theater survived in its most successful afterpieces, it is not surprising that he treats *The Romance of an Hour* harshly. He dislikes the sentimental afterpieces, believing that they "show no agreement on how to achieve their effects; they gesture at romance, patriotism, comedy of manners, and melodrama, sometimes all at once" (105). One can agree that *Romance* is not particularly successful, and one can also agree that it fails as an organic whole; yet I must point out once more that the potpourri of feelings, the multiple modal and generic gestures, that Bevis notes, although appearing from one perspective—formalistic organicism—to be contradictory, are in actuality representative of Kelly's traditional practices. They are the generic and emotive gestures that he employed to be popular, to be marketable. That combination seems to be what the reviewer for the *London Packet* referred to when he called the play a "hash."

To be popular, Kelly did not merely aim at embodying cultural fads and trends, although he did do that too. Rather, I argue, he was not above mixing those generic elements that Robert Hume defines in his useful essay "The Multifarious Forms of Eighteenth-Century Comedy." Hume suggests that, instead of organizing comedy around substance or plot, we look at it from its effects on the audience. He further identifies five main comic forms in the century—farcical, satiric, humane, reform, and exemplary—that produce reactions, respectively, of amused contempt, superiority or disdain, benevolence and goodwill, strong approval, and outright admiration (13–14). I maintain that Kelly's plays and certainly *The Romance of an Hour* contain elements of several of the subgenres Hume identifies.

The farcical elements in *Romance* are provided by Sir Hector's and Lady Diana's madcap son, Orson, a character rightly pointed out by one contemporary reviewer as owing much to Goldsmith's Tony Lumpkin; Orson's crudeness places him at odds with his genteel mother, and his nautical jargon exceeds his father's. Satire is another ingredient of this afterpiece: the play abounds with allusions to contemporary social maladies. Early in act 2, Pillage comments on young British women of marriageable age who, having been seduced, must journey to the colonies to find husbands. His remarks are directed at Zelida's desire to return to India, and he is wrong, of course, about the status of her virtue; yet there is certainly contemporary social satire in what he says: "The lady has been kept by one of the India captains, I suppose, and designs to enter herself in the cargo of damag'd virginity, which, for the honour of English delicacy nowdays, makes so considerable an article in our exports to Bengal." The humane element enters when Brownlow nobly gives up Zelida, whom he loves, because she has been already promised to Col. Ormsby, while Ormsby, once he discovers Zelida's true affections, just as nobly returns her to Brownlow. Finally, the reform genre of comedy plays itself out in Kelly's condemnation of one of his favorite targets—the duel; the folly of dueling is exposed by the moral Bussora, who notes the debased code of honor in England that "oblige[s a] gentleman to kill friend without cause." This assault against dueling, part of what Barker-Benfield calls the "repression of violence" (80–81), represents another instance of Kelly's interest in reforming male culture.

Again, I maintain that, as a reasonably popular writer, Kelly knew what he was doing and was not concerned with standards of generic purity: *I will mix genres—and gladly so* might have been his Derridean-like cry. Whether such a generic mixture could be successful in the long run is another question. Bevis feels that Kelly, even in *False Delicacy*, weakened his work because of "the pressure to include diverse modes" (*Laughing* 94–95). But it may have been insufficient strength in executing such diversity rather than diversity itself that limited the long-term effectiveness of Kelly's plays.

Market-oriented practicality is what Kelly seems to point to in the prologue to *Romance*:

> Let critics proudly form dramatic laws,
> Give me, say I, what's sure to meet applause;
> Let them of time, and place, and action boast,
> I'm for a devil, a dungeon, or a ghost—
>
> (*Plays, Romance,* lines 19–20)

Kelly is simply announcing the professional's creed: use what works. Later in this prologue, he notes that the Bussora character in his play will nevertheless be original:

> Yet tho' he calls his trifle a romance,
> He does not treat you with a single dance,
> Nor use one hackney'd, one eccentric art,
> To lull your judgment, or to cheat your heart—
> He brings, indeed, a character to view,
> From Indian climes, he trusts entirely new—
> A poor Gentoo, compos'd of virtues all,
> Tho' fresh from English nabobs at Bengal;
> His face, perhaps, too swarthy you may find;
> "Yet see Othello's visage in his mind—"
> And 'till you've fairly tried our trembling Bays,
> Forbear to blame—but do not fear to praise.

(lines 55–66)

The character of Bussora, played by Lee Lewes, was not new, but he was surely timely.[10] Although the noble savage figure of Restoration and eighteenth-century primitivism goes at least as far back as Aphra Behn's *Oroonoko* (1688), Kelly probably capitalized on a current noble savage, Omai, the South Sea prince, visiting England during 1774.[11] More culturally immediate would have been associations with India; the East India Co. had been in the news for months, and the nabobs referred to in the prologue had also been in the news and on the stage, as Foote's play *The Nabob* illustrates.[12]

The occasion of *The Romance of an Hour* is of some interest. In the "Advertisement" to the first edition, Kelly explains the piece's genesis by relating that he wrote it for Mrs. Abington, long a favorite of his, who once wished to "perform a character of perfect simplicity." This desire, says Kelly, inspired him to write *Romance* and to create Zelida, the daughter of an Indian aristocrat, as noble as her servant Bussora. But Frances Abington never played the part, according to Kelly, because she "generously refused to hazard any little reputation which I might possess, upon her account." Perhaps the real reason Mrs. Abington declined can be found in her fear that Kelly was still a marked man because of Wilkite prejudice, and since the piece was to be acted for her benefit night, she did not wish to risk losing her income.[13] Mrs. Abington possibly had reason to be wary of the Patriots. If a report in the *Middlesex Journal* for 8–10 December 1774 is accurate, Kelly himself worried that the play might be disrupted:

> Mr. Addington, who stood proxy for Mr. Kelly last year for his *School for Wives,* was asked to perform the same friendly office this season, for *The Romance of an Hour;* the Justice did not at first refuse it, but

asked to see the child, when, after examining its several features, he returned it, and begged to be excused. The poet modestly desired to know the reason, when he received for answer,—*A Word to the Wise!*

Given that Kelly's politics could still jeopardize his plays, it is surprising that *The Romance of an Hour* was advertised as his work soon after its first night. Acted first on 2 December, by 17 December it was advertised in the *General Evening Post* as by Kelly. There is a long puff for the play, featuring an entire scene, and additional advertisements for all of Kelly's other plays: two full columns are given over to the promotion of Hugh Kelly, an extensive space compared to that normally allotted to playwrights.[14] Despite Kelly's having been publicly associated with *Romance,* Wilkite wrath was withheld, and it ran four times during the season without incident.

Had the Wilkites known that Kelly was Numa, the staunch defender of colonial policies, however, they might have received *Romance* more harshly, for soon after the press activity surrounding that play ceased, Kelly resumed publishing the Numa letters. This propaganda campaign for 1775 exceeded by far his 1774 activity; by the end of 1775, he had published thirty-three letters under Numa, more than three times the number in the previous year's campaign, which, it will be recalled, did not commence until late June 1774. The length of these letters varied from roughly one-half column to two and one-half columns. Assuming the average letter was one and one-half columns—a reasonable estimate—and was fifteen hundred words long, then in 1775 alone Kelly's Numa letters totaled nearly fifty thousand words, enough to make a tidy volume had they been collected and reprinted.

All of the Numa letters appeared in Henry Sampson Woodfall's *Public Advertiser.* Woodfall had a long history of publishing sensitive political material: his paper had published the original Junius letters.[15] Woodfall's *Advertiser* was also known for living up to its editorial motto—"Open to all parties"—even though at least one correspondent (18 Sept. 1775) was to attack it for being the outlet of ministerial writers while noting that John Miller's *London Evening Post* was reserved for the Patriots. Woodfall adamantly denied partiality; and indeed, if one studies the entire run of the paper for 1774–75, immediately preceding the final breech between the colonies and Great Britain, one concludes that, if anything, the editorial slant was pro-American. That slant does not signify that Woodfall supported the City Patriots in all matters, but he did allow them their voice.

As we have seen, Kelly's 1774 Numa letters primarily defended the Quebec Bill. The 1775 letters, often appearing for a series of Saturdays, focused on two general targets.[16] One was the perfidy of the Americans; the other was the pro-American London Patriot movement. Within these two broad topics, Kelly almost always articulated a set of specific themes in the current debate: the right of Great Britain to tax its colonies, the question of a standing army, and the Catholic issue in North America as symbolized by the Quebec Bill. These themes were emphasized before June 1775, when it still appeared possible that relations between the colonies and Great Britain might be repaired. After Lexington and Concord, however, Kelly's Numa themes changed, and in addition to those above included the inevitability of the king's military victory over the rebels (Kelly refused to call the struggle, as some radicals did, a *civil war*); the harm caused the loyalists by the radical London press and by pro-American groups, like the SSBR; and a final theme with strong class conflict features: the false pretensions of the City Patriots to represent themselves as men of the first rank.

The Numa letters, more than forty in number and running from late June 1774 until November 1775, constitute Kelly's most sustained and unified body of political journalism. As such, it is important to examine a sampling of these letters to discover how Kelly supported the ministry's policies and attacked its enemies. I then look at the events surrounding exposure as the Numa writer in the late summer of 1775, when once again Kelly suffered personal attacks as he had in the days of the *Public Ledger* and the damnation of *A Word to the Wise*.

Kelly's most effective strategy in the 1775 Numa letters was to attack the self-interest of those merchants who supported the Americans. He contended that they supported the rebels only because their businesses depended upon the colonies. Such a charge would be difficult to disprove, even on a case-by-case basis, assuming that the particular merchant did trade with America. One supposes, furthermore, that for those who did not have financial ties to the colonies, such an argument, exposing motives not of political rectitude but of mere economic gain, would be effective. In the second Numa letter (14 Jan.), Kelly wonders how London merchants with American interests can place self-gain before the "general welfare of the Kingdom," and he constructs a parody of the radicals own device, the "Petition to the King," thus turning the tables on the Patriots:

> To the KING, LORDS and COMMONS of GREAT BRITAIN assembled in the present PARLIAMENT.
>
> The PETITION of divers MERCHANTS trading to AMERICA, HUMBLY SHEWETH,
>
> That the British Colonies beyond the Atlantic are at this Time engaged in an unnatural Rebellion against the MOTHER COUNTRY, which if not punished with proper Severity, must be destructive to the general interests of the BRITISH EMPIRE. That the Petitioners, however, having large Sums owing to them from the Colonies, and being promised large Orders, if they espouse the Cause of the Rebels, beg that the general Interests of the British Empire may be utterly neglected, and the Minister's Head cut off, for wishing to maintain the political Omnipotence of Parliament.

Kelly concludes this ironic "Petition" with the following:

> The Petitioners candidly acknowledge, that in the two Rebellions which raged in Scotland since the Elevation of the august House of Hanover to the British Crown, no Body even of Scotch Merchants, associated for the express Purpose of aiding the Rebels, nor once thought of a Petition to Parliament in favour of the Pretender.

This last paragraph introduces another line of attack Kelly employs in the Numa letters: the comparison of the Scottish rebellions of 1715 and 1745 with the American rebellion of the 1770s. Here he simply points out that the Scottish merchants never aided the Stuarts; in contrast, London merchants help the American rebels through appeals, fund-raising, and petitions. As his letter campaign wore on, Kelly returned to both themes to shame the London merchants into loyalty.

In August 1775, the propaganda battle between Kelly and the Patriots reached a climax; and before the month ended, Kelly had been identified publicly as Numa and had been accused of being "Palinurus," the author of still another series of pro-Court letters in the *Gazetteer,* a series that appeared in the spring and summer even as he was publishing his Numa pieces in the *Public Advertiser.* The assault began with a 5 August letter to the *Public Advertiser,* signed "Regulus," that arraigns Kelly, whom the writer identifies as Numa, for attempting to intimidate the Patriot press through his appeals for unity against the colonies. Specifically, Regulus accuses Kelly of addressing newspaper printers in a preface to the Numa letter of 28 July in which he warned the printers that publishing materials in support of the colonies has already been interpreted as treasonous by the Crown lawyers. The letter continues by daring Kelly to produce examples from among those treasonous publications, claiming that the charge by Numa/Kelly is a "very scandalous and infamous Falsehood." In essence, Regulus, quoting from most of Kelly's previous letters of the summer, accuses him of unfair attacks on the Patriot press's veracity. It is rather the ministerial press, and particularly the government's own *London Gazette,* maintains Regulus, whose truthfulness is suspect, especially with regard to battle reports from North America. Much of Regulus's attack is aimed at Kelly's rhetoric. He points to the obscurity of some of the rhetoric in Kelly's letter of 26 July, ridiculing in particular such phrases as "retrograde propensity" and "obscure sublime." These infelicities and one or two others, Kelly later claimed, were due to poor proofreading; and to be sure, Woodfall later confessed that the piece was not proofread at all.

The paper war heated up as August drew to a close, and both Regulus and Numa had letters in the 26 August issue of the *Public Advertiser.* The former continued to assail Kelly, more with ad hominem insults than with reasoned analysis of his arguments. Regulus complains of the "Incorrigible Stupidity of the Hackney Stager" and later calls Kelly "this rotten Irish Bog, the very Emblem of Sterility." Numa's own letter of 26 August does not reply to Regulus but turns back to consider colonial political issues, specifically focusing on the absence of close ties among the various colonies and noting that their constitutions are quite different. Kelly's design, one presumes, is to suggest that their alliance will prove to be unstable. Turning to the offense, Kelly partially exposes Regulus's identity in a 2 September letter. He addresses Regulus as the "Rev. Mr. N," but not until another letter, written by a Kelly partisan and signed "An Old Correspondent" (7 Sept.), is Regulus fully identified as Mr. Northcote. In all probability, Regulus was the Rev. Thomas Northcote, chaplin in the Royal Artillery, who in 1781 published *Observations on the Natural and Civil Rights of Mankind*.[17] He does not appear to have played any role in previous periodical wars, but Kelly clearly knew something of the man, for he addressed him mockingly as the "Rev. Adonis Mr. N———."

The letter exposing Regulus was published only five days before Kelly's private letter to David Garrick on 7 September in which Kelly admitted that Numa was his and "many others besides." But the controversy was dying down, and after 13 September, when "R.G.S." wrote to defend Kelly's right to "assume a Signature, and to reserve his Name as long as he pleases," the Northcote–Kelly paper war was over. Numa's career had also nearly run its course. Only one letter appeared during the remainder of September (on the thirtieth), when Kelly again arraigned the Middlesex Patriots for supporting the Americans and ridiculed their press's description of them as "significant" and "respectable" citizenry.

12

The Final Year: *The Man of Reason,* Law Career, and Fatal Illness

Ironically, in the same letter that Kelly wrote to Garrick announcing his responsibility for the Numa letters in the *Public Advertiser,* he also mentioned a new play. In the 7 September 1775 note, after briefly touching on his Numa persona, Kelly wrote of his new play: "The piece I hinted at my dear Sir, is not [a] petite piece; it is a full five act piece, and I flatter myself most egregiously if you will not find the *Cub* (to use a good humoured expression of your own upon a former occasion) extremely *lickable*" (Garrick Correspondence 5:no. 26).[1] I have been unable to determine when Kelly began to work on the play that when submitted to the licenser was entitled "The Reasonable Lover" but was produced under the title *The Man of Reason.* Certainly by 7 September 1775, the letter implies, he had nearly completed the first draft. Sometime within the next five weeks, Kelly sent Garrick what he had written to date, for Garrick's disappointing response to Kelly's letter of 7 September suggests that Garrick read a completed work. How much further work Kelly might have completed in the fall is not clear, but the Numa letters were few after early September, so he had time to pursue playwriting, more time than he had had for many months.

When Kelly received Garrick's 16 October 1775 reply, he learned that Garrick felt that the play could not be salvaged:

> Indeed, my dear Sir, You have put into my hands a performance of very great hurry, & which cannot possibly be Represented with Success. I never read More dangerous Scenes in all my life. An Audience in my opinion, would immediately take offence at Mr. & Mrs. Buzzard & particularly at the last—her culinary jokes when alter'd and made less strong, would be dangerous Even in a farce— but his peculiarity, & desire of lying with the Widow Keenly, in the Spartan manner would never be borne—Wellwood has marks of a Character but surely his being Kick'd & sent to Bridewell is carry-

ing the joke much too far—and the Widow, which seems the favourite female Character has a most abandon'd Mind, & tho she does not forge bonds, Yet she forges falsehoods to carry on her Schemes, & falls but little short of what is suppos'd of Mrs. Rudd: Commodore Sulky is rather a trite Character, and little use made of him hitherto—the idea of a Fribble officer and Foxhunting Girl (tho the last is in another play) is a good one, but there are no circumstances, no Comic incidents to shew them off. (Garrick Correspondence 5: no 28)[2]

This letter does not throw much light on *The Man of Reason* as it was produced because Kelly took Garrick's criticisms to heart and rewrote the play to a considerable extent. He made many changes in character and situation, for none of the names mentioned in Garrick's letter appear in the Larpent copy, the only original copy presumably extant.[3] Hence Garrick's specific criticisms cannot be traced in the final product, although some of his complaints are general enough to warrant speculative commentary. First, it is noteworthy that Garrick points to a lack of "Comic incidents," an old failing of Kelly's and one that his revisions only partially remedied. Second, Garrick in two different contexts expresses his belief that the play is "dangerous," a surprising analysis of the work of a leading sentimentalist. Yet, in the final version, Kelly satirized, among other things, the practice of medicine, the legal system as it applied to debtors, and the patronage of smugglers and their consumer goods by aristocratic London. Perhaps the number of his victims was larger and his tone sharper in the version Garrick saw.

In any case, Kelly responded on 20 October. The letter suggests that Kelly knew better than to propose revisions, as he did with *The School for Wives*. Instead, he accepted Garrick's judgment of the play, perhaps because he knew that the 1775–76 year would be Garrick's final one and his friend would not welcome the hard work an extensive revision would require. As O'Leary notes (178), Kelly's response was respectful:

> Don't be frightened when you see my name; for this is not a letter of importunity but of apology. Pardon me for re-agitating the business of the play in my note of yesterday, and believe me, I am not only satisfied, but obliged by the liberality as well as the friendship which you have manifested on this occasion. I was hurt at disappointing your expectations; therefore wished to recover my credit with you, and though I shall be uneasy till that is done, you shall undergo no further persecution this winter. Pray be composed, and get well for everybody's sake. (Garrick Correspondence 24: no. 30)[4]

How quickly Kelly began to rewrite his final play cannot be determined, but in the middle of October when these exchanges with Garrick occurred, some final political shots in the Numa campaign were fired.

On 19 October, one day before his final letter about "The Reasonable Lover" was sent to Garrick, Kelly struck again as Numa in the *Public Advertiser* in a letter that questioned the degree of support the City radicals actually possessed among the Middlesex freeholders and that claimed it did not run deep. On 21 October, the *Public Advertiser* printed an attack on Kelly from "Monitor" that mentioned Kelly's vanity. Kelly had challenged the social status of some of the radicals, and now Monitor mockingly alluded to Kelly's own possessions, when he ironically suggested to Wilkes that in assessing each freeholder's status he not "forget their Sideboards, to the Splendor of which their very Silver Spurs may occasionally contribute" (Sat., 21 Oct.). In striking at what Monitor perceived to be Kelly's own insecure status, he echoed Johnson's comment about Kelly, found in Boswell as he received it from John Nichols:

> Speaking one day of a person for whom he had a real friendship, but in whom vanity was somewhat too predominant, he observed that "Kelly was so fond of displaying on his sideboard the plate which he possessed, that he added to it his spurs." (qtd. in Boswell, *Life* 4: 407)

Friday, 9 February 1776, Kelly's final play was produced. *The Man of Reason* played for a single night and does not seem to have been produced again. The prologue is a lament about how difficult it is to gauge the fickle and changing taste of the audience, a succinct summation of the plight of the popular writer. In sounding the theme of escape from authorship, the prologue connects this last play to his earliest journalism. Addressing his audience, Kelly complained that a writer can never be sure "your humour to discern" (*Plays* 11; Prologue) and commented on the unpredictable taste for either laughter or sentiment. To the end, Kelly remained aware of the burdens of the professional writer.

The play is difficult to summarize, as two newspaper notices admitted.[5] Act 1 discloses that Capt. Cleveland, the disguised son of Dr. Wilmington, one of the play's comic villains, has fallen in love with Flavella Freemore as a consequence of having rescued her in a coach accident and having taken up lodging where she and her parents live. Cleveland confesses his true identity to Flavella, but his father, Dr. Wilmington, does not recognize him because he has been raised in Ireland by his grandfather. Consequently, Wilmington makes Cleveland a confederate in his plots, one of which is to marry off his own daughter, Urania, to the villainous Lestock, the other is to have Cleveland himself marry Flavella Freemore to prevent her from marrying the man of reason, Sir James Clifford. Wilmington feels that he will settle his estate upon his nephew, Lestock, and Lestock's wife, Wilmington's daughter, Urania, if Sir James does not marry.

In the first act, Dr. Wilmington is visiting the Freemore's home and we meet Flavella's parents, Mr. and Mrs. Freemore. Mrs. Freemore is a termagant ruthlessly pursuing her own self-interest in attempting to wed Flavella to Sir James, thereby securing the older man's wealth to help her husband out of debt. Mr.

Freemore, a sentimental benefactor, is nearly bankrupt, in part from aiding others less fortunate; he is also victimized by his wife's bullying tactics. Lady Winterly, Dr. Wilmington's sister, also visits the Freemore home in act 1. She is a comic widow who tries to aid her niece, Urania Wilmington, to escape Lestock, whom Urania detests. Urania loves Wyndam, supposedly exiled to France after nearly killing a man in defending Flavella Freemore, though at the time she was a stranger to him. Wyndam, disguised as William, a servant in Lady Winterly's household, becomes the object of Lady Winterly and her maid, Gloworm.

The exposition in act 1 necessary to clarify these intertwined plots is excessive and does not always succeed, even for readers; it is only later that we learn why Wyndam had to flee to France: for most of act 1, we and the other characters think he merely fought a duel over a streetwalker. Near the end of act 1, the villainous Lestock, the last major character, save Wyndam, to appear, tells us why he has announced (falsely) Wyndam's death (so he can marry Urania) and how he will also obtain Sir James's estate. He also reveals that he has bribed Dr. Crisis so that Crisis will keep Wyndam's injured dueling victim incapacitated, thus frightening Wyndam into remaining in France. Before the act concludes, the scene shifts to Lady Winterly's home, where Wyndam and Urania discuss his return to England disguised as Lady Winterly's footman and the villainy of Lestock. He relates that the duel was fought to save a lady's honor and not over a whore. Lestock and Wyndam have a great deal to explain during the course of this first act, some of which would have been unclear even to an experienced theater audience.

In act 2, the major business has to do with Dr. Wilmington, Cleveland, and Lestock attempting to persuade Sir James to test Flavella Freemore's love for him, presumably so he will learn how little she cares for him and give her up. Before Sir James's scene with Flavella, a comic interlude occurs in which Gloworm demonstrates her affection for William/Wyndam; Lady Winterly discovers them in an embrace; and we learn both she and Gloworm, like Lady Booby and Slipslop in *Joseph Andrews,* desire William/Wyndam. The Flavella–Sir James confrontation begins with Sir James indelicately asking her to confess her affection for him above all men in the world, to which she responds in an appropriately evasive way. She exits without satisfying Sir James's request, and he vows to the others to give her up, thinking it the reasonable course of action.

The third act begins and concludes with the Lady Winterly–Wyndam plot, as Lady Winterly confesses to Urania, her niece, that she loves Wyndam and asks the younger woman to intercede for her. Meanwhile, Sir James resigns Flavella, much to her father's joy, but his wife is upset at losing the Clifford money. Not satisfied with the five thousand pounds that Sir James promises to settle upon Flavella, providing she be allowed to select her own husband, Mrs. Freemore exits to consult a lawyer. Flavella and her father meet in the most sentimental scene in the play and promise to sacrifice for each other, she vowing to turn the Clifford money over to his debtors and he saying he would rather go to debtor's prison than have her marry against her inclination. The scene ends in mutual tears. When Mr. Freemore leaves, Cleveland enters and in an equally sentimental fashion tells Flavella to use the five thousand pounds to rescue her father because he will marry her anyhow, dowry or not. She consents but says he must first obtain her father's permission. The act ends with Gloworm and Lady Winterly overhearing Urania Wilmington and William/Wyndam declare their mutual love; Lady Winterly locks up Urania and drives William from her house.

Act 4 begins with a dispute between the Freemores, as Mrs. Freemore has convinced Sir James that Flavella really does love him and that he should repropose. Mr. Freemore urges Sir James against such an attempt, but Flavella is now bound to accept him, determined to use his money to save her father. Cleveland enters but refuses to push his claim, and in a moment of false delicacy, he gives up Flavella, saying he would never force a woman against her will. Finally determined to oppose his wife's schemes, Mr. Freemore vows never to speak with Flavella again if she accepts Sir James. She persists, and her sacrifice of both Cleveland and her father convinces Sir James that she does indeed love him. Meanwhile, Lady Winterly aids her brother, Wilmington, in his scheme to match Lestock with Urania; Lady Winterly is driven by jealousy of her niece, who possesses William's affection. Lestock plots with Dr. Crisis to have Sir James declared mentally incompetent to prevent his marriage to Flavella. There follows a farcical scene in which Dr. Crisis and three other doctors harass the surprised Sir James with silly questions about his health and finally have him committed. Sir James exits, crying that he has received what he deserves for living in a "country of fools."

The final act opens with Dr. Wilmington shown fast becoming a victim of his own plots, for he is persuaded by Cleveland, his disguised son, not only to agree to his marriage to Flavella but also to assume responsibility for her father's debts. Flavella, her father saved, agrees to elope with Cleveland, thinking that the son has told the father all. Of course, he has not. At Lady Winterly's home, Wyndam enters in his true identity, claims Urania, and forces Lestock to leave when he exhibits the bond with which Lestock attempted to bribe Dr. Crisis. The doctor has turned out to be a good soul and has helped foil Lestock's schemes. The would-be lovers, Gloworm and Lady Winterly exit in embarrassment. When the final scene opens at Sir James's home, Sir James has just been told the true story about his two nephews, Lestock and Wyndam, by Crisis. Enter Wyndam and Urania, whose marriage is consented to by Dr. Wilmington, who thinks Sir James's money will yet go to his daughter because Wyndam has become the favorite nephew. Sir James is told of Flavella's marriage to Cleveland, which he accepts with good grace, and Dr. Wilmington is told of Cleveland's true identity, which he does not accept well. Finally reconciled, he confesses that he became "the dupe of my own designs." The play ends with Sir James Clifford, the man of reason, deciding to accept society's customs after all.

The modern reader of *The Man of Reason* will readily agree with contemporary reviewers who found the play too complicated in its exposition and plotting for a theater audience. William Watt was correct when, in summing up the play's faults, he pointed to Kelly's "inability to organize the intricacies of his plot" (309), and even closet readers have problems in comprehending the action and the motivation. Watt is also correct, I believe, in stating that in general Kelly experienced difficulties in his plays with the exordium. Kelly simply found beginning a play a formidable task, and in this play the exposition is more complicated and more clumsily handled than in his earlier efforts. As alluded to earlier, only at the very end of the play, for example, do we learn the full story of Wyndam's duel: it was fought to save Flavella from a rape, and she had kept the incident quiet for fear of alarming her family, a singularly unconvincing explanation.

Other factors contributed to the play's failure. Had Garrick taken an interest in the piece, it might well have been spared some structural weaknesses. The slow-moving scenes in which far too much dialogue and far too little action occur would have been tightened. But the reviews, although not terribly detailed, also suggest problems in ethics and ideology that needed to be reconsidered. I mentioned Kelly's hit at the situation of the debtor, his satire of doctors, at least unethical ones, and his suggestion that the aristocracy abets criminality by purchasing smuggled goods. Kelly withdrew the piece after the house had responded negatively to the announcement that it would be played again on Monday, 12 February. The *Morning Chronicle* for 10 February reported that the author, not yet identified, canceled the Monday performance at the end of the afterpiece, "declaring that he wished not on any consideration to disturb the Theatre." *The Man of Reason* thus passed quietly into oblivion with barely a response from the press.

Cooke maintained that after the play's failure Kelly turned his entire attention to the law ("Hugh Kelly," Jan. 45), but careful study of the newspapers suggests that Cooke was incorrect. Evidence shows Kelly's pen active in the ministry's campaign against Warren Hastings, although he seemed mute in causes that would have previously demanded his attention. Apart from the anti-Hastings campaign, there is no evidence that Kelly wrote for other, more local political situations. His pen was not involved in the heated contest between John Wilkes and Alderman Benjamin Hopkins for the City post of chamberlain, even though Hopkins was the ministerial candidate supported by the son and son-in-law (Walter Rawlinson) of Kelly's old patron, Sir Robert Ladbroke. The banking house of Ladbroke, Rawlinson, and Parker provided the necessary financial backing that Alderman Hopkins needed to run for the post.[6] Although mentioned once or twice in general attacks on ministerial writers, Kelly on other occasions throughout the winter and spring of 1776 was not included among those actively writing.

Yet even after the failure of his last play, theater politics continued to hound Kelly. He was mentioned in a letter printed in both the *Morning Chronicle* on 1 April and the *Middlesex Journal* of 30 March–2 April that complained about the "mean passions prevalent in the literary world today." The writer was unhappy that Cumberland abused other writers, that Goldsmith quarreled with Kelly because "*False Delicacy* succeeded better than the *Good-natured Man,*" and then that Kelly had "joined the herd of scribblers who wondered at the success of the *Duenna*." On 2 April, William Woodfall editorialized that Kelly denied attacking the comic opera; Kelly claimed, said Woodfall, that the report was "totally without foundation" and said that he had "assisted in the applause of some authors, who have repeatedly made the most illiberal attacks upon his character." Woodfall implied that Kelly esteemed the author of the *Duenna,* Richard Sheridan, but it is unclear whom Kelly meant when he complained of attacks by brother authors. Goldsmith comes to mind, but the piece provided no specifics. Kelly's response here is another of the gaps in the story of his professional life, particularly his relationships with other writers.

The incident reminds us again that, in the new commodity world of print, the author was an intellectual worker, a producer who competed with others: understandably, this competition yielded animosity toward one's fellows. Also understandably, it was in the press that this competitive tension found expression, recalling again the politics of literary journalism. Interestingly enough, in this final year of Kelly's life, two plays were produced that seemed to highlight this complex relationship among literature, politics, and journalism. On 7 March at Drury Lane, Colman's *Spleen: or, Islington Spa* was produced; this afterpiece featured a journalist-bookseller, Rubrick, an apothecary who also had interests in several newspapers. But the possibility that the Newbery family inspired Rubrick is not as relevant to my purposes as the representation of a journalist in a play is.[7] This farce makes fun of Rubrick, who plans to bring out a new newspaper called the *Noon Post,* so it can serve as a morning paper at the west end of town and an evening paper at the east. Journalists and journalism may have become important enough to be targets of satirical wrath, thus joining the ranks of other satirized professionals, such as doctors and lawyers. If journalists could use the pages of their magazines and newspapers to comment, often adversely, on the world of drama, it seems reasonable that eventually the comic and satiric dramatists would find enough in the practices of the newly emergent field of journalism to return the favor. In either case, marketable wares were turned out for a knowledgeable reading public aware of the ways in which both fields, theater and journalism, were now so situated as to create discourses about each other.[8]

Colman in his February 1767 work, *The English Merchant,* had depicted a vile journalist hack called Spatter, whose name indicated someone who covered another with obloquy.[9] In 1776, Arthur Murphy's *News from Parnassus* was staged at Covent Garden on 23 September. Like Colman's play, it makes fun of booksellers who sell quack medicines, and the bookseller-journalist character, Vellum, explains how news is "made" (like quack medicines?) by revealing how much fiction gets into the newspapers. Another character involved in the intersecting worlds of journalism and literature is Catcall, who relates how he became a theater critic.[10] Not only playwrights saw the growing importance of journalism; others clearly saw it becoming more complicated and controversial as a discourse, as seems apparent with the early 1770s appearance of such anonymously authored works as *The News-Readers Pocket Book* (1773) and *An Essay on the Art of Newspaper Defamation* (1775).

In the *Gazetteer* of 19 July, an attack on Kelly appeared, signed by one "Regulus," accusing him of leading the government's assault on the governor general of the East India Co., Warren Hastings. Who Regulus was is unclear; Northcote, Kelly's enemy, had earlier used that pen name to expose Kelly as Numa. But the editor of the *Morning Chronicle* in the summer of 1776, William Woodfall, had accused Wilkes of employing the name in some letters to the press. Corroboration of Regulus's accusation can be found in a letter written to Hastings by his agent in England, Col. Laughlin MacLeane, dated from Portsmouth on 10 November 1776.[11] The letter deals with MacLeane's perception of the political activity surrounding the East India Co. and specifically mentions that a paper war against Hastings was "conducted under the immediate orders of the Treasury. This business was managed by the person employed in it (a Mr. Kelly) with the most illiberal scurrility, but with very little ability" (qtd. in O'Leary 152). The motivation for the hostility toward Hastings in Lord North's ministry is not altogether clear: one modern account states that Hastings was in the minority on the council that governed India and that George III wanted Hastings's rival, Gen. John Clavering, to be governor general. Why Regulus, assuming he wrote for the Patriots, supported Hastings is also cloudy, especially given the Patriots' feeling that Scotsmen had been given too much patronage and that Hastings appointed a large number of Scots to posts within the East India Co.[12] Other than maintaining that Hastings was "an honest man, and an able servant of the India Company," Regulus provides no extensive rationale for his support.

Kelly's assault on Warren Hastings was the briefest of his major propaganda campaigns on behalf of the ministry of Lord North. Only seven letters, all appearing in the *Public Advertiser,* seem to have been written, the first appearing on Monday, 27 May 1776, and the last printed on 16 July. The full details of Kelly's charges against Hastings need not concern us, but the essence of Kelly's argument seems to have been that Governor Hastings had violated his own rules when he allowed Cantoo Baboo, a collector of revenue for the company government, to rent farms from the company, thus creating a potential for conflict of interest. Kelly, then, first charged that Hastings allowed such a conflict to be created in violation of his own rules and then accused him of letting Cantoo escape from his farm leases when Cantoo found that he could not meet the rental fees. It is doubtful that many readers of the *Public Advertiser* could have followed the legal intricacies that both Kelly and the defenders of Hastings cited in their elaborate arguments presented in the several letters of June and July that made up the paper war. It is equally doubtful that they would have cared very much about the issue. Certainly, no other voices were raised in this brief summer debate, unlike Kelly's earlier campaign on the Quebec Bill. Although the issue soon disappeared from the pages of Woodfall's paper, Kelly's name remained before the public.

In its 16–18 July issue, the *Middlesex Journal* noted that Kelly attended the recent pastoral masquerade at Carlisle House, a social activity we know he enjoyed because of earlier reports in the *General Evening Post*.[13] Near the end of the summer, the first indication that Kelly was indeed pursuing his law career is given in a *Middlesex Journal* story of 3–5 September. We learn that Kelly had been hired by three London citizens accused of perpetrating a fraud upon a physician, Frederick Sherico, lately arrived from the West Indies. The three pretended, argued the prosecution, they were city officials who had to collect three guineas from Sherico for a ticket admitting him to Court and providing several other privileges. Thinking the men actual officials, Sherico complied and later discovered he had been duped.

Kelly had been retained to act in the three men's defense, which he did by arguing that technically the men did not insist upon the fee but merely said it was customary for them to be paid a gratuity for celebrating the arrival of foreigners. Kelly tried to prove that the men were guilty of telling a lie but not of fraud, the difference being, in Kelly's view, that the men did not demand the money as their right. Kelly lost his case, and his clients were bound over for prosecution. The *Middlesex Journal* story stated:

> Mr. Kelly now addressed himself to the auditors, saying, that some murmurs and hisses of disapprobation had made it necessary for him to say, that the practice of his honourable clients he utterly abhorred; but that in his official capacity, it became necessary for him to urge every possible argument in extenuation of the offence alledged against them. This entirely reconciled those persons who had judged of him as a gentleman, when he was acting in the character of an advocate.

This incident is revealing, and it is revealing apart from the possibility that the *Middlesex Journal* was ironically reinforcing the image the radicals had of Kelly as a hireling who would argue any position in print or in court if he were paid to do so. Kelly had always been accused of vanity but here seems justified in explaining a situation that allowed him his self-respect. The distinction between what he might have thought as a private citizen and how he had to act as an advocate on behalf of his clients is not only sound but also one that again demonstrates the distinction between a professional and a private person. The professional must do things in his capacity that are not necessarily self-expressive. The professional lawyer is thus like the professional writer. This telling anecdote dramatizes Kelly's rhetorical knowledge that one wishing to earn his living through arguing for others cannot afford to express his own beliefs. The lawyer, like the popular writer, is audience centered.

That he stoops to explain this to yet another audience, those attending the sessions at Bow Street, suggests that something of the self-conscious young journalist who wrote journalism about journalism was still alive in Hugh Kelly the barrister. It also suggests that his explanation represented a kind of professionalism not everyone in the society either understood or accepted. In his study of the professions in early-eighteenth-century England, Geoffrey Holmes discusses the problems involved in forming professional identity (1–18). He describes the development of what he terms "corporate self-awareness" (9) and mentions, among other manifestations, the distinctive dress within professions. But surely another form of self-awareness can be seen in the need Kelly obviously felt to explain his practices to the skeptical who observed his courtroom behavior. Holmes points to the increase of status among lawyers from the late seventeenth through the early eighteenth century, but that increase could only have been relative, and possibly part of Kelly's motive in this incident had something to do with the ambivalence some felt toward lawyers. Holmes also notes the importance of the services professionals provided their society (7–8), and what we observe in Kelly's statement to the court is Kelly explaining the very nature of a legal defense, a key element of the service barristers rendered.

The last of Kelly's cases that I have located was heard in the middle of October 1776. From the 17–19 number of the *London Evening Post,* we learn of Kelly's involvement in a forgery trial.[14] The accused, William Davis, a London merchant involved in marketing spices imported by the East India Co., was charged with forging warrants on another merchant. It appears from the testimony of other brokers and merchants that warrants were sometimes used as a substitute for money. Davis, it seems, had one of his new employees forge the signature of another merchant, Benjamin Barbaud, on the warrants with the intent to defraud another merchant, Samuel Drybutter, of the sum of forty-three pounds. As with many cases reported in the newspapers, the roles of the counsels involved were often so briefly noted that one cannot always know, for instance, what specific lines of interrogation were employed by any given barrister.

The Davis trial may have been Kelly's last case worthy of note: in less than four months, he would be dead. As already noted, some contemporaries felt that he had done reasonably well as a barrister and that, had he lived, he would have had increasing success.[15] William Cooke, a barrister himself, did not assess Kelly's legal career quite so positively; and it is with his view that I begin my evaluation of Kelly's law career. Cooke felt that Kelly's income suffered considerably once he gave up his literary and journalistic pursuits for the law:

> Kelly from his Editorship, the Theatre, and holding in a variety of other respects "the pen of a ready writer," could make little less than one thousand pounds per year (at least in such years as he brought out a new play). Here was a kind of certainty for himself, his wife, and a family of five or six children, and this he altogether relin-

quished for a profession in which neither his natural inclination, his education, or even occasional studies, had fitted him. ("Hugh Kelly," Jan. 45–46)

Cooke further observes that Kelly was beginning his legal career in competition with younger men who had more time to achieve success than Kelly. Yet, says Cooke, Kelly entered his new profession with skills in language and speaking that in some ways compensated for what he lacked in the study of law itself. Forgetting that he had already said, erroneously, that Kelly only pursued the law after *The Man of Reason* failed, Cooke concludes his narrative of Kelly's legal fortunes by suggesting that, after a year or two of "unremitted attention" to the law, Kelly found that his income suffered by comparison to the sum he had earned as an author:

> Kelly's income from his profession the last year of his life has been computed by the late Mr. Akerman, who knew it almost to exactness, to be from two to three hundred pounds per year. This, with two hundred per year pension, which it is said he enjoyed, ought to have kept him out of debt particularly as his original habits could not lead him to any extravagance; but he had imprudently, a few years before, set out upon a certain scale of expence, on the accidental profits of some lucky hits, and vanity (though necessity afterwards enjoined it) would not let him retrench. (46)

Cooke's analysis provides the only contemporary estimate of Kelly's finances. I am inclined to trust it in the main even though some contradictions are apparent. That Cooke was a longtime friend of Kelly's and a dramatist, journalist, and barrister lends weight to his view. But what is to be made, for example, of his claim that Richard Akerman knew Kelly's income from the law "almost to exactness" and Akerman's general assessment of Kelly's income as between two and three hundred pounds? The figures, hardly specific, call into question the "exactness" of Akerman's knowledge. And there is some confusion in Cooke's account about how active a law career Kelly had from his admission to the bar in May 1773 until the failure of his last play in February 1776. He says that Kelly gave the law his full attention only after February 1776, and yet he also claims that Kelly had, prior to his stage failure, pursued law "for a year or two with unremitted attention."

It is hardly likely that Kelly pursued his legal career assiduously from the end of 1773, when he was still presumably involved in the Lord Boyne case, until the end of 1775. During this two-year period, after all, he brought to the stage two plays, *The Romance of an Hour* and *The Man of Reason,* and wrote the Numa letters on behalf of George III's colonial policies. Then, too, no newspaper accounts of his legal work appear during this two-year period. The absence of such reports does not mean Kelly had no legal clients during this term, but the lack of press attention coupled with his work in journalism and drama call into question Cooke's assertion that Kelly practiced law with "unremitted attention."

If Akerman's estimate of Kelly's income is correct—that he made between two hundred and three hundred pounds in his last year—then Kelly's career must be considered a modest success, assuming that his legal income in previous years was approximately the same as or lower than his income in 1776. This possibility seems likely because, as we have seen from his journalism on Warren Hastings, he could not have practiced law exclusively even in 1776. Compared to Arthur Murphy, Kelly appears to have made a reasonable amount of money, given his late entry into the field. Jesse Foot, Murphy's biographer, estimated his subject's total income from his law career, which began in 1762 and ended in 1787, at £10,744 (356–68).[16] Murphy evidently had one extraordinarily fine year—1773—when, Foot claims, he earned £3,863. If we accept Foot's figures and omit the singularly successful year of 1773, then Murphy's average income from his legal work was approximately two hundred seventy-five pounds. Comparing that to Akerman's estimate of between two hundred and three hundred pounds per year for Kelly, we can conclude that Kelly did fairly well. Murphy, after all, was a more experienced lawyer who had a formal education and who began his law practice more than a decade before Kelly. Somewhat ironically, the last year of Kelly's life saw a substantial reduction in London criminal case work. According to a report in the *Morning Chronicle* (9 Sept. 1776), few prisoners were to be tried in the September sessions, and the editor reasons that "the American disputes have taken off a great many idle fellows."

Given the importance of his legal practice during the last few years of Kelly's life, it is not surprising that a number of people in law should have become his acquaintances, if not his friends. That shift seems clear enough from an examination of the subscription list to his collected *Works* (1778). Among the dozen names of those connected to the law in some fashion are several fellow barristers: Serjeant James Adair, Serjeant Davy, Edward Bearcroft, and Sampson Wright are among the most interesting of these names. Serjeant Adair was a leading Wilkite and perhaps the most important radical lawyer in the City after Serjeant Glynn. Adair later became recorder of London (1779) and had a long career in Parliament before his death in 1798 (Valentine 1: 7–8).[17] Adair's name on the subscription list suggests perhaps that political opponents might be professional friends, or at the very least obtain the professional respect of colleagues. Davy was an active lawyer who practiced with Kelly at the Old Bailey: he was involved with him in the William Davis case of October 1776. Edward Bearcroft's name appears in the reports of trials throughout the early and middle 1770s: he often prosecuted libel cases for the king. Sampson Wright was doubtless well known to Kelly, as he was one of the three magistrates, along with Fielding and Addington, working at Bow Street in the Public Office during the 1770s.

Additional friends of Kelly's from the field of law not on the subscription list were John Day and Henry Howarth, who served as pallbearers at his funeral.

John Day, appointed advocate general for Bombay at three thousand pounds per year in November 1776, was one of Kelly's "truest friends in England," says O'Leary (154) who gives no explanation for his estimate. Because Day was an Irishman and also a friend of Goldsmith's, he and Kelly may have been old friends.[18] Henry Howarth, king's counsel, was a very active lawyer in the 1770s in both civil and criminal cases.[19] He had worked with Kelly in the recent Davis case and often was counsel for the prosecution in cases where Wilkites were being tried. He later became an MP.

I am not certain when Kelly first realized he was ill and began the futile treatments for the disease that ended his life. Cooke, as usual, provides the fullest picture of Kelly's last weeks and theorizes that Kelly's illness was brought on in part by the general decline in his prosperity, which in turn led to heavy drinking before bedtime to "recover that composure which his waking thoughts denied him" ("Hugh Kelly," Jan. 47). Cooke continues:

> The effects of this, a natural corpulency, and a sedentary life, early brought on by habits of business, induced an abscess in his side about the latter end of January 1777, which he rather neglected in the beginning, till becoming more painful, his physicians, amongst other things, advised the hot bath, as apprehensive of a mortification. As they were bringing him in a sedan from Newgate-street Bagnio after this operation, the writer of this account had the last nod from him, which he gave with his usual complacency and friendship, though he had evidently the hand of death on him at the time. Soon after he arrived at his house in Gough-square he became speechless, and next morning, on the 3rd day of February, he died, in the thirty-eighth year of his age.

Other contemporary reports are perfunctory and add nothing to Cooke's narrative. Of modern accounts, only O'Leary's adds much of interest. William Watt, unsympathetic to the end, merely sums up Kelly's last weeks by noting that he "seems to have paid as little heed to his own homilies on intemperance as he did to his sermons on vanity" (315), while Lacroix follows Cooke's account without adding anything new (1: 66–68). O'Leary suggests that the illness was "tuberculosis of the bone" (187) but does not explain the grounds for his diagnosis. The fullest obituaries were carried by those newspapers that late in his career Kelly had been extensively involved with, Mary Say's *Gazetteer* and *General Evening Post*. The *Gazetteer* on 5 February printed the longest death notice; and on the following day, the *General Evening Post* reprinted it in full:

> The late Mr. Kelly was one of the few that nature honoured with her confidence and tuition. The ability of his works prove his divine preceptor, and the greatness of his knowledge the sacred library from whence he had it. He could shine in the dazzling illu-

mination of genius among men of parts, or be the affable, unassuming companion with those of inferior merit. Nor was he less informed of the duties of a man, than tenacious of the performance. He displayed the highest polish of urbanity, without the least tincture of the sycophant, and had just arrived at the full meridian of genius when death eclipsed the lustre. His enemies (if he had any) cannot call this the mere effusion of friendship, or a tribute of false adulation, when they consider that Mr. Kelly, by the strength of his abilities, worked through the numberless obstacles that stood between an obscure beginning, and the respectable rank in which he died. He has left an amiable wife, four lovely children, and a long list of respectable and sorrowing friends.

Several other papers contained brief notices of Kelly's death with a sentence or two about his career. The *Morning Chronicle,* no doubt in part due to its theater interest, published on 5 February an extensive tribute, noting that Kelly "is deservedly lamented by a numerous circle of acquaintance" and then summarizing his success story, which placed him in intimacy with men whose "friendship did him the highest credit. As an author, although his abilities did not entitle him to rank in the first class, they certainly enabled him to figure with some *eclat.*" William Woodfall, if it was Woodfall, admits that Kelly's plays have "different degrees of merit" but claims that his writing deserved support because Kelly labored for the "best of purposes—the support of an affectionate wife and a numerous offspring." Recall that Kelly in his defense against Horne Tooke in the preface to *A Word to the Wise* himself used the image of the faithful family man as a means of gaining audience sympathy. In another piece on Kelly (6 Feb.), the *Chronicle* looked once again at Kelly's career and focused on his relationship with Goldsmith, defending Kelly's sincere feelings that prompted his attendance at Goldsmith's funeral and commenting that Kelly had "at the time expressed to many of his friends his earnest wish to have a trifling difference made up."

Kelly's own funeral, occurring on Saturday, 8 February, was summarized in the *General Evening Post* for 8–11 February on its front page. Kelly was buried at

> St. Dunstan's Church, in the same vault in which his children were buried. Mr. Kelly's corpse was attended to the grave by eight of his friends, viz Counsellors Day and Howarth, William Strahan, Esq. and his son, William Addington, Esq., Mr. Glover, Mr. Shepherd, and Mr. William Murphy.

The mention of Kelly's children prompts the observation that we know little of Kelly's family and of their life together, for there are no extant records of Kelly's private life. One can piece together, as I have demonstrated, some sense of his life of writing, his public career, but the letters, diaries, and other personal writings that might illuminate his private family life simply do not exist. Contemporary accounts of his death are ambiguous and sometimes contradictory about his family. One newspaper reported that two of Kelly's children had died of the same infection that killed him, and Cooke later reported that his entire family, save one son, had died before 1794 ("Hugh Kelly," Jan. 47). John Taylor, however, in his *Records of My Life*, reported meeting Mrs. Kelly "after more than forty years' separation" in his editor's office at the *Sun*, where he "found her a very pleasant and intelligent old lady, her mental powers unimpaired, and full of anecdotes of Dr. Johnson, Goldsmith, Garrick and the chief literary characters of her day" (1: 101).

Jean-Michel Lacroix has assiduously searched public records to estimate the number of Kelly's children and to trace Kelly's family after his death. He has found that few definite records exist; there are no baptismal records of infants that are clearly Kelly's in his parish church, St. Dunstan-in-the-West.[20] Examining burial records, he concluded that there were possibly, but not certainly, five daughters and two sons, at least five of whom were buried in the North Vault of St. Dunstan's Church: Clementina, born 2 September 1771 and died sometime after 1791; Caroline, born 3 December 1772 and buried 8 April 1773; Matilda, born 15 February 1774 and interred 30 January 1777; Emma, born 23 February 1776 and buried 20 December 1779; and Benedicta, born 23 March 1777 and interred 8 September 1778. Lacroix's Guildhall Library researches also yielded the names of John Kelly, buried at the age of one or two years in St. Dunstan's on 10 August 1763; Catherine Bickerstaff Kelly, buried 28 April 1768; and Michael Ladbroke Kelly, interred 31 December 1769. He notes Frederick Kelly, buried 30 November 1771 and Eliza Kelly, buried 25 March 1779 as possible Kelly children. Certainly Lacroix's suggestion that all of the children with the Kelly surname buried in the North Vault of Hugh Kelly's church would seem to be his is sound. Of the other, earlier children, Catherine Bickerstaff Kelly was named after Hugh Kelly's good friend and fellow dramatist Isaac Bickerstaff, and Frederick Calvert Kelly, who died on 26 November 1771 and who was identified in the *London Evening Post* (27 Nov. 1771) as Hugh Kelly's second son, was surely named after Lord Baltimore, Frederick Calvert, whose relationship to Hugh I discussed earlier. And surely Lacroix is correct in assuming Michael Ladbroke Kelly was named after Kelly's patron, Sir Robert Ladbroke. Because several newspaper reports of Kelly's own death mentioned that two of his children died of the same fever that took him, it is probable that Matilda Kelly was Hugh's child. Finally, given that these reports noted that Mrs. Kelly was expecting another child at the time of Hugh's death, that child was probably Benedicta, born on 23 March 1777, only a few weeks after her father's death.

Lacroix has traced the history of another of Kelly's sons, Bartlett Hugh Kelly, whose career as an officer in the army of Bengal ended with his death on 19 October 1818. He had reached the rank of lieutenant colonel and left a married daughter, who eventually returned to England with her husband; she was probably the one whom Mrs. Kelly referred to in her conversation with John Taylor when she related that she did not get along well with her granddaughter and her husband (1: 101). Records of other surviving children and their offspring, however, do not seem to have survived. Several sources, Taylor among them, indicate that Mrs. Kelly married a second time and that her husband, a Capt. Davis, reportedly could not "bear to hear her first husband had been a staymaker" (101).

My researches have been mainly aimed at illuminating Kelly's public life; and I can add little to the Kelly family story after Hugh's death. In William Strahan's ledger for 1 January 1780, an entry shows Strahan owed Mrs. Kelly seventeen pounds, two shillings, two pence but provides no further details. Strahan had been one of Kelly's pallbearers and was perhaps helping his friend's family.[21] A few years later, Capt. Edward Thompson, Kelly's 1778 editor, noted in his diary under 16 December 1784 that he was "bleeding to hear of the apostasy of human nature," the cause of which remark was the detection of Mrs. Kelly in an act of theft. According to Thompson, Mrs. Kelly had been befriended by a Mr. Halet and his family of Berwick Street with whom she had been living, "cherished and protected." For her misdeed, she was turned out of the family.[22]

Thompson printed in the *General Evening Post* (13–15 Feb. 1777) the following elegy:

> Sacred to the Memory of Hugh Kelly, Esq.
> Who, tho' he could not boast the noblest ancestry,
> Yet his conduct taught to shew, that birth
>> Was not the highest honour:
> For complacency of temper, benignity of heart,
> Rectitude of manners, and liberality of sentiment,
>> (of all which he was eminently posses'd)
>> Placed him in a sphere, second to none,
>> However descended, however distinguished,
> In apprehension lively, in judgement profound,
> Entertaining by the former, by the latter instructing.
> So amiable his temper, so benevolent his mind,
>> That he never made an enemy:
> Admired whilst living, lamented now dead.
> From his presence he never turned the suppliant unheard;
> Nor did the mendicant's cry reach his ears in vain:
>> For he diffused his kindness to all alike.
>> As he was courted when alive
>> So at his obsequies myriads of his friends
>> Manifested their friendship, by paying the last tribute,
>> And pouring forth their sorrow, to the memory
>> Of so good, so just, and noble a character.

Epilogue: Kelly in His Own Time

As noted earlier, one of the many anecdotes about Kelly to have survived concerns his first attendance on Samuel Johnson. After listening to Johnson for a while, Kelly rose to depart, remarking to his host that a longer stay might be inconvenient, whereupon Johnson curtly replied, "Not in the least, sir, I had forgotten that you were in the room" (Boswell, *Life* 2: 48).[1] Indeed, in his time, as well as in our histories of his time, Kelly has seemed to be a man who was not there, an absent presence. Kelly would have appreciated the irony that the anecdote, often told to his disadvantage, has become a source of our knowledge of him and of the ways in which his own time perceived him or failed to perceive him. As a journalist who himself retailed anecdotes, sometimes even inventing them and at other times, as with his stories about Israel Pottinger, his old publisher, relating them to listening friends like William Cooke, Kelly would have understood. The question I want to consider before concluding this study is why Kelly was, despite his considerable achievements, either neglected or scorned in his own time.

Accounting for the scorn, insofar as it is politically motivated, is not difficult. In attempting to defend King George III and his ministers to London middle-class, mercantile audiences who felt that the government opposed their interests both at home and abroad, Kelly incurred their anger. These feelings perhaps intensified among those Patriots who presumably resented his "outsider" status as an Irishman from humble beginnings. Because Kelly was often assailed for his Irishness and accused of being a Catholic when he was an Anglican, I believe the sort of ultranationalist feeling that Newman considers one of the key ingredients in later eighteenth-century English radicalism was behind some of the antagonism the City radicals felt for Kelly (177–79). Whatever else the Wilkites were, they were not tolerant of ethnic and religious differences.

Certainly, class consciousness and status anxiety enter the picture as well. Kelly's class and status disadvantages are reflected in the persistent reminders by his enemies that he was once a staymaker, and his humble origins are noted even in the friendly biographical accounts that have come down to us. The writer in the *Hibernian Magazine* for March 1777, after discussing Kelly's being the son of a Dublin tavern keeper, went on to remark that Kelly "never attempted to conceal any part of his history, and with conscious merit soared above the little prejudices of a mean parentage, or a confined education" (175). But after reviewing the evidence, one must conclude that soar as he might, Kelly could never escape such prejudices, particularly those related to his lack of education. These prejudices were found in and were a part of the world of writing he inhabited. Johnson once said, after being asked to talk with Kelly, "I never desire to converse with a man who has written more than he has read." I would not deny Johnson's assertion, for Kelly probably did write more than he read. As one of the most prolific journalists of his era, as a man who relied on his pen for his livelihood, he had no time to do otherwise, a situation not lost on others besides Johnson. William Cooke, who wrote biographies of Hugh Kelly and Charles Macklin and who edited a book of Samuel Foote's conversation, noted the following incident in *The Table Talk and Bon Mots of Samuel Foote:*

> Hugh Kelly, the author of *False Delicacy* dining with Foote one day, in passing through the drawing room looked into the library, and being surprised at the smallness of the collection (the principal part of his books being at North End), rather triumphantly exclaimed, "Why, hey-day! I have got almost as many books myself!" "Perhaps you may, sir," said the other, "but consider, you read all that you write." (*Foote* 45)

Kelly's lack of formal learning clearly put him at a disadvantage with his fellow writers of the 1760s and 1770s. In discussing Kelly's legal career, I noted Colman's and Murphy's university educations; one can add Kenrick, Cumberland, Johnson, and Goldsmith to the list of Kelly's peers who had more formal learning. Cooke, generally sympathetic to Kelly, was not above implying that Kelly in leaving the life of an author for that of a barrister might be at risk, for he had to "exchange light congenial reading for the severer studies of the law" ("Hugh Kelly," Jan. 45). Moreover, the anonymous enemies who spouted against Kelly in the London press would often point to errors in grammar or diction as a way of triumphing over a man whose arguments they had difficulty refuting.

Some felt Kelly a vain man. I noted the incident of the silver spurs that Kelly placed on his sideboard with his plate for all to see: Johnson rightly viewed this display as vanity. Wilkites thought Kelly vain for daring to address his Patriot betters in rhetorical combat. They attacked his presumption for writing a public letter in the spring of 1770 to one of their heroes, Lord Mayor William Beckford. And it did not help when Kelly pointed out in Johnsonian fashion, as he did more than once, that the radicals wished to level only down to themselves. Nor was Kelly reluctant to make himself an object of social interest, for in more than one instance in newspapers for which he wrote, he is the likely author of reports on his own social life, noting himself and his wife in attendance at a ball or a masquerade.

Yet if Kelly did possess some vanity, it may well have been understandable, for, as I have demonstrated, Kelly's life may be viewed as a sentimental tale of "rising," where the hero, in spite of a poor family and a lack of education, overcomes obstacles to achieve middle-class respectability. That thematic is embedded as well in a number of contemporary biographical summations of Kelly's life.

Kelly's not being much regarded in his own time has inevitably contributed to his obscurity in ours. Nor has he helped himself: surely one of the reasons Kelly is not better known today is because he left no easily followed paper trail. There are no letters to speak of, no treasure trove of archival materials, and no journals or diaries. Ironically, the man who lived by his public writings nearly vanished because he left few private ones.

Yet now that the full extent of his considerable achievement as a professional writer has been established, we may be willing to view Kelly more favorably than people in his own time did. We can admire the man who overcame ethnic and class prejudices. Aware of market forces, we can understand Kelly's commercial orientation: we can see his mixing of comic modes to appeal to his audiences and his securing of a livelihood by writing propaganda for the government as moves necessary for survival. We are, in sum, more likely than his fellows were to appreciate the professional skill that allowed Hugh Kelly to succeed in the new commodity marketplace of writing.

And succeed Kelly did. His magazine and newspaper work placed him at the center of London cultural life; he became a force in the political and theater conflicts of the 1760s and 1770s. His political journalism situated him in the midst of the nation's key issues, both domestic and foreign, while his dramatic journalism allied him with the most powerful theater person of the age, David Garrick. The sentimentalism he espoused in his plays and in his popular "Babler" essay series meant that Kelly played a serious role in sentimentalism's effort to reform British manners, specifically the hard male culture. In sum, Kelly was an important voice in his own time, one whose contributions to the nation's cultural conversations deserve to be better known.

Notes

Bibliography

Index

Notes

1. Beginnings

1. For these contemporary accounts, see Thompson, "Life"; Cooke, "Hugh Kelly," Nov.–Jan.; J. Taylor; and "Memoirs," *Town and Country* 85–86.

2. Walpole produced two important works employing the anecdote, *Royal and Noble Authors* (1758) and *Anecdotes of Painting in England* (1762–71); Seward published his *Anecdotes of Some Distinguished Persons* in 1795; *Almon's Anecdotes* came out in 1797; while *Percy's Anecdotes* did not appear until 1821–23. Thrale published her *Anecdotes of the Late Samuel Johnson* in 1786. John Nichols's seventeen volumes, *Literary Anecdotes* and *Illustrations of the Literary History of the Eighteenth Century,* came out over a number of years beginning in 1812; most volumes were published by 1817 except for the last, which did not appear until 1858. See Hart, Introduction xxvi, for further details on the Nichols material.

3. All biographers mention the staymaker apprenticeship. See J. Taylor 1: 95–96; and Cooke, "Hugh Kelly," Nov. 337.

4. Although W. W. Watt was primarily interested in Kelly's plays, he provides a good bit of biographical information. O'Leary and Lacroix consulted a number of public records, efforts that I did not duplicate once I found their work was to be trusted. For the records consulted by O'Leary, see esp. 1–10; additional sources are noted throughout his chap. 1, 1–55. For Lacroix's records, see his chap. 1 (1: 77–113).

5. See O'Leary (315–16) for a complete list of the biographical accounts of Kelly's peers in which he is mentioned.

6. Bateson's *Cambridge Bibliography of English Literature* lists twenty-two magazines that began publishing from 1760 until the end of 1762. From the start of 1763 through the end of 1765, fourteen more publications began. That variety was important, especially in a magazine, is suggested by the criticism of the *Universal Visiter,* edited by Christopher Smart, in the *Critical Review* 1 (1756): 85–87. The reviewer criticizes it for having "less variety" than other magazines.

7. The occasional moral tale excepted, the typical length of a magazine piece in the 1760s was two to four pages.

8. Gans feels that popular culture fulfills the needs of the audience—it is used by such audiences for information, fantasy, and the like—while he sees high culture as essentially fulfilling the needs of its creators.

9. Plomer (201–2) notes a James Pottenger, or Pottinger, but not an Israel Pottinger.

10. George Robinson's *Lady's Magazine* of 1770 was the first magazine devoted primarily to women readers that endured for any time. Previously there had been, for instance, the *Lady's Curiosity* (1738), Eliza Haywood's *Female Spectator* (1744–46), and several variations on the "ladies' magazine" title, such as Jasper Goodwill's *Ladies Magazine* (18 Nov. 1749–10 Nov. 1753), but they were short-lived. Other periodicals, such as the successful *Ladies Diary* catered to women, but the *Diary* was an almanac, strictly speaking, even though it exhibited some features characteristic of magazines.

11. See Pat Rogers, chap. 6, "The Grub Street Myth." Rogers suggests that the Grub-Streeters of the early part of the century did not have a self-conscious self-perception (280), but I argue here and in chap. 2 that Kelly possessed such self-consciousness to a high degree.

12. See, for example, Johnson's 1756 essay "Reflections on the Present State of Literature" in the *Universal Visiter* (Bloom, *Samuel Johnson* 123–24).

13. That is, as Paul Fussell puts it, one was expected to "write badly" (17).

14. W. W. Watt calls the "Green Room" after Apr. 1763 "a mere calendar of plots and players" (19).

2. Newspaperman and Essayist: The *Gazetteer* and "The Babler"

1. The first poem, "Epistle from a Lady in the Country," also appeared in Kelly's *Court Magazine* for Aug. 1762 (578), and although the poem is not signed "H. K." as a number of Kelly's poetical pieces were, it appears in the poetry section of this number where all the other poems are either signed or were later reprinted in Kelly's *Works* (1778) by his editor, Edward Thompson. Thompson's selection of Kelly's poems followed no consistent pattern: sometimes he reprinted poems from the *Court* that were signed; sometimes he ignored other signed poems; and occasionally he reprinted poems from the *Court* that were not originally identified as Kelly's. "Epistle from a Lady" bears a close resemblance in theme, diction, and imagery not only to the third poem in the *Gazetteer* series, "Flavella to Beverley, An Epistle from the Country," but also to "Theodosia to Cornelia, An Epistle from the Country." And, as "Theodosia to Cornelia" appears in Kelly's *Works* (427–34), "Epistle from a Lady" is presumably Kelly's too. "Flavella to Beverley" itself was printed in the *Court* for July 1762 (530–31), as well as in the *Gazetteer* and, again like "Epistle from a Lady in the Country," appears in a context of three other poems, all of which are either signed by Kelly or are identified as his by Thompson. "Spatter's Rambles" came out in the Sept. number of the magazine (623–24) and was later reprinted by Thompson (Lacroix [1: 143] first located "Spatter's Rambles" in the *Gazetteer*). That this poem was printed first in the newspaper before appearing in the magazine suggests that

the *Gazetteer* was not simply reprinting random pieces of Kelly's that had first appeared in the *Court*. Indeed, the paper did not print much poetry at all, averaging about five poems per month from July through Sept.; and with few exceptions, Kelly's poems among them, the poems that were reprinted from their original sources were identified as such.

2. Kelly wrote in his final "Babler" (Sat., 5 June 1767) that he was about to publish a selection of the work in book form. That selection became *The Babler*, a two-volume edition published by John Newbery that contained 123 numbers. He also claimed to have "committed to the flames" a number of dull papers. I have arrived at the 220 figure by calculating the number of weeks between 12 Feb. 1763, when the series began, and 5 June 1767, when it ended.

3. For a listing of the many successors to the *Tatler* and *Spectator* in the essay-series tradition, see Woodruff 393–400.

4. For some American reprints of "Babler" essays, see Pitcher, "Some Emendations" 143–45.

5. One needs to keep in mind that Kelly had admitted in one of his *Court* pieces on journalism that he wrote letters to himself, the editor, and later many antagonists were to accuse him of this very practice.

6. W. W. Watt examines at length Kelly's debt to the *Spectator*, in particular (see 20–29).

7. Barker-Benfield suggests the importance of rural simplicity to sensibility's ideology; he locates this tendency to idealize the rural poor in fiction, but it occurs occasionally in drama as well (228–29). *Love in a Village* (1762) and *The Maid of the Mill* (1765; this last owing something to Samuel Richardson's *Pamela*) by Kelly's friend Isaac Bickerstaff (no connection to the Bickerstaff pseudonym used by Steele), are cases in point. In Kelly's own work the city-country polarity is not a major theme. R. F. Brissenden also discusses the relationship between rural idealism and sensibility (69–77).

8. See Carver, "Babler" 16. Larry Carver and I are in substantial agreement that Kelly aimed at a middle-class audience and not at the "Town."

9. L. Stone 217–24, discusses the difference between the old-style, arranged marriage and the more modern practice that Kelly supported—hardly surprising given his general sentimentalism—which urged parents to employ love, not merely their authority, to win a young woman's consent to a marriage.

10. I am indebted to Jacques Ellul's *Propaganda: The Formation of Men's Attitudes* for what I say about propaganda theory in this study, including the way(s) in which popular culture may be said to perform propaganda functions. One way in which propaganda and popular culture flatter their audiences is by being timely (see Ellul 43). O. B. Hardison also discusses the way in which professional rhetoricians, oriented toward the marketplace, design their products to court their audiences; their language is disguised flattery (137–39). Another commentator who stresses the connection between propaganda and popular culture is Todd Gitlin.

11. I am thinking of Davis's contention that the news-novel discourse brings the reader "closer to the events being described than earlier readers and auditors might have been" (L.J. Davis 66), as well as a "decreasing of the perceptual distance between reader and text" (67). With the news-novel discourse, there is an increase in temporal and spatial intimacy.

12. For a discussion of the male public culture of tavern and alehouse, see Barker-Benfield 38–51.

13. Kernan addresses at length the professional writer and how he was constructed by the demands of that culture; see esp. chap. 3, "Making a Writer's Role in a Print Culture."

14. Kernan (5–6) notes Johnson's attempt to maintain dignity for the professional writer even though he was at the mercy of the marketplace; yet Johnson was at other times keenly aware of the need for the professional writer to appeal to his audience, as is evidenced by his famous lines in his "Prologue Spoken at the Opening of the Theatre in Drury-Lane, 1747."

15. Purdon (1729–67) was an Irishman who may have met Kelly through Goldsmith, with whom he attended Trinity College. I do not know to what magazine Kelly refers, and the *Dictionary of National Biography* (47: 46) only associates Purdon with newspapers. He may have been a member, with Goldsmith and Kelly, of the Wednesday Club, for Goldsmith wrote Purdon's epitaph for the Club when he died on 27 Mar. 1767.

16. Robert Lloyd ran the *St. James's Magazine* from Sept. 1762 through June 1764 almost entirely on reader-contributed material. In the initial number, a section entitled "To the Reader" discusses the use a journal may make of its readers as writers. Lloyd may be said to have presided over a "vanity" press. Ellul argues that an organization's ability to influence its members and secure their loyalty depends upon their active participation in the life of the organization itself (see esp. 25–30, under "Orthopraxy"). I similarly maintain that a periodical that allows its members (readers) to participate by writing to it and in it has a better chance to secure reader loyalty than one that does not. Popular-culture productions are propagandistic insofar as they flatter their audiences' needs and fantasies.

17. The essay periodical seems to have been a great wellspring of the author's lament tradition, for in the series Kelly mentioned in his preface to *The Babler,* there are, if not laments for the journalist, at least analyses of the difficulties of employment. Space in this study does not permit a full discussion of the variations on this tradition, but a sampling may be found in the *Spectator* (nos. 124 and 442 for 23 July 1711 and 28 July 1712), the *Rambler* (no. 145 for 6 Aug. 1751) the *Adventurer* (nos. 35 and 115 for 6 Mar. and 11 Dec. 1753), the *World* (nos. 152 and 155 for 28 Nov. and 18 Dec. 1755), the *Connoisseur* (nos. 71, 96, 114, and 116 for June and 27 Nov. 1755, and for 1 and 15 Apr. 1756). Newspapers were also contributors to this self-reflexive discourse about their own authors, genres, and operations.

18. The more serious romantic self-construction of such writers as Thomas Chatterton and James Macpherson is discussed by Kernan 84–90.

19. For the literary and political implications of "independence," see Bertelsen, chap. 7, esp. 223.

20. Kernan (22) refers to the heroic qualities that Boswell endows Johnson with as a kind of gladiator of print.

3. Kelly in Transition: *Thespis* and *Memoirs of a Magdalen*

1. Price (126–33) notes the development after 1756 of more extensive theatrical criticism in periodicals than had appeared previously; he relies in part on Charles Harold Gray. Gray is useful, but his dating of critics' associations with periodicals cannot always be trusted: he is wrong in assuming that Kelly wrote the theatrical criticism for the *Public Ledger* in 1772. Price (6–42) cites "actor" poems in his discussion of acting. Earlier J. M. Beatty traced many of these poems and included Kelly's *Thespis* (see "Battle"). Robert Lloyd, Churchill's friend, wrote *The Actor* (1760), a poem perhaps most immediately central to *The Rosciad*. On this matter, see Bertelsen 75.

2. Beatty ("Battle" 458–61) suggests *The Rosciad* as the main element in the tradition, but surely the intertextuality of many titles points to Pope; see Bond. The original *Rosciad* may well have been Richard Rolt's: see Rizzo on this matter.

3. Bertelsen (220) discusses Churchill's insistence on literary independence in connection with the theme of independence in Churchill's work. O'Leary (45) suggests that Kelly too was aware of the "financial possibilities of another controversial cannonade of the theatre in the Churchillian manner," but he cites no evidence of this awareness.

4. Bertelsen (83) notes the Churchill–Garrick tie, and O'Leary (56) argues that Kelly's poem helped him too gain acquaintance with Garrick.

5. Bertelsen (75) suggests that Churchill attended the theater consistently for less than a full season before composing *The Rosciad* in 1761.

6. W. W. Watt calls *Thespis* a "stepping stone in the path of his rapid rise to prominence in the theatrical world" but says little more (chap. 3, 40–64).

7. Brownsmith was prompter at the Haymarket Theatre. All of these poems are discussed briefly by W. W. Watt (53–56) and by O'Leary (48–49). Neither Watt nor O'Leary concerns himself with the economic advantages of this small discourse explosion to Kelly's career.

8. O'Leary (50) feels that Kelly turned to the novel in the winter of 1766–67, but newspaper dates advertising its publication suggest an earlier start, even when one considers that publication dates given in the papers were often premature.

9. See Baker (94–95) and Foster (152–53), for traditional assessments. Baker said that Kelly wrote his novel "as the masculine rejoinder to *Clarissa*" (95).

10. For other valuable commentaries on Kelly's relation to sensibility, see Carver, Introduction; and Rawson.

11. Todd (117) calls such relationships "emotional tableaux" and feels that this friendship reduces familial importance. While the familial bonds are somewhat weakened in Kelly, I find the female relationships to be more rational and pragmatic than emotional, enabling the women to aid each other in necessary and specific ways.

12. Of the 123 "Babler" essays reprinted by John Newbery in *The Babler,* twenty-eight are on the interrelated subjects of courtship, marriage, and sexual morality.

13. Auerbach borrows the term *watchers* from a story by Sarah Orne Jewett.

14. For a full treatment of Hanway's life (1712–86), see Hutchins. A modern consideration of his role in the charity movement is found in J. S. Taylor. Hanway's first pamphlet, *Letter,* was dated 18 Feb., while the second pamphlet, *Plan,* was dated 7 June. The *Plan* too contains a short, introductory letter to Dingley.

15. See Saxe; and see especially Mahood, who deals only with the Glasgow institution of the nineteenth century.

16. Kelly's own *Court Magazine* reported on the Society's activities with some frequency in the mid-1760s. In the Feb. 1765 number, Kelly reports that the queen had agreed to become patroness of the Magdalen charity; while, oddly, on the same page (614), he noted that a William Mildmay was created a baronet. Coincidentally, a Robert Dingley was involved in Hanway's original proposal for the Magdalen charity. For the prior novel, see Blondel.

4. From Journalism to the Theater:
The *Public Ledger* and David Garrick

1. For a full discussion of the evidence of his start as *Ledger* editor, see Bataille, "Hugh Kelly, William Jackson."

2. William Owen, bookseller and publisher, was active from 1748 to 1793 in his shop near Temple Bar. What further association Kelly may have had with him is unknown.

3. O'Leary makes the claim that no other periodical seems to have republished "Babler" essays (29, note 64), and I have found no evidence to dispute it.

4. This amusing piece of what I take to be self-propaganda can be found in the *Ledger* for Wed., 3 July 1765; it appears in a letter signed, appropriately enough, "Gregory Grubb."

5. The Burney Collection contains approximately twenty numbers of the *Ledger* for the months of June–July 1766 but possesses no others until June 1771.

6. Charles Green Say's paper, the *Gazetteer,* had a similar column, and of course Kelly had worked for Say's paper.

7. Two letters from Kelly to Garrick concern the writing of *False Delicacy,* but they provide little information about Kelly's life and nothing at all about his ongoing journalism (Garrick Correspondence 24: nos. 17 and 19).

8. The *North Briton* ran from 10 May 1768 until 11 May 1771; after 11

May, it was incorporated into *Bingley's Journal* until 22 June, when it ceased to exist. *Bingley's Journal* (9 June 1770–85) was a weekly distributed throughout Great Britain.

9. Throughout the late 1760s and early 1770s, Bingley's editorial comments focused on the threat to the freedom of the press stemming from the ministerial attempt to prosecute newspaper publishers and printers for various libels. The number of such prosecutions between 1768 and 1776 involved at one time or another many of the important London printers.

10. The first extant letter from Kelly to Garrick in the Garrick Correspondence (24: no. 19) is dated—but not in Kelly's hand—24 Nov. 1767; but see O'Leary (57, note 124), who argues for a 24 Nov. 1766 date instead. Certainly the 24 Nov. 1767 date is in error, for the 27 June 1767 letter, no. 17, from Kelly to Garrick in Kelly's hand mentions a play already drafted and ready for Garrick's perusal. Thus no. 19 must have been written much earlier than no. 17.

11. The relationship between Kelly and Kenrick remains uncertain. Kelly knew Kenrick as early as Mar. 1765 when he and Kenrick dined with Richard Rolt (Percy Papers, BM ADD MS 32,336; I am indebted to Betty Rizzo for this reference), and Kenrick was to defend Kelly against those who felt that Kelly was too critical of Goldsmith's *She Stoops to Conquer* (Percy Papers, BM ADD MS 42,516), but their relationship was most likely an unstable one, especially after Kenrick's attack on Garrick and his hit at the Irish playwrights in his poem *Love in the Suds* (1772). Dampening any long-lasting friendship was Kenrick's tendency to write on behalf of the Patriots, as revealed in a letter to the *Public Advertiser* (30 Nov. 1773). Many details about Kenrick's life are in George Brewer's unpublished ms.

12. "Ferrula" makes a similar charge in *Bingley's Journal* (6 Oct. 1770).

13. The original title, as reported to Garrick by Kelly in his 27 June 1767 letter, was "Fortune with Eyes" (Garrick Correspondence 24: no. 17).

14. For a somewhat different version of this subject, see Bataille, "Kelly–Garrick."

15. The letter is in Kelly's hand and is dated by him 12 Sept. 1770 (Garrick Correspondence 24: no. 21).

16. For instance, the review of Bickerstaff's comic opera *The Maid of the Mill* in the Feb. 1765 issue of the *Court Magazine* was highly laudatory; at five pages it was one of the longest reviews published in the *Court* during its four-year run. *The Maid* was based on *Pamela,* and soon Kelly would publish his own imitation of Richardson, his *Memoirs of a Magdalen.*

17. For details of the conger that controlled the *Packet,* see Minutes of the Meetings.

18. Stone and Kahrl (340), quoting Robert Haig's study of the *Gazetteer,* note that the *Gazetteer's* contracts prohibited shareholders from owning interests in other papers. But clearly that contractual situation was unusual and did not prevent conflict of interest elsewhere. Kelly, while owning a share in the *Packet,* still

edited the *Ledger*. Henry Baldwin and Henry Sampson Woodfall were also involved in other papers.

19. The original letter from Kelly to Garrick is dated Oct. 1775, but the date is not in Kelly's hand and is probably incorrect. The letterhead states that it was written "Thursday morning," and the text of the letter itself says "last night." As Garrick first played in *The Chances* on Wed., 21 Apr. 1773, the letter was probably written on Thurs., 22 Apr. 1773, and not in Oct. 1775. No performance of *The Chances* in Oct. 1775 is noted by G. W. Stone in *The London Stage*, pt. 4.

20. Kelly, in telling Garrick he would send the notice to either the *Morning Chronicle* or the *Morning Post*, obviously knew his editors. William Woodfall of the *Chronicle* and Henry Bate of the *Post* were both important figures in the theater journalism of the 1770s.

21. Kelly wrote for the *General Evening Post* after leaving the *Ledger* early in 1772 and remained an important political journalist until very nearly the end of his life.

22. Addington, a London magistrate working out of Bow Street and later a playwright himself (*The Prince of Agra*, 1774), pretended to have written *The School for Wives* to protect it from being banned as *A Word to the Wise* had been in 1770.

23. In a letter dated 7 July 1773 found in the Garrick Correspondence (6: no. 145) addressed to Spranger Barry, Murphy claims that he has not written "one word of politics" since 1763 and expresses a desire to avoid all such writing. Murphy alludes to a conversation he had with Garrick during the summer of 1770 when "Roscius" (Garrick) tried to recruit him for political propaganda. Murphy says Garrick told him that Kelly was "only a flea-bite" to the Patriots, a description laughably understated, given the relentless attacks on Kelly by the Patriots.

5. *False Delicacy* and Its Reception

1. Mrs. Yates's fine performance in Kelly's only tragedy, *Clementina* (1771), enabled it to run nine nights.

2. Yet the writer Ferrula was to claim that Garrick did use his "theatrical pruning knife" to make *False Delicacy* ready for the stage (*Bingley's Journal* 6 Oct. 1770).

3. Kelly's letter is dated from the Middle Temple, 27 June 1767, in Kelly's hand.

4. See especially Cooke's "Hugh Kelly" and Thomas Davies's *Memoirs of the Life of David Garrick* (vol. 1, chap. 40).

5. For the sections that deal with Kelly and Goldsmith, see Forster, bk. 3, 271–72, and bk. 4, 212–14, 463; and Prior 2: 172–78.

6. Kelly had praised both women highly in *Thespis I*, and he later wrote his only afterpiece, *The Romance of an Hour* (1774), with Mrs. Abington in mind for the female lead.

7. There may have been some unrecorded provincial performances; one such is recorded by Boswell's friend William Temple at Newcastle on 19 Mar. 1768. See Boswell, *Boswell* 136. See also Hare 232–49. For these and all other citations to Kelly's plays as they appeared in Dublin theaters, I am indebted to Prof. John C. Greene; the Dublin dates for 1770 were as follows: 26 Feb., 5 Mar., 23 Mar., and 22 Dec.

8. A note dated 1787 in a copy of the fourth edition of 1768 found at the University of Texas says that the play was "acted at Blenheim, Oct. 25" and lists the presumably amateur cast.

9. As O'Leary (218) notes, Riccoboni translated *False Delicacy* and included it in her *Nouveau theatre anglais*. See Lacroix (2: 1188–89) for additional information about French translations; French translations are noted in Lacroix and in Rochedieu 175.

10. Both Sherbo and Bevis (*Laughing* 95) make essentially the same point about Kelly's plays; that is, they recognize his tendency to both embrace and parody a form. The difference between them and myself is that Sherbo and Bevis feel such a contradiction cannot work. I contend it works as long as the audience is not troubled by it.

11. Rawson provides a fine discussion of the complexities of both sensibility and delicacy.

12. For the context of Churchill's criticism of Davies, see Bertelsen 75, esp. note 26.

13. O'Leary may have been repeating what Cooke said, who also cites £700. See Cooke, "Hugh Kelly," Jan. 43.

14. See Forster (bk. 3, 270–71) for the Macklin–Kelly anecdote. The Wednesday Club is shrouded in mystery. A journal of the Club's meetings that contained a number of anecdotes was supposedly kept by William Ballantyne; his journal is mentioned by Forster (270), who used it as the basis for much of what he wrote about Kelly, Goldsmith, and the Wednesday Club that met in the mid-1760s. The journal may have been a part of the "Newbery Papers," whose subsequent disappearance has distressed a few scholars.

15. William Oxberry claims that Kelly read very "musically, though with little or no foundation in the science" (2: 206).

16. Goldsmith biographer Samuel Woods Jr. kindly shared his view of the Goldsmith–Kelly relationship with me: Woods felt that Garrick, for his own purposes, kept alive the tensions between the two men.

6. Confrontation with the Wilkites

1. Bingley began to publish what he called "Part II" of the *North Briton* on 10 May 1768; it ran until 11 May 1771. He published several additional political journals, but the most important of these later periodicals was his weekly newspaper, *Bingley's Journal*.

2. Part of my consideration of the *Elegy* and the pamphlet on Pitt follows O'Leary here; see 85–89.

3. For details of Pulteney's career, see Speck 221–23, 240–48; and Rudé, *Hanoverian London* 151–56. For Pulteney's relationship to George Colman the Elder, see Bertelsen 37, 196, 213; and Page 3–11. Barnard was a nominal Whig who allied the City with the Patriots and Tories against Walpole; see Rudé, *Hanoverian London* 149.

4. Colman was disappointed by Pulteney's will, which left his large estate to the management of his brother, Henry Pulteney, who disliked Colman (see Page 96–98). Colman, however, still continued to receive £900 per year from the estate.

5. For the full title, see O'Leary 87, note 196.

6. Cooke ("Hugh Kelly," Nov. 339) also mentions Chesterfield's approval. I have not seen this pamphlet.

7. Andrews places Kelly and Almon on Charles Green Say's *Gazetteer* at the same time (1: 220). Haig repeats Andrews's assertion that Kelly and Almon supplied material for the paper (70–71). But as Almon, who became a leading Wilkite bookseller (see D. Rogers) and Kelly were in opposite political camps, it is not surprising that no later association has been recorded, though both remained important journalists. Kelly is not mentioned in Almon's *Memoirs*.

8. For details of the trial of Lord Baltimore, see *Gentleman's Magazine* 38 (Apr. 1768): 180–87.

9. O'Leary favors the "Memoirs," *Town and Country,* account of the Baltimore incident and maintains that it was through such activities that Kelly "built up his personal contacts and his fortune" (90).

10. The extent of the relationship between Kelly and Frederick Calvert (1732–71) is difficult to determine. Kelly was not mentioned in Baltimore's will (*Lloyd's Evening Post* 16–18 Dec. 1771), but in Lord Baltimore's *Gaudia Poetica,* published privately in 1770, an "H. K." is addressed in the text, which is a poetical description of Holland. This "H. K." may have been Hugh Kelly. A copy of this rare work can be found in the Houghton Library, Harvard University. Kelly's attachment to Baltimore resulted in his naming his second son after Baltimore: Frederick Calvert Kelly died in Nov. 1771.

11. Lacroix notes this date but says little else about Kelly's legal career.

12. W. W. Watt (149–50), for instance, merely summarizes what can be found in Cooke, "Hugh Kelly," Nov.–Jan.

13. The event was noticed in the newspapers. See, for example, the *Morning Chronicle* for Mon., 24 May 1773. O'Leary (183) notes that the Register of Admissions for the Middle Temple also lists the date as 21 May.

14. See J. Brewer, esp. 22–23 and chap. 9, 163–85. On the slow erosion of the stability established under the first two Georges, see J. Brewer 3–8; also described in Speck, esp. chap. 6, "The Making of the English Ruling Class." My notions about the interconnections of politics, theater, and journalism that un-

dermined this stability have been influenced by J. Brewer and by Bertelsen. Recent studies have shed further light on these interconnections: although dealing with different time periods than I deal with, both Backscheider and Baer, at least in part, investigate the complicated relationships between theater, theatrical popular culture, politics, and propaganda in London culture.

15. See Bertelsen, chap. 7, esp. 227–28, where he links the action of Charles Churchill's poem *Gotham* with Wilkite political theater and the carnivalesque. In his chap. 7, "Independence," Bertelsen demonstrates the ramifications that the key political terms *dependence* and *independence* had for the City radicals in the 1760s. Dependence in both politics and literature was of course associated with detested patronage.

16. In Rudé's view, martyrs are exactly what the Wilkites were given by this government violence. Ellul (29–30) argues that the committed partisan can only be constructed through action calling for him or her to endure hardships and self-sacrifice.

17. However, J. Brewer argues in *Party Ideology* and elsewhere that the press was the single most important factor in "obtaining any degree of national political consciousness . . . and in providing political grievance with a common focus" (16).

18. No discussion of Wilkes and the Wilkites mentions Kelly; he has vanished from the twentieth-century political historian's investigation of the Wilkite years to 1775; and yet, as I demonstrate, Kelly was a staunch adversary of the London radicals for nearly a decade.

19. In general, I agree with J. Brewer as he describes the use of propaganda and popular culture by the Patriots. However, he does not present a theory of propaganda; I have tried to do that by employing Ellul.

20. Bertelsen's illuminating study, like J. Brewer's, does not present a theoretical assessment of propaganda.

21. The radical *Middlesex Journal* first appeared on 4 Apr. 1769. It had a number of different printers and publishers in its early months, the first being Isaac Fell.

22. J. Brewer notes how Wilkes used the media to make propaganda for himself and discusses Wilkes's self-dramatizing propensity (163–66); but others, like Wheble, took advantage through print media of the heady combination of carnivalesque street theater and popular politics.

23. See Newman, especially the sections headed "Radical Ideology and Saxon Legitimacy" and "The Norman Yoke" (183–91), for Newman's interpretation of the cultural nationalism of Horne Tooke and friends.

24. The Patriots' hatred for all things Scottish owed much to their belief that Court party policy ultimately derived from the earl of Bute. Less noticed, however, was the anti-Irish prejudice found in the Wilkite press. Fueled in part by anti-Catholicism, this hostility increased when, in the Dec. 1768 parliamentary election for Middlesex, Irish chairmen were found to be working for the Court party as election bullies. As Linda Colley demonstrates, the Wilkite antipathy for

the Scots who took part in George III's government had complex roots. The hostility had much to do with the king's desire to integrate the Highlanders into mainstream political and economic life to secure their loyalty. Some Englishmen resented this move; and Wilkes himself, in Colley's view, went into opposition journalism primarily because he lost his fight to become governor of Quebec to James Murray, a Scot. See Colley 117–32.

25. This charge is unclear as Turner was a Court supporter; nor is it clear why Kelly would attack him, if in fact he did so.

26. This charge can be found in a letter signed "Sub Rosa."

27. Ladbroke in particular deserves notice because he was in essence Kelly's patron until he died in Nov. 1773. Sir Robert was a banker, a former lord mayor, the "Father of the City" (a title given to the senior alderman), and an MP for London. Proctor was a political rival of Wilkes's and a pro-Court MP candidate who in Dec. 1768 ran against Serjeant John Glynn in the election during which the Irish chairmen Lawrence Balfe and Edward McQuirk were involved in the riot that led to their being indicted for murder.

7. Friends, Enemies, and the Damnation of *A Word to the Wise*

1. I do not know when Kelly moved to Knight-Rider Street from the Middle Temple, where he had lived at least since the fall of 1766; but in an attack on Kelly in the *Public Advertiser* for 2 June 1770, the writer suggests that Kelly had not been long in the City, so perhaps his move occurred at the end of 1769 or early in 1770. He was living in Doctor's Commons by early Apr. 1770.

2. For a detailed look at the politics of the City Council during the Wilkite years, see Rudé, *Wilkes* 149–51, and *Paris* 47–49.

3. William Beckford, wealthy MP for London and a leading anti-Wilkite radical before his death in June 1770 while lord mayor, would be attacked by Kelly later in the spring.

4. Sir Robert's London home was at St. Peter's Hill, Doctor's Commons; his country seat was located at Mt. Maskall in Kent. In 1771, the Wilkite *London Evening Post* of 31 Aug.–3 Sept. 1771 would accuse him of seeking a peerage and would mock his humble origins. There is a brief notice of him in Valentine 2: 517.

5. It is in the 4–6 Nov. number where we learn that Ladbroke left a son, four daughters, and an estate estimated at £200,000.

6. Baldwin and Kelly exchanged testy notes over Kelly's offer to review Garrick's *Chances* in 1773. Kelly told Baldwin that, were he capable of literary prostitution, then perhaps they would still be working together (Garrick Correspondence 24: no. 36).

7. Thomas Becket was Garrick's "personal bookseller-publisher-agent" by 1760, according to Stone and Kahrl 171.

8. This was probably John Harris, chief assistant to Thomas Evans; Evans would print the *Packet* in 1771.

9. That it was a week later is what the evidence seems to suggest; however, the date is unclear in the manuscript.

10. In his "Numa" letter of 7 Sept. 1775, Kelly refers to his journalistic efforts on behalf of Lord North and tells Garrick that his "friends" should appreciate his productivity (Garrick Correspondence 24: no. 26).

11. He was fined on 17 Dec. 1776.

12. The attack on Woodfall by Northcote came in the *Public Advertiser* (17 Oct. 1775). William Bingley also ran for public office in Apr. 1772; he attempted to win election to the post of clerk to the commissioners of the land tax but, like Woodfall, he lost.

13. For the details of Strahan's holdings, see Strahan, Papers. For his political stance in Parliament, see Valentine 2: 832–33.

14. Valentine (2: 924) claims that Whitefoord was a writer of "witty political squibs critical of the North ministry," but he was more anti-Patriot than he was anti-North, judging from his private papers. His correspondence reveals his antipathy for the radicals (see Whitefoord Papers). The names under which he wrote are listed in the *Monthly Review* for July 1813 and include "Papirius," "Cursor," "Ship News Extraordinary," and "Errors of the Press."

15. Scott, according to the *Public Advertiser* (21 Nov. 1775), also wrote under the names "Cinna" and "the State Tinker." He published under this last name alongside Kelly (as Numa) in the *Public Advertiser* during 1775, although not nearly as often as Kelly did.

16. Curiously, Woodfall says that he does not want to use the *Packet* to counter Johnson's attacks on the Scots, fearing that Johnson will find out that Macpherson is a *Packet* shareholder. Instead, he suggests that Whitefoord write to the *Morning Chronicle*, his brother's paper. See Whitefoord Papers.

17. Some sense of the increase in propaganda of all kinds in the late 1760s and early 1770s can be gleaned from Henry Sampson Woodfall's account book for the *Public Advertiser* in 1765: he was printing from 1,950 to 2,050 copies of his paper each day; but by Dec. 1771, he was printing 3,200–3,300 copies. Surely some of this increase in circulation had to do with the intense propaganda wars in the press that accompanied the Patriots' opposition from 1768 until the mid-1770s. See Woodfall. Theater politics interested William Woodfall as much as, if not more than, normal politics; in the *Morning Chronicle* (18 Dec. 1776), he calls his paper a "professedly theatrical paper."

18. In an editorial for 3–6 Aug. 1771, the Wilkite *London Evening Post* claimed that the *Middlesex Journal* was "chiefly written, and entirely managed by Mr. Horne."

19. Griffin published Goldsmith's *Essays* in 1765, *The Good Natur'd Man* in 1768, and *The Deserted Village* in 1770.

20. The years it appeared at Bath are 1772, 1773, 1778, 1782, 1783, 1786, 1789, 1790, 1796, 1797, 1801, and 1802. See Hare 233–49.

21. These performances occurred at the New Theatre on 1 and 8 Jan. 1779 and 23 Mar. 1781, and at the Theatre Belfast on 21 Apr. 1783. Clark (318) notes these same Belfast productions.

22. Auburn suggests that Dormer's "sexual rapacity" is his most believable trait (15–16), but I believe he is uncomfortable in his rakedom; he refers to himself more than once as a sentimental rake. *Self-conscious* and *guilt-ridden* are more apt terms to describe Capt. Dormer

23. Barker-Benfield (52–53) specifically discusses a shift toward the consumption of goods rather than tobacco and drink.

24. *Honor* is discussed on 85–86 and 288–89; the term does not yet mean "goodness of character" for Capt. Dormer but is still tied to rank.

25. Barker-Benfield (esp. 85–88) notes the new traits, such as reputation, needed by those in the new business-consumer culture.

26. Barker-Benfield (80–81) discusses the causes of the suppression of forms of private violence, such as dueling, by the state.

27. For examples of the anti-dueling theme in Kelly's didactic journalism, see the *Court Magazine* (Apr. 1764 and Oct. 1766) and "The Babler" (nos. 29 and 74). In "Babler" no. 23, Kelly attacks both toasting and dueling, arguing, as Sir George Hastings does, that the former often causes the latter.

28. The discussion of public sites of male culture, their interrelationships, and their changing functions can be found in Barker-Benfield 88–91.

8. Politics after *A Word to the Wise* and the Staging of *Clementina*

1. Thomas Harley was an important friend of Kelly's: Harley, according to Cooke, obtained some portion of Kelly's pension for his widow ("Hugh Kelly," Jan. 47). A Court party MP and alderman, Harley was an inveterate anti-Patriot. He had been lord mayor in 1768.

2. The cost of the government's propaganda effort was an abiding concern for the *Middlesex Journal*: in its 2–4 Apr. 1776 number, it attacked the ministerial writers' pensions, naming Samuel Johnson, John Shebbeare, and Sir John Dalrymple, who were said to receive £600, £400, and £700, respectively; and when it recorded the death of David Hume in its 3–5 Sept. 1776 issue, it reported a rumor that the government paid Dr. James Beattie £200 to refute Hume's skepticism. When the *Public Advertiser* noted Hume's death, it satirically suggested a contest be held to see which of the other ministerial writers should obtain Hume's pension. Kelly was mentioned as one of the contestants.

3. In Jan. 1770, Johnson published *The False Alarm*, in which he argued that the House of Commons had the right to bar Wilkes.

4. Langford (521) notes that Beckford's Remonstrance had by implication

compared George III's behavior to James II's and feels that the Patriot stance verged on the republican, even the revolutionary.

5. Kelly may be alluding to such peers as James Caulfeild, Lord Charlemont; and Hervey Redmond, Lord Mountmorres, who, according to Sutherland (51, note 45), were pro-Patriot Irish peers. For the anti-Irish feeling during the Wilkite years, see Langford 453–57; and Rudé, *Wilkes* 13–14, 60–61.

6. The instances of publishers and printers who were brought to trial, often for libel, during the Wilkite years are too many to enumerate, but a thorough narrative can be found in Rea, esp. chaps. 10–12. Ironically, Woodfall's *Public Advertiser* (1774–75) became the vehicle for Kelly's greatest propaganda effort, the Numa letters in defense of the ministry's American policies.

7. Bankes supported the ministry consistently. See Rudé, *Wilkes* 151.

8. This issue of the *Middlesex Journal* also reports one of the legal troubles facing Patriot publishers during the second Wilkite period of 1768–75: the former publisher of the *Middlesex Journal*, Isaac Fell, was reported imprisoned for libeling Lord Irnham, Simon Luttrell.

9. Grey Cooper was the undersecretary of the treasury; loyal to North until North's fall in 1782, Cooper could estimate Kelly's propaganda talents because he himself had written pamphlets in the mid-1760s in favor of the Rockingham ministry. See Valentine 1: 202.

10. And Garrick's biographers say so little about his private relationship with Kelly that no help in deciding the matter can be found in that quarter.

11. Tooke was a leading City radical; after he broke with Wilkes, the *Middlesex Journal,* a paper in which Tooke had some influence (Rea [204] claims Horne attempted to "direct the conduct of John Wheble of the *M[iddlesex] J[ournal]*"), consistently attacked Wilkes. Anyone reading the pages of the *Journal* after the Wilkes–Tooke split will realize the degree to which the paper had become anti-Wilkes while still maintaining a general radical outlook. During a clash between Wilkes and John Sawbridge in the fall of 1770, Tooke took Sawbridge's side; and later, in Feb. 1771, Tooke allied himself with another anti-Wilkes Patriot, James Townsend.

12. The papers of the day also printed the American clergyman story.

13. See Brissenden's chap. 4, "Virtue in Distress: The Emergence of a Theme," esp. 83–85.

14. Hawkesworth's review is perhaps the severest.

15. Prof. John Greene's unpublished research shows that the play was performed in Dublin on 19 and 29 Apr. 1771 and on 2 May and 3 June 1771; performances were at the Crow-Street Theatre. Another Dublin appearance occurred on 27 Mar. 1776. Theatre Belfast saw productions on 19 Nov. 1773 and 6 Feb. 1774 and on 27 Mar. 1776. The Lishburn and Cork productions are noted in Clark 318.

16. According to Forster (bk. 4, 119), these four editions of *False Delicacy* ran to ten thousand copies altogether.

17. The normal price was £150 (Collins 267). If we compare *Clementina* with Johnson's *Irene*, which also ran but nine nights, the sum of £400 seems reasonable. Johnson earned £195 for his three nights plus £100 for the copyright (Price 155); Kelly received £200 for his copyright alone (Cooke, "Hugh Kelly," Jan. 1794, 44).

9. Politics before and after *Clementina* and Departure from the *Public Ledger*

1. Serjeant is a title applied to the highest rank of barrister.

2. Who among those men associated with the production of the *London Evening Post* was responsible for its avid support of Wilkes is uncertain. John Miller was the *Post*'s registered publisher, but John Almon reported the parliamentary debates in its pages, and Almon was Wilkes's man. Deborah Rogers (9) points out that the degree of Almon's involvement in the *Post* is unclear, although he claimed to be an owner of the paper.

3. In its 14–16 May 1771 issue, the Wilkite *London Evening Post* castigated the Constitutional Society for breaking with the SSBR and for failing to support Wilkes above all others.

4. After 1766, no extant numbers of the *Ledger* exist until 1771; and because only twenty-eight issues are available from 24 June 1771 through 26 Dec. 1772, it is difficult to trace themes in the paper, revealing why we must rely on the radical papers to learn even the little we do about Kelly's John Hampden.

5. Indeed Newman (182) says that Wilkes had been warned by Horne Tooke about the former's cultivation of French ton.

6. For the problem in identifying the *Ledger*'s editors, see Bataille, "Hugh Kelly, William Jackson." Who had ultimate control of the *Ledger* in the early 1770s is unclear. Aspinall (227–28) lists Francis Newbery as the publisher until 1774, when Henry Randall is named as Newbery's successor. William Faden had been the paper's printer at least since 1765.

7. The *St. James's Chronicle* (18–20 May 1769) and the *Middlesex Journal* for the same date report these events, although the *Journal* credits the *Chronicle* as its source.

8. Bleackley's chronology must be faulty here, for Allen was not arrested until mid-May.

9. The speech Allen delivered to the Common Council as reported in the *London Evening Post* for 8–10 Oct. 1771 is a case in point. He spoke too long, implied the paper, and delivered Wilkite sentiments to an audience of Courtiers who were basking in the victory of their lord mayor candidate, William Nash.

10. Additional evidence that Kelly left the *Ledger* in the winter of 1772 and began to work for the *General Evening Post* is contained in the *Middlesex Journal* for 24–27 Oct. 1772. A letter writer states that Kelly had left the *Ledger* and "now writes for the *General Evening Post*" and claims that Kelly was forced to leave

because he attacked the *Ledger* in the *Post;* but because even his enemies never made this charge, I assume that if Kelly did attack his old paper he did so well after his departure from it. Under William Jackson, the *Ledger*'s editor after Kelly, the paper became radical.

11. The Bickerstaff scandal had to do with Isaac Bickerstaff's homosexuality, the discovery of which forced him to flee to the continent in May 1772. Kenrick then published in late June a poem, *Love in the Suds,* suggesting that Garrick had had a sexual relationship with Bickerstaff. This scandal created its own paper war during the Kelly–Allen conflict. See Tasch 221–43.

12. Ladbroke's family affairs are noted in the 9–12 May issue, and Mrs. Kelly's masquerade costume—she was dressed as a "Lady Abbess"—was noted in the 7–9 May number.

13. For Kelly and the *Packet,* as discussed in chap. 7, see "Minutes of the Meeting." The *Packet*'s conger included (in addition to Kelly) Lockyer Davis, Thomas Becket, Thomas Lowndes, and Richard Baldwin, but the group agreed to offer shares to Charles Say, William Strahan Jr., and Henry Sampson Woodfall. The *General Evening Post* was under the control of Kelly's old employer from his days on the *Gazetteer,* Charles Green Say.

14. For a defense of Garrick against newspaper attacks see the 18–20 June 1772 *General Evening Post,* but the paper did not touch the Garrick–Bickerstaff–Kenrick scandal. Bickerstaff and Kelly had been friendly; Bickerstaff was instrumental in bringing Kelly and Garrick together prior to *False Delicacy.* The only comment the paper made about Bickerstaff appeared in its 12–14 May 1772 issue where appeared a covert note on Bickerstaff's acknowledgment of guilt; his actual name is not mentioned, however.

15. See Foucault, *Discipline,* esp. "Hierarchal Observation" 170–77. See also Popkin (132–36), who notes that in prerevolutionary eighteenth-century French society, even more than in England, the newspaper gave "private members of civil society the raw material for critical judgments of their rulers" (136).

16. Townsend, the leader of the Shelburne faction in the City, had been allied with Horne Tooke since late 1770. See Rudé, *Wilkes* 161–65.

17. Goldsmiths' Hall was often the location of meetings of the City Courtiers; as a banker, Sir Robert Ladbroke, Kelly's friend and patron, belonged to the Goldsmiths' Co.

10. The *General Evening Post,* Kelly as Barrister, and *The School for Wives*

1. At the beginning of 1773, Kelly probably had no more than three living children: Bartlett Hugh, Clementina, and Caroline, and Caroline would die in early Apr. Frederick Calvert Kelly had died in Nov. 1771.

2. The publishing history of the *General Evening Post* is complicated. In an advertisement inserted in the 28–30 Mar. 1771 issue, the publisher of the *Post*

asserted that the paper was printed by Mr. Edward Say up until his death, the paper remaining in the family. New orders for the paper, the advertisement continued, would be taken by Edward's son, Charles Say. The notice stated that the printer would be Roger Thompson, also printer of Charles Green Say's *Gazetteer*. This information was probably printed because Samuel Bladon was selling a version of the *General Evening Post* that the advertisement called "an impostor." Edward and Charles Green were brothers, and Kelly's association with the family was an old one: he had worked for Charles's *Gazetteer* in 1762.

3. He could see both Foote's and Murphy's productions during that summer, for the two playwrights had leased Drury Lane from Garrick. See Spector, *Arthur Murphy* 74.

4. Samuel Reddish played Arnolph in this tragedy by Dorothea Celisia; first produced at Drury Lane on 12 Jan. 1771, it ran nine nights.

5. This 1728 work by Sir John Vanbrugh and Colley Cibber was one of the century's most popular comedies.

6. Price's observation holds true not only for Kelly's *General Evening Post* but also for Woodfall's *Morning Chronicle,* as noted earlier.

7. Murphy offers this view in his "Advertisement" to the first edition of *Alzuma;* the date was 23 Feb. 1773. In this connection, see Spector, *Arthur Murphy* 153–54.

8. That Murphy may have resented Kelly is Dunbar's opinion (186), but he gives no substantial evidence that the Kelly–Murphy relationship was unfriendly.

9. Dunbar (107–21) blames Colman and his ambitious friends for some of the hostility directed at Murphy because Colman's friends were said to want him to replace Murphy as resident dramatist at Drury Lane. Bertelsen (84–90, 188–89) also discusses Murphy's conflicts with the Nonsense Club but emphasizes Murphy's political journalism rather than theater jealousies for the troubles his plays suffered at the hands of Colman and friends.

10. Besides, sentimentalism was alive and well, if one judges from the periodical industry. On 1 Apr. 1773, *The Sentimental Magazine* was successfully launched, suggesting that the mode was still very popular with the common reader.

11. The usual number of columns in the London newspaper of the late 1760s and early 1770s was four; each column had roughly one hundred twenty lines, and each line, conservatively estimated, contained eight to ten words. A single-column review, such as Kelly's on *She Stoops to Conquer,* would run approximately one thousand words.

12. In "Babler" no. 70, Kelly attacks the Restoration dramatists for their immorality and defends the didacticism of present dramatists. In no. 85, he argues that even modern songs ought to be instructive, as well as entertaining.

13. Kelly makes a similar comparison in *The School for Wives* when Miss Walsingham compares a stage-set carpenter's talent to a comic poet's.

14. In Goldsmith, *Collected Works* (209), the editor, Arthur Friedman, notes that the "essay has frequently been described as an attempt to prepare the town for *She Stoops to Conquer.*"

15. Hume argues that "genteel" comedy is not a useful distinction when discussing serious comedy because the category in turn can be broken down into satiric, reform, and exemplary ("Multifarious Forms" 18–20).

16. Tasch (106–9) discusses the problems Bickerstaff's play encountered. Ironically, *The English Merchant* opened at Drury Lane the same night (21 Feb. 1767) that *Love in the City* did, but it was very flattering to merchants.

17. Prof. B. H. Davis, in a letter to me, suggests that Hawkins's opinion of Kelly's legal success need not be considered authoritative.

18. See a study of this case in Wright 90–91.

19. The *General Evening Post,* in its 4–6 Nov. 1773 issue, provided a synopsis of Ladbroke's will and in its next number a report on his funeral.

20. W. W. Watt (241) quotes a letter by Walpole giving his opinion that Garrick has the "chief hand in it." The letter is in Walpole 6: 29.

21. Testimony to the drawing power of the play even in 1800 can be found in G. W. Stone (pt. 5): for its 4 June 1800 production at Drury Lane, *School* earned £420; during the same week, the *Clandestine Marriage* earned £127 and the *School for Scandal* £213.

22. O'Keeffe says that the new scene that featured Torrington calling the bailiffs "Danzig traders" was not printed in the Dublin edition of the play with which the Cork audience was familiar (1: 234–35). See also W. W. Watt 268.

23. For the Dublin theater rivalry involving Dawson and Ryder, see Stockwell 135–42.

24. The Library Company of Philadelphia houses a copy of a sixth edition (Philadelphia: Reprinted and sold by John Dunlap, 1774).

25. But the title was changed to *The East Indian,* according to Seilhamer (2: 242–43) to take advantage of the popularity of Cumberland's *West Indian* (1771).

26. As noted earlier in this chap., similar language in praise of the set designer was employed in Kelly's review of Goldsmith's *She Stoops to Conquer.*

27. It is also possible to explain Kelly's practice by recalling that, as Richard Ohmann points out, ideology tends toward contradiction; see Ohmann 106–15.

28. Bevis does not cite a particular passage in Sherbo that he says makes this claim, but he may be referring to his impression of Sherbo's entire chap. 4, "Eschewal of Humor and the Bawdy," where he takes up the question of humor in the sentimental play; see Sherbo 72–99.

11. The Aftermath of *The School for Wives* and *The Romance of an Hour*

1. As noted earlier, a comparison of the manuscript with the printed version of each of Kelly's plays shows that the sentimental elements were not always prevalent in the printed version. With both *A Word to the Wise* and *The Romance of an Hour,* not only is the printed version shorter than the copy submitted to the licenser, but each is also no more sentimental than the performed version.

2. The letter reminds one of the incident in a Cork theater, as reported by O'Keeffe (1: 234–35), where the audience held the players strictly accountable to the printed version of *The School for Wives* with which they were familiar.

3. The *Middlesex Journal* was published by William Griffin in 1774; whether he was also the editor is not known, but the paper maintained its traditional hostility toward Kelly.

4. The complaint about Wilkes's lack of enthusiastic resistance to the Quebec Bill came in the *Middlesex Journal* for 23–25 June 1774.

5. For the conflict, see Sainsbury (56), who explains that the trouble was rooted in Franklin's role in exposing how the unsympathetic attitude of the British government was due to British officials in Massachusetts. Wedderburn attacked Franklin for his role, and the matter received press attention in the late winter and early spring of 1774. For his thorough discussion of the Wilkite perception of the Quebec Bill, I am indebted to Sainsbury 58–62. Newman (208) observes that radicals considered this bill a "sinister expression of anti-national influence" in George III's government.

6. Modern scholarship has tended to side with Kelly: Keith Perry (77) calls the bill a "statesman-like measure in its grant of legislative power, of free exercise of the Roman Catholic religion, and in its recognition of Quebec's separate civil law tradition"; while James E. Bradley (18) interprets the bill as "a sensible attempt to provide good government."

7. See W. W. Watt (288), who feels that Colman's attack was in part motivated by Kelly's denouncing in his epilogue the French borrowings of his peers.

8. It appeared at Kilkenny (24 June and 17 July 1776) and at Waterford (22 Oct. 1787; see Clark 318); it was given at Edinburgh at least twice between 1786 and 1788. (The Library Company of Philadelphia has the prompter's copy from these Edinburgh performances.) In 1792, a new edition of the play came out in Edinburgh. Henderson is probably John Henderson.

9. W. W. Watt (290) suggests that "[p]robably by analogy with Cumberland's greatest success, it masqueraded at the performance as *The East Indian: or, The Romance of an Hour.*"

10. Lewes, who appeared as Capt. Savage in *The School for Wives* (1776–77), was one of the few actors to subscribe to Thompson's edition of Kelly's *Works* in 1778. His sixteen-year career at Covent Garden ended with the 1782–83 season. See Highfill, Burnim, and Langhans 9: 269–76.

11. Omai was used by a number of satirists of the 1770s to attack British corruption, as Sambrook notes (194).

12. Foote's *Nabob* had dominated the stage in the summer of 1772; it was a timely thrust at the immense fortunes made in India. Indian affairs had been a prominent part of the news since the investigation of Robert Clive in the spring of 1771 (see Trefman 203–4) and continued to be important in the middle years of the decade. Kelly was to become involved in the attempt to discredit Warren Hastings, the governor general of the East India Co. in 1776.

13. As noted in chap. 7, as late as 1775, Mrs. Abington was fearful of playing in *The Sultan* (which appeared on 12 Dec.) because of a rumor that Kelly was its author; see Little and Kahrl 3: 1052, no. 3.

14. This allotment suggests that Kelly maintained some connection to the *General Evening Post*. When, if ever, he ceased to work for this paper I have not been able to discover.

15. The first Junius letter was published by Henry Sampson Woodfall on 21 Jan. 1769.

16. Seven of the Numa letters were published on seven consecutive Sats., from 7 Jan. through 18 Feb. 1775.

17. Northcote is not mentioned in Valentine; nor is he mentioned in Baylen and Gossman. He is mentioned, however, in Robert Watt's *Bibliotheca Britannica* 2: 710. Northcote's letters clearly indicate his radicalism.

12. The Final Year: *The Man of Reason,* Law Career, and Fatal Illness

1. See also Boaden 2: 102. Little and Kahrl (3: 104, note 2) date this letter 7 Sept. 1775, a date I accept for reasons previously stated.

2. See also Boaden 2: 103. The original is fully dated in Garrick's hand.

3. In the Larpent Collection, it is entitled "The Reasonable Lover." All of my references to the play are to *The Man of Reason* in Kelly, *Plays*.

4. This letter is dated in Kelly's hand. See also Boaden 2: 103.

5. The review in the *Middlesex Journal* for 8–10 Feb. 1776 is identical to that in the *Public Advertiser* for 10 Feb. Both complain, "[T]he story of this piece is so very complex and intricate, that it will be a matter of some difficulty to make it intelligible." The *Morning Chronicle* reviewer states: "To attempt to give the outline of the story with any sort of precision is out of our power, for we honestly confess we did not ourselves perfectly comprehend it."

6. Since the office of chamberlain is essentially that of city treasurer, bonds of surety were needed; the Ladbroke firm provided £15,000 for this purpose, as reported in the *London Evening Post* (22–24 Feb. 1776).

7. John Newbery had founded the *Public Ledger* in 1760; he and then his son, Francis, also sold the famous medicine Dr. James's Powders. John had also been part of the conger that published the collected edition *The Babler* in 1767.

8. Two other plays relevant to the antijournalism mode are *The Man of Business* (Colman, 1774) and *The Bankrupt* (Foote, 1773). In Colman's piece, one character, Tropick, confesses that he has been corrupted by reading too much gossip in the papers and too readily believes the worst of people. In the dedication, Colman berates newspapers for abusing the liberty of the press, observing that such abuse is a proper "object of comedy." Foote opened the 1776 season with *The Bankrupt* because, according to Trefman, he had been attacked by William Jackson's *Public Ledger;* Foote could obtain some revenge as his play satirized the "scandalmongers of the press" (see Trefman 249).

9. Ironically, Kelly's friend Thomas King played the journalist in both of Colman's plays.

10. Dunbar (265) suggests that the Catcall story came from Murphy's journalism in the *Gray's-Inn Journal*.

11. O'Leary discovered this letter; see O'Leary 152.

12. See Riddy 45. A similar view is expressed in Turnbull (98–100), although Turnbull is more sympathetic to North, who had to placate the king and his party.

13. Located in Soho Square, Carlisle House was occupied in the 1760s and early 1770s by Theresa Cornelys, a singer and courtesan who provided rooms for dancing, cards, operatic music, and masquerades. Declared a bankrupt in 1772, Mrs. Cornelys lost her property, but masquerades continued to be held there until 1783 (see Weinreb and Hibbert 121–22). As noted earlier, several times during his work for the *General Evening Post* Kelly reported his and his wife's attendance at masquerades: see, for example, the issues for 7–9 May 1772 and 18–20 Feb. 1773.

14. The case was also covered by the *Morning Chronicle* of 19 Oct. 1776.

15. Modern students of Kelly say next to nothing about his legal career. O'Leary (183) repeats Cooke's "Hugh Kelly" and claims to have found nothing in the sessions books of Middlesex County and Old Bailey housed in the Middlesex County Record Office. As usual, most of my new information has been gleaned from the newspapers.

16. Dunbar (252) appears to accept Foot's statistics.

17. In the Adair Papers in the British Library are letters indicating a friendship between Adair and Sir Nash Grose, another Kelly acquaintance who also subscribed to the 1778 edition of Kelly's *Works*.

18. See Forster (bk. 4, 463) for Day's attendance at Goldsmith's funeral.

19. A king's counsel or a queen's counsel is a senior barrister.

20. St. Dunstan's Church was located on Fleet Street; its churchyard contained a number of stationers shops. Lacroix discusses his search of public records concerning Kelly and possible Kelly family members (1: 69–73).

21. The nature of the Kelly–Strahan relationship itself remains unclear. In Cochrane, *Dr. Johnson's Printer*, a study about Strahan, there is no mention of Kelly. In a personal letter to me, Cochrane said he had found nothing concerning the friendship between the two. There were connections besides the political tie; both knew Johnson and were heavily involved in London journalism. Kelly worked for Charlotte Lennox on the *Lady's Museum*, and her husband worked for a time in Strahan's printing shop.

22. For details, see Thompson, Diary (1783–84). Thompson's handwriting is not clear here, so I cannot be certain about the name "Halet," which could be "Hales." At any rate, I cannot find either name associated elsewhere with Hugh Kelly.

Epilogue: Kelly in His Own Time

1. O'Leary notes that other biographers, mainly of Goldsmith, have repeated this anecdote with "mischievous delight" (80).

Bibliography

Works by Hugh Kelly

Drama

Clementina. London: Dilly, 1771.
False Delicacy. London: Baldwin, 1768.
The Man of Reason. Kelly, *Plays.* 1–130.
"The Reasonable Lover" Larpent Collection, Ms 401. Henry E. Huntington Library, San Marino, CA.
The Romance of an Hour. Larpent Collection Ms 401. Henry E. Huntington Library, San Marino, CA.
The Romance of an Hour. London: Kearsly, 1774.
The School for Wives. London: Becket, 1774.
A Word to the Wise. London: n.p., 1770.

Prose

The Babler. 2 vols. London: Newbery, 1767.
Memoirs of a Magdalen: or, The History of Louisa Mildmay. 2 vols. London: Griffen, 1767.
A Vindication of the Conduct of the Late Great C——. London: Bladon, 1766. (Apologia for Pitt.)

Separately Published Poems

An Elegy to the Memory of the Right Honourable William, Late Earl of Bath. London: Nicoll, 1765.
Thespis: or, A Critical Examination into the Merits of All the Principal Performers Belonging to Covent-Garden Theatre. Book the second. London: Kearsly, 1767.
Thespis: or, A Critical Examination into the Merits of All the Principal Performers Belonging to Drury-Lane Theatre. London: Kearsly, 1766.

Journalism

Newspapers
Gazetteer. From Aug. 1762.
General Evening Post. 1772–?.
Owen's Weekly Chronicle. Feb. 1763–June 1767.
Public Ledger. 1765–72.
Royal Chronicle. Jan.–Mar. 1762.

Bibliography

Magazines
Court Magazine. Sept. 1761–Nov. 1765.
Court Miscellany. July 1765–late 1766?.
Gentlemen's Journal. Nov. 1768.
Lady's Museum. Mar. 1760–Jan. 1761.

Collections of Primary Works

The Babler. London: Harrison, 1786.Vol. 6 of *Harrison's British Classicks.* 8 vols. 1785–87.
The Plays of Hugh Kelly. Ed. Larry Carver. New York: Garland, 1980.
Works of Hugh Kelly. 1778. Ed. Edward Thompson. London: Cadell; New York: Verlag, 1973.

Eighteenth-Century and Early-Nineteenth-Century Works

Adair Papers. British Library. BM ADD MSS 53,500, 53,811–14.
Addison, Joseph. *The Spectator.* 5 vols. Oxford: Clarendon, 1965. (Orig. pub. London, 1 Mar. 1711–20 Dec. 1714.)
Almon, John. *Memoirs of a Late Bookseller.* New York: Garland, 1974.
Baltimore, Lord [Frederick Calvert]. *Gaudia Poetica.* n.p., 1770.
———. Will of Frederick Calvert. *Lloyd's Evening Post.* 16–18 Dec. 1771.
Bickerstaff, Isaac. *Love in the City.* London, 1767.
Bingley's Journal. London, 1770–72.
Boaden, James. *The Private Correspondence of David Garrick.* 2 vols. London, 1831–32.
Boswell, James. *Boswell in Search of a Wife, 1766–1769.* Ed. Frank Brady and F. A. Pottle. New York: McGraw, 1956.
———. *The Life of Samuel Johnson, LL.D.* 1791. Ed. George Birkbeck Hill and L. F. Powell. 6 vols. Oxford: Clarendon, 1934–50.
Burney Collection. British Library, London.
Review of *Clementina,* by Hugh Kelly. *Critical Review* 31 (Apr. 1771): 311–12.
Review of *Clementina,* by Hugh Kelly. *Monthly Review* 44 (Mar. 1771): 252–54.
Colman, George. *The English Merchant.* London, 1767.
———. *The Man of Business.* Vol. 2 of *The Dramatic Work of George Colman.* 4 vols. London: Becket, 1777.
———. Review of *The Romance of an Hour,* by Hugh Kelly. *Monthly Review* 52 (Jan. 1775): 91.
Colman, George, the Elder. *Some Particulars of the Late George Colman, Esq.* n.p., 1795.
Cooke, William. "Hugh Kelly." *European Magazine* 24 (Nov. 1793): 337–40; 24 (Dec. 1793): 419–22; 25 (Jan. 1794): 42–48.
———. *Memoirs of Charles Macklin, Comedian.* London, 1804.
Davies, Thomas. *Memoirs of the Life of David Garrick.* 2 vols. London, 1779.
Dibdin, Charles. *The Professional Life of Mr. Dibdin, Written by Himself.* 4 vols. London, 1803.
Foot, Jesse. *The Life of Arthur Murphy.* London: Faulder, 1811.
Foote, Samuel. *Piety in Pattens.* 1773. Bogorad and Noyes 1–129.
———. *The Table Talk and Bon Mots of Samuel Foote.* Ed. William Cooke. London, 1889.
Garrick, David. Correspondence. Forster Collection. Victoria and Albert Museum.
———. Diary for 1767. Harvard Theatre Collection. Cambridge.
Gazetteer. London, 1760–62; 1766–69; 1775–77.
General Evening Post. London, 1770; 1772–77.

Bibliography

Genest, John. *Some Account of the English Stage*. 10 vols. Bath, 1832.

[Gentleman, Francis.] *The Dramatic Censor*. 2 vols. London, 1770.

[————]. *The Theatre: A Poetical Dissection*. London, 1771.

Gentleman's Magazine. London, 1767–68.

Hanway, Jonas. *Letter to Robert Dingley, Esq., Being a Proposal for the Relief and Employment of Friendless Girls and Repenting Prostitutes*. London: Dodsley, 1758.

————. *A Plan for Establishing a Charity-House, or Charity-Houses, for the Reception of Repenting Prostitutes*. London, 1758. (Introductory letter to Robert Dingley dated 7 June 1758.)

Hawkins, Sir John. *Life of Johnson*. 2nd ed. London: Buckland, 1787.

Hibernian Magazine. Dublin, Mar. 1777: 174–75.

Hiffernan, Paul. *The Recantation and Confession of Doctor Kenrick, L.L.D.* London: Allen, 1772.

Johnson, Samuel. "Prologue Spoken at the Opening of the Theatre in Drury-Lane, 1747." Vol. 6 of *The Yale Edition of the Works of Samuel Johnson*. New Haven: Yale UP, 1964. 87–90.

————. "Rambler No. 208." *The Rambler*. Ed. W. J. Bate and Albrecht B. Strauss. Vol. 5 of *The Yale Edition of the Works of Samuel Johnson*. New Haven: Yale UP, 1969. 315–20.

Juryman's Touchstone: or, A Refutation of Lord Mansfield's Lawless Opinions on Crown Libels. London: Almon, 1771.

The Larpent Ms Plays. Henry E. Huntington Library, San Marino, CA.

A Letter to the Jurors of Great Britain. London, 1771.

Lloyd's Evening Post. London, 1768–70.

London Chronicle. London, 1772.

London Evening Post. London, 1771–72; 1774–77.

London Magazine. London, 1767–77.

"Memoirs of the Late Hugh Kelly, Esq." *Town and Country Magazine* 9 Feb. 1777: 85–86.

"Memoirs of the Life and Writing of Hugh Kelly, Esq." *Westminster Magazine* 5 Mar. 1777: 115–18.

Middlesex Journal. London, 4 Apr. 1769–19 Dec. 1776.

Minutes of the Meetings of the Conger Controlling the *London Packet*. London, Jan. 1770. British Library. BM ADD MS 38,729, f. 165; 38,728, f. 130.

Monthly Review. July 1813.

Morning Chronicle. London, 1772–77.

Murphy, Arthur. *The Life of Garrick*. 1801. New York: Blom, 1969.

O'Keeffe, John. *Recollections of the Life of John O'Keeffe, Written by Himself*. 2 vols. London: Colburn, 1826.

Oxberry, William. *Dramatic Biography*. 2 vols. London, 1825–26.

Parliamentary Spy. London, 21 Nov. 1769–25 May 1770.

Peake, Richard B. *Memoirs of the Colman Family*. 2 vols. London: Bentley, 1841.

Percy Papers. British Library. BM ADD MS 32,336 and 42,516.

Piozzi, Hester Lynch [Thrale]. *Anecdotes of the Late Samuel Johnson*. 1786. Ed. S. C. Roberts. Westport, CT: Greenwood, 1971.

Prior, James. *The Life of Oliver Goldsmith*. 2 vols. London, 1837.

Public Advertiser. London, 1769–77.

Public Ledger. London, 1765–66; 1771–72.

Reed, Joseph. "Theatrical Duplicity." Unpublished ms. Harvard Theatre Collection. Cambridge.

Bibliography

Riccoboni, Jeanne Marie. *Nouveau theatre anglais.* Paris, 1768.
Review of *The Romance of an Hour,* by Hugh Kelly. *Critical Review* 38 (Dec. 1774): 480.
Sentimental Magazine. London, Apr. 1773.
Stephens, Alexander. *Memoirs of John Horne Tooke.* London, 1813.
Strahan, William. Ledgers. BM ADD MS 48,809, p. 32. The Ledgers and Other Business Papers of William Strahan. British Library. BM ADD MS 48,800–48,919.
———. Papers. BM ADD MSS 48,805, p. 8, and 48,809, p. 6. British Library. The Ledgers and Other Business Papers of William Strahan. British Library. BM ADD MS 48,800–48,919.
Taylor, John. *Records of My Life.* 2 vols. London, 1832.
Theatrical Monitor. London, 1767–68.
Thompson, Capt. Edward. Diary, 1783–84. British Library. BM ADD MS 46,120.
———. "The Life of the Author." *Works of Hugh Kelly.* London: Cadell, 1778. iii–xi.
Trial of John Almon, Bookseller. London, 1771.
Underwood, Thomas. *Poems.* Bath, 1768.
Review of the *Universal Visiter,* ed. Christopher Smart. *Critical Review* 1 (1756): 85–87.
Watt, Robert. *Bibliotheca Britannica.* 4 vols. Edinburgh: Constable, 1824.
Whitefoord Papers. British Library. BM ADD MS 36,593, f. 83.
Wilkinson, Tate. *The Wandering Patentee.* 4 vols. York: 1795.
Woodfall, Henry Sampson. Account Books for the *Public Advertiser.* British Library. BM ADD MS 38,169.

Modern Secondary Sources

Adburgham, Alison. *Women in Print.* London. Allen, 1972.
Allan, D. G. C. "Caleb Whitefoord: Merchant, Diplomat and Art Patron." *Connoisseur* 190 (1975): 194–99.
Andrews, Alexander. *The History of British Journalism.* 2 vols. 1859. New York: Haskell, 1968.
Aspinall, Arthur. "Statistical Accounts of the London Newspapers in the Eighteenth Century." *English Historical Review* 63 (1948): 201–32.
Auburn, Mark S. *Sheridan's Comedies: Their Contexts and Achievements.* Lincoln: U of Nebraska P, 1977.
Auerbach, Nina. *Communities of Women: An Idea in Fiction.* Cambridge: Harvard UP, 1978.
Backscheider, Paula. *Spectacular Politics: Theatrical Power and Mass Culture in Early Modern England.* Baltimore: Johns Hopkins UP, 1993.
Baer, Max. *Theatre and Disorder in Late Georgian London.* Oxford: Clarendon, 1992.
Baker, Ernest A. *The History of the English Novel.* Vol. 5. London: Witherby, 1934.
Barker-Benfield, G. J. *The Culture of Sensibility: Sex and Society in Eighteenth-Century Britain.* Chicago: U of Chicago P, 1992.
Basker, James G. *Tobias Smollett, Critic and Journalist.* Newark: U of Delaware P, 1988.
Bataille, Robert R. "Hugh Kelly, Goldsmith, and *The Court Miscellany* of 1765: Some Conjectures." *American Notes & Queries* 19 (1980): 38–40.
———. "Hugh Kelly's Journalism: Facts and Conjectures." *Journal of Newspaper and Periodical History* 1 (1985): 1–10.
———. "Hugh Kelly, William Jackson, and the Editorship of the *Public Ledger.*" *PBSA* 79 (1985): 523–27.
———. "The Kelly–Garrick Connection and the Politics of Theatre Journalism." *Restoration and 18th Century Theatre Research* 4 (Summer 1989): 39–48.

Bibliography

Bateson, Frederick W., ed. *The Cambridge Bibliography of English Literature*. Vol. 2. Cambridge, UK: Cambridge UP, 1969.

Baylen, Joseph O., and Norbert J. Gossman, eds. *Biographical Dictionary of Modern British Radicals*. Vol. 1. Atlantic Highlands, NJ: Humanities, 1979.

Beatty, J. M. "The Battle of the Players and Poets, 1761–1766." *MLN* 35 (1919): 449–62.

——. "Churchill's Influence on Minor Eighteenth Century Satirists." *PMLA* 42 (1927): 162–76.

Bender, John. *Imagining the Penitentiary: Fiction and the Architecture of Mind in Eighteenth-Century England*. Chicago: U of Chicago P, 1987.

Bernbaum, Ernest. *The Drama of Sensibility*. Boston, 1915.

Bertelsen, Lance. *The Nonsense Club: Literature and Popular Culture, 1749–1764*. Oxford: Clarendon, 1986.

Bevis, Richard. *English Drama: Restoration and Eighteenth Century*. New York: Longman, 1988.

——. *The Laughing Tradition: Stage Comedy in Garrick's Day*. London: Prior, 1981.

Bleackley, Horace. *Life of John Wilkes*. London: Lane, 1917.

Blondel, Madeleine. "A Minor Eighteenth-Century Novel Brought to Life: The Life and Adventures of a Reformed Magdalen (1763)." *Notes and Queries* ns 31 (Mar. 1984): 36–37.

Bloom, Edward A. "Joseph Addison: The Artist in the Mirror." *Educating the Audience: Addison, Steele, and Eighteenth-Century Culture*. Ed. Edward A. Bloom and Lillian D. Bloom. Los Angeles: Clark Library, 1984. 3–48.

——. *Samuel Johnson in Grub Street*. Providence: Brown UP, 1957.

Boas, Frederick. *An Introduction to Eighteenth Century Drama*. Oxford: Clarendon, 1968.

Bogorad, Samuel N., and Robert G. Noyes. *Samuel Foote's* Primitive Puppet Show Featuring Piety in Pattens: *A Critical Edition*. Theatre Survey 14 (Fall 1973): whole vol.

Bond, Richmond P. "-IAD: A Progeny of the *Dunciad*." *PMLA* 44 (1929): 1099–1105.

Bond, Richmond P., and Marjorie Bond. "The Minute Books of the *St. James Chronicle*." *SB* 28 (1975): 17–40.

Bradley, James E. *Popular Politics and the American Revolution in England*. Macon, GA: Mercer UP, 1986.

Brewer, George. "The Black Sheep of Grub Street: William Kenrick, LL.D." Unpublished ms. Boston Public Library.

Brewer, John. *Party Ideology and Popular Politics at the Accession of George III*. Cambridge, UK: Cambridge UP, 1976.

Brissenden, R. F. *Virtue in Distress: Studies in the Novel of Sentiment from Richardson to Sade*. New York: Barnes, 1974.

Carretta, Vincent. *The Snarling Muse: Verbal and Visual Political Satire from Pope to Churchill*. Philadelphia: U of Pennsylvania P, 1983.

Carver, Larry. "The Babler." Sullivan 15–18.

——. Introduction. Kelly, *Plays* ix–liv.

——. Textual Notes. Kelly, *Plays* lvii–lxx.

Chatten, Elizabeth N. *Samuel Foote*. Boston: Twayne, 1980.

Churchill, Charles. *The Poetical Works of Charles Churchill*. Ed. Douglas Grant. Oxford: Clarendon, 1956.

Clark, William Smith. *The Irish Stage in the Country Towns, 1720–1800*. Oxford: Clarendon, 1965.

Bibliography

Cochrane, James Aikman. *Dr. Johnson's Printer: The Life of William Strahan.* Cambridge: Harvard UP, 1964.

————. Letter to the author. 8 May 1983.

Colley, Linda. *Britons: Forging the Nation, 1707–1837.* New Haven: Yale UP, 1992.

Collins, Arthur Simons. *Authorship in the Days of Johnson.* London: Routledge, 1928.

Corvasce, Diane. "Hugh Kelly: A Critical Edition of *False Delicacy.*" Diss. New York U, 1976.

Crozier, Alice E. "An Old-Spelling Edition of *False Delicacy.*" Diss. Catholic U of America, 1974.

Davis, Bertram H. Letter to the author. 13 May 1983.

————. *A Proof of Eminence: The Life of Sir John Hawkins.* Bloomington: Indiana UP, 1973.

Davis, Lennard J. *Factual Fictions: The Origins of the English Novel.* New York: Columbia UP, 1983.

Dircks, Richard J. *Richard Cumberland.* Boston: Twayne, 1976.

Donohue, Joseph W., Jr. *Dramatic Character in the English Romantic Age.* Princeton: Princeton UP, 1970.

Dunbar, Howard Hunter. *The Dramatic Career of Arthur Murphy.* 1946. New York: Kraus, 1966.

Ellis, Frank H. *Sentimental Comedy: Theory and Practice.* Cambridge, UK: Cambridge UP, 1991.

Ellul, Jacques. *Propaganda: The Formation of Men's Attitudes.* New York: Vintage, 1973.

Fineman, Joel. "The History of the Anecdote." *The New Historicism.* Ed. H. Aram Veeser. New York: Routledge, 1989. 49–76.

Forster, John. *The Life and Times of Oliver Goldsmith.* 4 bks. London: Ward, 1890.

Foster, James R. *The History of the Pre-Romantic Novel in England.* 1949. New York: Kraus, 1966.

Foucault, Michel. *Discipline and Punish: The Birth of the Prison.* New York: Vintage, 1979.

————. *The History of Sexuality.* Vol. 1. New York: Vintage, 1980.

Fussell, Paul. *Samuel Johnson and the Life of Writing.* New York: Harcourt, 1971.

Gans, Herbert J. *Popular Culture and High Culture.* New York: Basic, 1974.

Gitlin, Todd. "Television Screens: Hegemony in Transition." *Cultural and Economic Production in Education.* Ed. Michael W. Apple. London: Routledge, 1982. 202–46.

Gold, Joel. "Mr. Serjeant Glynn: Radical Politics in the Courtroom." *Harvard Library Bulletin* 29 (1981): 197–209.

Goldsmith, Oliver. *The Collected Works of Oliver Goldsmith.* Ed. Arthur Friedman. 6 vols. Oxford: Clarendon, 1966.

Gottlieb, Jean S. *An Old-Spelling Edition of Hugh Kelly's Comedy* The School for Wives. New York: Garland, 1987.

Graham, Walter. *English Literary Periodicals.* New York: Wilson, 1930.

Gray, Charles Harold. *Theatre Criticism in London to 1795.* New York: Columbia UP, 1931.

Greenblatt, Stephen. *Marvelous Possessions: The Wonder of the New World.* Chicago: U of Chicago P, 1991.

Greene, John C. Computer disk supplied to the author. 22 Oct. 1993.

Haig, Robert. *The Gazetteer.* Carbondale: Southern Illinois UP, 1960.

Hardison, O. B. "The Rhetoric of Hitchcock's Thrillers." *Man and the Movies.* Ed. W. R. Robinson and George Garrett. Baton Rouge: Louisiana State UP, 1967. 137–39.

Hare, Arnold, ed. *Theatre Royal Bath: A Calendar of Performances at the Orchard Street, 1750–1805*. Bath: Kingsmead, 1977.

Hart, Edward L. Introduction. *Minor Lives: A Collection of Biographies by John Nichols*. By John Nichols. Cambridge: Harvard UP, 1971. xv–xxxii.

Highfill, Philip H., Jr., Kalman A. Burnim, and Edward A. Langhans, eds. *A Biographical Dictionary of Actors, Actresses, Musicians, Dancers, Managers, and Other Stage Personnel in London, 1660–1800*. 16 vols. Carbondale: Southern Illinois UP, 1973–93.

Holmes, Geoffrey. *Augustan England: Professions, State and Society, 1680–1730*. London: Allen, 1982.

Hughes, Leo. *The Drama's Patrons: A Study of the Eighteenth-Century London Audience*. Austin: U of Texas P, 1971.

Hume, Robert D. "English Drama and Theatre, 1660–1800: New Directions in Research." *Theatre Survey* 23–24 (Winter 1982–83): 71–100.

———. "Goldsmith and Sheridan and the Supposed Revolution of 'Laughing' Against 'Sentimental' Comedy." *Studies in Change and Revolution*. Ed. Paul J. Korshin. Menston, UK: Scolar, 1972. 237–76.

———. "The Multifarious Forms of Eighteenth-Century Comedy." *The Stage and Page: London's "Whole Show" in the Eighteenth-Century Theatre*. Ed. George Winchester Stone. Berkeley: U of California P, 1981. 3–32.

———. *The Rakish Stage: Studies in English Drama, 1660–1800*. Carbondale: Southern Illinois UP, 1980.

Hutchins, John Harold. *Jonas Hanway*. London: Soc. for the Propagation of Christian Knowledge, 1940.

Isles, Duncan. "The Lennox Collection." *Harvard Library Bulletin* 18 (1970): 317–44.

Jay, Martin. "In the Empire of the Gaze: Foucault and the Denigration of Vision in Twentieth-Century French Thought." *Foucault: A Critical Reader*. Ed. David Couzens Hoy. Oxford: Blackwell, 1986. 175–204.

Kaminski, Thomas. *The Early Career of Samuel Johnson*. Oxford: Oxford UP, 1987.

Kaufman, Paul. "The Reading of Plays in the Eighteenth Century." *BYNPL* 53 (1969): 562–80.

Kernan, Alvin. *Printing Technology, Letters, & Samuel Johnson*. Princeton: Princeton UP, 1987.

Ketcham, Michael G. *Transparent Design: Reading, Performance, and Form in the Spectator Papers*. Athens: U of Georgia P, 1985.

Knight, Charles A. "Bibliography and the Shape of Literary Periodicals in the Early Eighteenth Century." *Library* 8 (1986): 232–48.

———. "The Writer as Hero in Johnson's Periodical Essays." *PPL* 13 (1977): 238–50.

Lacroix, Jean-Michel. *L'oevre de Hugh Kelly (1739–1777): Contribution à l'étude du sentimentalisme anglais*. 2 vols. Diss. U de Paris. Talence: PU de Bordeaux, 1984.

Langford, Paul. *A Polite and Commercial People: England, 1727–1783*. Oxford: Clarendon, 1989.

Lemmings, David. *Gentlemen and Barristers: The Inns of Court and the English Bar, 1680–1730*. Oxford: Clarendon, 1990.

Little, David M., and George M. Kahrl, eds. *The Letters of David Garrick*. 3 vols. Cambridge: Harvard UP, 1963.

Lockwood, Thomas. *Post-Augustan Satire: Charles Churchill and Satirical Poetry, 1750–1800*. Seattle: U of Washington P, 1979.

Loftis, John. *Sheridan and the Drama of Georgian England*. Cambridge: Harvard UP, 1977.

Bibliography

Lynch, James J. *Box, Pit, and Gallery: Stage and Society in Johnson's London*. Berkeley: U of California P, 1953.

Macklin, Charles. *Four Comedies by Charles Macklin*. Ed. J. O. Bartley. Hamden, CT: Archon, 1968.

Mahood, Linda. *The Magdalenes: Prostitution in the Nineteenth Century*. London: Routledge, 1990.

Mayo, Robert. *The English Novel in the Magazines, 1740–1815*. Evanston, IL: Northwestern UP, 1962.

Mullan, John. *Sentiment and Sociability: The Language of Feeling in the Eighteenth Century*. Oxford: Clarendon, 1988.

Nettleton, George. *English Drama of the Restoration and the Eighteenth Century*. New York: Macmillan, 1914.

Newman, Gerald. *The Rise of English Nationalism: A Cultural History, 1740–1830*. New York: St. Martin's, 1987.

Nichols, John. *Minor Lives: A Collection of Biographies by John Nichols*. Ed. Edward L. Hart. Cambridge: Harvard UP, 1971.

Nicoll, Allardyce. *A History of Late Eighteenth-Century Drama, 1750–1800*. Cambridge, UK: Cambridge UP, 1927.

Odell, George C. D. *Annals of the New York Stage*. 15 vols. New York: Columbia UP, 1927–44.

Ohmann, Richard. "Doublespeak and Ideology in Ads." *American Media and Mass Culture*. Ed. Donald Lazere. Berkeley: U of California P, 1987. 106–15.

O'Leary, Thomas K. "Hugh Kelly: Contributions toward a Critical Biography." Diss. Fordham U, 1965.

Ong, Walter. "The Writer's Audience is Always a Fiction." *PMLA* 90 (1975): 9–21.

Page, Eugene R. *George Colman, the Elder*. 1935. New York: AMS, 1966.

Paulson, Ronald. *Satire and the Novel in Eighteenth-Century England*. New Haven: Yale UP, 1967.

Perry, Keith. *British Politics and the American Revolution*. British History in Perspective Ser. Basingstoke: Macmillan, 1990.

Pitcher, Edward. "Edward Thompson (d. 1786) and the *Westminster Magazine*." *PBSA* 79 (1985): 527–29.

———. "Some Emendations for Lyle B. Wright's *American Fiction, 1774–1850*." *PBSA* 74 (1980): 143–45.

Plomer, Henry Robert. *A Dictionary of the Booksellers and Printers Who Were at Work in England, Scotland and Ireland from 1726 to 1775*. Oxford: Oxford UP, 1968.

Pollock, T. C. *The Philadelphia Theatre in the Eighteenth Century*. 1933. Westport, CT: Greenwood, 1968.

Popkin, Jeremy D. *News and Politics in the Age of Revolution*. Ithaca: Cornell UP, 1989.

Price, Cecil. *Theatre in the Age of Garrick*. Oxford: Blackwell, 1973.

Rawson, Claude. "Notes on 'Delicacy.'" *Order from Confusion Sprung: Studies in Eighteenth-Century Literature from Swift to Cowper*. By Claude Rawson. London: Allen, 1985. 341–54.

Rea, Robert R. *The English Press in Politics, 1760–1774*. Lincoln: U of Nebraska P, 1963.

Riddy, John. "Warren Hastings: Scotland's Benefactor?" *The Impeachment of Warren Hastings*. Ed. Geoffrey Carnall and Colin Nicholson. Edinburgh: Edinburgh UP, 1989. 30–57.

Rizzo, Betty. "Richard Rolt and David Garrick: Rolt's 1750 *Rosciad,* Other Attributions, and his Drury Lane Career." *PBSA* 79 (1985): 489–98.

Rochedieu, Charles A. *A Bibliography of French Translations of English Works, 1700–1800.* Chicago: U of Chicago P, 1948.

Rogers, Deborah. *Bookseller as Rogue: John Almon and the Politics of Eighteenth-Century Publishing.* American University Studies; ser. 4, English Language and Literature 28. New York: Lang, 1986.

Rogers, Pat. *Grub Street: Studies in a Subculture.* London: Methuen, 1972.

Roscoe, Sydney. *John Newbery and His Successors, 1740–1814.* Wormley, Hertfordshire: Five Owls, 1973.

Rudé, George. *Hanoverian London, 1714–1808.* Berkeley: U of California P, 1971.

———. *Paris and London in the Eighteenth Century: Studies in Popular Protest.* New York: Viking, 1970.

———. *Wilkes and Liberty.* Oxford: Clarendon, 1962.

Sainsbury, John. *Disaffected Patriots: London Supporters of Revolutionary America, 1769–1782.* Kingston: McGill–Queen's UP, 1987.

Sambrook, James. *The Eighteenth Century: The Intellectual and Cultural Context of English Literature, 1700–1789.* London: Longman, 1986.

Saxe, Victoria. *Le culte de Marie Madelein en occident.* Paris, 1959.

Schorer, Mark. "Hugh Kelly: His Place in the Sentimental School." *PQ* 12 (1933): 389–401.

Seilhamer, George. *History of the American Theatre.* 3 vols. Philadelphia: Globe, 1888.

Shattuck, Charles H. "Playhouse Politics: William Woodfall and the Haymarket Theatre, 1777." *Studies in Theatre and Drama: Essays in Honor of Hubert C. Heffner.* Ed. Oscar Brockett. The Hague: Mouton, 1972. 120–37.

Sherbo, Arthur. *English Sentimental Drama.* East Lansing: Michigan State UP, 1957.

Shevelow, Kathryn. "The Productions of the Female Writing Subject: Letters to the *Athenian Mercury.*" *Genre* 19 (1986): 385–407.

Small, Miriam R. *Charlotte Ramsay Lennox.* New Haven: Yale UP, 1935.

Smith, Charles Daniel. *The Early Career of Lord North the Prime Minister.* London: Athlone, 1979.

Speck, W. A. *Stability and Strife England, 1714–1760.* Cambridge: Harvard UP, 1977.

Spector, Robert D. *Arthur Murphy.* Boston: Twayne, 1979.

———. *Political Controversy: A Study in Eighteenth-Century Propaganda.* Westport, CT: Greenwood, 1992.

Stevenson, John, ed. *London in the Age of Reform.* Oxford: Blackwell, 1977.

Stockwell, La Tourette. *Dublin Theatres and Theatre Customs.* New York: Blom, 1968.

Stone, George Winchester, ed. *The London Stage, 1660–1800: A Calendar of Plays, Entertainment, and Afterpieces Together with Casts, Box-Receipts, and Contemporary Comment, Compiled from the Playbills, Newspapers, and Theatrical Diaries of the Period.* Pt. 4: 1747–1776; pt. 5: 1776–1800. Carbondale: Southern Illinois UP, 1965–67.

Stone, George Winchester, and George M. Kahrl. *David Garrick: A Critical Biography.* Carbondale: Southern Illinois UP, 1979.

Stone, Lawrence. *Family, Sex, and Marriage in England, 1500–1800.* Abr. ed. New York: Harper, 1979.

Sullivan, Alvin, ed. *British Literary Magazines: The Augustan Age and the Age of Johnson, 1698–1788.* Westport, CT: Greenwood, 1983.

Bibliography

Sutherland, Lucy. "The City of London and the Opposition to Government, 1768–74." Stevenson 30–54.

Tasch, Peter A. *The Dramatic Cobbler: The Life and Works of Isaac Bickerstaff.* Lewisburg, PA: Bucknell UP, 1971.

Tave, Stuart. *The Amiable Humorist.* Chicago: U of Chicago P, 1960.

Taylor, James Stephen. *Jonas Hanway: Founder of the Marine Society.* London: Scolar, 1985.

Taylor, Richard C. *Goldsmith as Journalist.* Rutherford, NJ: Fairleigh Dickinson UP, 1993.

Thorndike, Ashley. *English Comedy.* New York: Macmillan, 1929.

Todd, Janet. *Sensibility, an Introduction.* London: Methuen, 1986.

Trefman, Simon. *Samuel Foote, Comedian, 1720–1777.* New York: New York UP, 1971.

Turnbull, Patrick. *Warren Hastings.* London: New English Library, 1975.

Valentine, Alan. *The British Establishment, 1760–1784.* 2 vols. Norman: U of Oklahoma P, 1970.

Walpole, Horace. *The Letters of Horace Walpole.* Ed. Peter Cunningham. 9 vols. London: Bentley, 1886.

Wardle, Ralph M. *Oliver Goldsmith.* Lawrence: U of Kansas P, 1957.

Watt, William W. "Hugh Kelly and the Sentimental Drama." Diss. Yale U, 1935.

Weinbrot, Howard D. *The Formal Strain: Studies in Augustan Imitation and Satire.* Chicago: U of Chicago P, 1969.

Weinreb, Ben, and Christopher Hibbert, eds. *The London Encyclopedia.* London: Macmillan, 1983.

Williamson, Aubrey. *Wilkes: 'A Friend to Liberty.'* London: Allen, 1974.

Wilt, Judith. "He Could Go No Farther: A Modest Proposal about Lovelace and Clarissa." *PMLA* 92 (1977): 19–32.

Woodruff, James F. "Contemporaries of the *Tatler* and *Spectator*." Sullivan 393–400.

Woods, Leigh. *Garrick Claims the Stage.* Westport, CT: Greenwood, 1984.

Woods, Samuel, Jr. Letter to the author. 7 Apr. 1992.

Worth, Katharine. *Sheridan and Goldsmith.* Basingstoke: Macmillan, 1992.

Wright, Rev. William B. ["Lord Boyne Case"]. *Genealogical Magazine* 4 (1900): 90–91.

Index

Index

edition of, 139; comic subgenres in, 137–38; concealed authorship of, 139–40; Larpent copy of, 136; performances of, 136–37; plot of, 135; printed version of, 131, 136, 183n1; prologue to, 138–39; reviews of, 130–31, 134–36; Wilkites and, 139–40

Rosciad (Churchill), 7, 25, 26, 27, 55

Ross, David, 95

Rous, Thomas Bates, 133

Rudé, George, 62, 68, 73, 105

Ryder, Thomas, 125

satire, 9–10, 26, 53, 111, 150

Savage, Richard, 22, 24

Say, Charles Green, 3, 5, 12, 77, 78–79, 80, 182n2

School for Rakes, The (Griffith), 99

School for Wives, The (Kelly), 71, 83, 101, 114, 121; concealed authorship of, 45, 132, 172n22; contemporary criticism of, 126–27; Irish theme in, 124, 126; performances of, 125–26; plot of, 123–24; printed version of, 127–28, 184n2; reviews of, 124–25; success of, 122–23, 130

Schorer, Mark, 51–52, 83, 126–27

Scott, James, 79, 88, 177n15

Seilhamer, George, 50, 82, 98, 99, 126

Sense and Sensibility (Austen), 52, 53

sensibility, 31–33, 83–85, 106–7

sentimentalism, 14–15, 30, 49, 51–52, 83, 116, 162, 167n9; changes in meaning of, 129; criticism of, 127, 173n10; hard male culture and, 15, 84–85, 126, 162; printed versions of plays in genre of, 127–28, 131, 136, 183n1, 184n2

Seven Years' War, 109

Shakespear, John, 79

Sherbo, Arthur, 52, 129, 137, 173n10, 183n28

Sherico, Frederick, 152

Sheridan, Frances, 11

Sheridan, Richard, 53, 122, 150

She Stoops to Conquer (Goldsmith), 102, 116–18, 136

Smart, Christopher, 24

Smollett, Tobias, 53, 79, 136

Society of the Supporters of the Bill of Rights (SSBR), 66, 67, 78, 86, 91, 95, 100–101, 105, 141, 170n16, 180n3

Spectator, 16, 23

spin-offs, 26, 64, 65, 66

SSBR. *See* Society of the Supporters of the Bill of Rights

Stamma, Louis, 26

Stanhope, Philip Dormer, 58

Steele, Richard, 13

Stephens, James, 108

Sterne, Laurence, 16

St. George's Fields massacre (1768), 64, 68, 76, 91, 104

St. James's Chronicle, 44, 79, 80, 107, 108, 124, 136

stock companies, 77–80

Stone, George Winchester, 7, 42, 44, 98, 125

Stone, Lawrence, 14, 50, 96

Strahan, William, 74, 78, 79, 80, 159, 186n21

Strahan, William, Jr., 44, 77, 79

Sultan, The (Bickerstaff), 76

surveillance, 111, 113

Swift, Jonathan, 8, 16

Tasch, Peter, 43, 56

Taylor, John, 1, 4, 58, 59, 122, 123, 158, 159

theater, 9, 50; criticism of, 25–29, 48, 93–96, 109–10, 114–18, 172n20; intersection of, with journalism and politics, 65, 73–74, 77–81, 86, 97, 174–75n14; politics of, 110, 116, 149–50

Theater, The: A Political Dissection (Gentleman), 97

theater managers, 38–39, 75, 108, 110

Theatrical Monitor, 38–42, 44, 46, 57, 58, 59, 75, 80

Thespis (I) (Kelly), 7, 11, 25–29, 36, 48, 57, 93, 110, 115

Thespis (II) (Kelly), 27, 28, 95–96

Thompson, Edward, 1, 4, 5, 25, 55, 58, 115; collected *Works* and, 6, 58, 80; and elegy on Kelly, 159; *The Romance of an Hour* and, 137; stock companies and, 77, 79

Robert R. Bataille is a professor of English at Iowa State University where he teaches courses on eighteenth-century British literature and is the director of Undergraduate Studies. He has a particular interest in the history of British journalism in the second half of the eighteenth century and has published notes and articles in, among other journals, the *Library,* the *Publication of the Bibliographical Society of America,* and the *Journal of Newspaper and Periodical History.*